MYSTICAL DIMENSIONS OF ISLAM

MYSTICAL DIMENSIONS OF ISLAM

A R Khan

MD Publications Pvt Ltd
New Delhi
www.mdppl.com

Published by :

MD Publications Pvt Ltd
"MD House", 11, Darya Ganj,
New Delhi-110 002
Phone : +91-11-45355555
E-mail : contact@mdppl.com
Website : www.mdppl.com

ISBN : 978-81-7533-291-1

Published and Printed by Mr. Pranav Gupta on behalf of **MD Publications Pvt Ltd** at Printext, New Delhi.

Preface

Sufism or tasawwuf also spelled as *tasavvuf* and *tasavvof,* is generally understood to be the inner, mystical dimension of Islam. A practitioner of this tradition is generally known as a sufi though some adherents of the tradition reserve this term only for those practitioners who have attained the goals of the Sufi tradition. Another name used for the Sufi seeker is dervish.

Classical Sufi scholars have defined Sufism as "a science whose objective is the reparation of the heart and turning it away from all else but God." Alternatively, in the words of the renowned Darqawi Sufi teacher Ahmad ibn Ajiba, "a science through which one can know how to travel into the presence of the Divine, purify one's inner self from filth, and beautify it with a variety of praiseworthy traits."

Sufism was considerably influenced by the Hindu discipline of Yoga in such areas as physical postures (asanas) and breath control (pranayama). During the primary stages of Sufism, Sufis were characterised by their particular attachment to *dhikr* "remembrance of God" and asceticism. Sufism arose among a number of Muslims as a reaction against the worldliness of the early Umayyad Caliphate (661-750 CE).

This is one of the most misunderstood terms in any language or culture. That is because of the extreme materialistic, rationalistic tendency that is in vogue. We believe in reason, materialistic reason. Reason that can deal only with reality through the five senses. That can deal only with the measurable. The immeasurable is outside its sphere. But let us look at human life: friendship, smiles, love of children, admiring a flower, hate of enemy, all of these is intangible. The materialistic mind cannot deal with it. Therefore it does not exist.

Mysticism is also one of these things that the materialistic mind cannot deal with, therefore it has maligned it. It has discredited it completely. It has been associated in the modern mind with hocus-pocus or magic. Mysticism in Arabic is Tassawuf. It comes from the root word "Suf" meaning wool. Donning of woolen clothes was a sign of withdrawing from the luxury of the world, not renunciation of the world. (compare silk which stands for luxury).

There is always a thin line dividing Islamic Mysticism from a lot of heresies that are anti-Islamic. Islamic Mysticism does not shun the world or renounce it, it simply withdraws from some of its luxuries. Islamic mystics have all three components. Islamic mystics have to live all religious experiences of all the religions - then the final flowering is not union with God, but better knowledge of God. Not becoming part and parcel of God. There is always a gap or field where interaction occurs. The more you know Him, the more you love him, the better you know Him. Knowledge here is not Union, - Wahidat Wujud, and Unity of Being. But Wahidat Ash-shuhud, Unity of Consciousness. To many Muslim mystics wahidat wujud- or union would be heretical, moving outside Islamic orthodoxy. In Islam it would be more of a consciousness of God not a union. It is a psychological not an ontological condition.

I am very grateful to Mr. Pranav Gupta, Director of MD Publications Pvt Ltd, New Delhi, for his kind cooperation and support for this book.

A R Khan

Contents

	Preface	*v*
1.	The Foundations of the Path	1
2.	Sufism	49
3.	Historical Outlines of Classical Sufism	89
4.	The Rose and the Nightingale: Persian and Turkish Mystical Poetry	117
5.	Sufism in Indo-Pakistan	157
6.	Sufi Orders and Fraternities	205
7.	Theosophical Sufism	241
	Bibliography	287
	Index	291

1

The Foundations of the Path

As approaching the twenty-first century, few challenges loom larger in the search for justice and world peace than the achievement of mutual understanding among nations, cultures, and religious traditions. For people who profess faith in a sovereign God, few responsibilities are more urgent than that of moving toward a sympathetic appreciation of other faiths. The more our world grows, the more rapidly it seems to shrink, so that we must at the very least learn to cope with the fact of diminishing religious and cultural elbowroom. One of the increasingly visible features on the international landscape is the religion known as Islam, with it's nearly three-quarters of a billion adherents. A major question for Christians with respect to Islam is this: How can we begin to learn about so massive and expansive a phenomenon without resorting to the convenient but unjust stereotypes one hears so often, caricatures that amount to little more than a new form of religious bigotry or racism?

Three more specific questions present themselves. First, what do Muslims have in common with other avowedly religious people across the world? Second, how do Muslims define themselves as a distinct community of faith unique among religions? And third, what possibilities for spiritual growth has Islam offered historically to the individual believer? The image of a spiritual journey will provide a framework within which to respond to these questions. As citizens of the world, Muslims discern God's signs in nature, the broad terrain on which they journey. As members of a unique community of faith, they discover God's signs preeminently in their scripture, the Quran, and in their history; this scripture and history map out for them the main road, the "straight way." As individual believers, Muslims look for God's signs within themselves, where the signs mark off the path each person must walk before God. In all three instances the signs are illumined by the light of God's all-encompassing revelation. Believers strive to respond to that revelation by taking one more step across the terrain of creation, down the "straight way" of Islam's special history, and along the path of personal sanctification and self-knowledge, all in a journey back to the Lord of the universe.

Both the imagery of God's threefold revelation and that of journey and light are rooted in the Quran. "We will show them our signs on the horizons and in their very selves, until it becomes clear to them that it is the Truth" (41:53). And: "On the earth there are signs for those of firm faith, and in your very selves. Will you not then see?" (51:20-21). In addition, the Arabic term that is used for "verse" of scripture (ayah) also means "sign," thus suggesting that the Quran also is one great sign replete with more specific signs. In response to each of the three questions I have posed above, I will introduce further texts of the Quran that unite all three elements of the imagery of journey, sign, and light. If readers are willing to accept the possibility that God has spoken, and continues to speak, to human beings who are not Christians, let them read on. My premise here is that, for reasons known only to the Creator, God has desired to make his word known to a faith community whose members call themselves Muslims. He is not some "other" God who speaks Arabic, Persian, Turkish, and a host of other tongues which Muslims speak all over the globe. For the Arabic word Allah simply means "God," the very Deity to whom we pray. Now to the first question: How do Muslims perceive and respond to God's signs on the horizons?

Signs on the Horizons

Behold, in the heavens and the earths are signs for those who believe. And in your creation, and all the wild creatures He has scattered over the earth, are signs for a people of firm faith. And the alternation of night and day, and the sustenance that God sends down from the sky, quickening thereby the earth after her death, and the ordering of the winds - these are signs for a people who understand. (Quran 45:3-5)

Divine revelation in nature appears in Islam's scripture as the "terrain" on which the journey of humanity takes place, the heavens and the earth as alluded to in the word horizons. Human response at this level we may characterize as a universal or cosmic experience expressed in a creation - inspired language and system of symbols that describe the journey of all creation from God and back to God. According to an Islamic tradition, called a "Sacred Saying," God once said: "I was a hidden treasure and I desired to be known, so I created the world." In that world all nonhuman creatures are essentially "*Muslim*" in that they "surrender" to God by their very nature. Human beings must make the choice as to whether they will surrender. Once they choose to submit and respond gratefully (thus becoming Muslims through their response of "Islam", human beings rather naturally express their response in ritual and symbol that are at once common to other religious traditions and also distinctively Islamic.

In themselves these practices are not uniquely Islamic, but they bear an Islamic stamp to the extent that they are integral to the faith-response of a community explicitly gathered by God's revelation as delivered through Muhammad in the Quran. This aspect of Islamic religious experience we will take up in the next segment of this discussion. For now, let us look at some of the ritual and symbolic ways in which Muslims express their response to the "signs on the horizons." Fasting is a nearly universal religious practice. Each year, during the lunar month of Ramadan (movable in relation to our calendar), Muslims break their regular life-patterns by abstaining from food and drink from dawn to sunset each day, a period that averages fifteen to seventeen hours. The discipline of refraining from creation's means of sustenance is a reminder of one's greater need of God, a need that even creation itself cannot fill. It presupposes that one is also refraining from forbidden words and actions and thoughts, such as envy or hatred. Compassion for those who habitually suffer from hunger, greater ability to go against one's own less noble tendencies, and the removal of obstacles in one's relationship to the Creator is among the most desired effects of the fast.

Almsgiving likewise is commonly practiced among religious people the world over. Muslims have the conviction that creation is not a permanent possession, but merely given to humankind as a "loan." That conviction prompts the response of sharing God's own wealth. Muslims "give God a loan" in return and seek to steward creation by giving freely what they have freely received. The root meaning of the word for almsgiving in Arabic, *zakat,* is "to purify oneself," in the sense that one must strive never to lay claim to what belongs only to God. One must not "overflow one's banks" by imagining he or she is the source or owner of created goods. Almsgiving is therefore meant not to give a person the good feeling of being generous, but to remind the Muslim of who first gave all to him or her. Before each of the five daily prayers, Muslims perform a ritual ablution. It is another facet of the purification that almsgiving presupposes. The action involves the use of that universal symbol of cleansing - water. But if water is not available, one may use sand or pebbles.

The important thing is to make use of some earthy object as a physical reminder of the overall, inner and outer, purification that is itself an integral part of a proper relationship with God and his creation. Daily ritual prayer with its orientation toward Mecca is another way of expressing a right relationship to the created world. Mecca is a symbolic axis of the world, a spiritual center, the meeting place of heaven and earth from which all creation radiates. Orientation to one of the cardinal points of the compass or to a particular "spiritual center" (such as Jerusalem in Judaism, for example) is evidenced in many major religious traditions. When Muslims pray together on Friday at noon, or whenever they gather in a mosque for congregational prayer, they express their right relationship with each other by lining up in rows as they face Mecca. Finally, the five daily ritual prayers sanctify time as well as space, as a round of concrete reminders that morning, noon, and night are a gift of God.

Pilgrimage to Mecca, ideally to be made once in a lifetime if one possesses good health and sufficient means, is meant to acknowledge the unity and absolute equality of all. It is the symbol par excellence of the journey of God's people back to the source. Including such rituals as change of garb and cutting of hair, the journey gives physical expression to the need for a change of heart and mind. Pilgrim goals vary from one religion to another, but they are all symbolic of the journey to the center of creation. According to Quran 6:39, "those who reject Our Signs are deaf and dumb and in profound darkness. God allows going astray whom He will, and He places on the Straight Way whom He will." One of the Quran's most beautiful images provides both a background and a foreground against which to appreciate the Muslim response to signs on the horizons:

> God is the Light of the heavens and the earth. The likeness of His Light is as a Niche [the symbol of orientation to Mecca on the back wall of every mosque, as well as a symbol of the human heart] in which there is a lamp. The lamp is within a glass which is like a shining star enkindled from a blessed olive tree, neither of East nor West, whose oil would glow almost of it even if no fire touched it. Light upon Light! And God guides to His Light whom He will. (Quran 24:35)

The Quran as Sign

These are the signs [verses] of the clear Scripture. We have sent it down as an Arabic Quran. Perhaps you will understand.

(Quran 12:1-2)

Muslims believe, as do Christians, that the most significant events in human history are precisely those events that define their history. If the "signs on the horizons" describe the terrain in which God reveals himself, the historical fact of the Quran as revealed to Muhammad between 610 and 632 is for Muslims the opening to the main road on which they as a community journey. "Lead us along the Straight Way," Muslims pray five times daily and on the many other occasions when they recite the opening chapter of the Quran. One might describe Muslims' response to God's revelation in "an Arabic Quran" as a communitarian experience expressed in a confessional (or kerygmatic) language and symbol-system. Their experience is that of being Muslims in a world where most people are not. Terms of membership are definitive; although there is a good deal of latitude in practice, for we are talking about a tradition that crosses many ethnic and cultural boundaries, they call for a deliberate choice either for or against membership.

How do Muslims define themselves as a unique community of faith? What is distinctively Islamic about Islam? Reduced to the most fundamental terms, to be a Muslim is to adhere to God's revelation in the Quran as spoken by the Prophet Muhammad. "We have sent a Messenger into your midst and from among you, to recite [that is, make a Quran, a recitation] to you Our Signs . . . and to teach you the Book and Wisdom" (Quran 2:151). But if the matter were all that simple, I would probably not have written this chapter, and surely no one would be reading it. History has a way of making life enormously complicated. During the course of nearly fourteen centuries, Islam has come to embrace a remarkable variety of cultural and ethnic entities.

As the world of Islam expanded, it became more and more evident to Muslims that neither the text of the Quran, nor the paradigmatic words and deeds of Muhammad enshrined in the community's collective memory, corresponded item for item with the new issues that surfaced with changing times and circumstances. Therefore, the two prime sources of Islamic tradition, the scripture and the Prophetic Example (called the Sunnah in Arabic), had to be adapted and reinterpreted continually. Islam's religious history is the composite story of how those adaptations and reinterpretations have unfolded. In order to appreciate something of the Islamic experience of unity in diversity, it will be necessary to explore some of the implications of Muslims' evolving understandings, first, of the Prophet Muhammad and the issue of leadership and authority as it arose after the Prophet's death; and, second, of the Quran and the problems attendant on the need to implement it in daily Islamic life. I shall introduce each of these considerations with an appropriate text from the Quran, so as to situate both the Prophet and the Quran in the context of our journey, sign, and light imagery.

We turn, then, to the role of the Prophet and the question of community leadership. He [God] is the One Who sends manifest Signs to His servants, that He might lead you from the depths of darkness into the Light.... O you who believe! Be mindful of your duty to trust in His Messenger, and He will bestow on you a double portion of His Mercy: He will provide for you a Light by which you shall walk and He will forgive you.... (Quran 57:9 and 28)

It was one thing to trust in God's messenger while he lived; it was yet another to know whom to trust as Muhammad's successor. Muhammad's death thrust the young Muslim community into a protracted debate over the criteria of legitimate succession, a debate that gave rise to a diversity of opinion that would also have serious implications for the practical implementation of Quranic legislation, as we shall see shortly. According to sources compiled as much as two or three centuries after the Prophet's death in 632, two predominant approaches to the problem of succession emerged. One group held that the Prophet had named his son-in-law Ali to be his caliph ("successor," "vicar"). The other, convinced that Muhammad had made no such appointment, opted for an elective procedure.

Abu Bakr, Muhammad's father-in-law, emerged as their choice. Ensuing developments are much too involved to detail here. In brief, the group that supported Ali came to be known as the Shi'ah (that is, party) of Ali. Those who backed Abu Bakr formed the nucleus of what is known now as the "People of the Sunnah and the Assembly," or the Sunni Muslims. The distinction between Sunni and Shiite is not the only mark of diversity within Islam. Within each of these groups there are significant subdivisions. I will mention the most important variations among Sunnis shortly, in the context of variant interpretations of the Quran. Here I would like to give a brief sketch of the two principal Shiite groups.

Major differences between the two largest segments of Shiite Islam crystallized around the second half of the eighth century. Until that time, both agreed that the authority to lead the community was vested in a hereditary succession of six descendants of Muhammad, beginning with Ali. In 765, the sixth Imam, or spiritual leader, died; and a dispute arose over who would be his legitimate heir. One group pledged allegiance to the sixth Imam's older son, even though he had died before his father did. They effectively terminated the official line of succession with this seventh Imam, and hence are known as "Seveners" (or Isma'ilis, after the seventh Imam, Isma'il). The Seveners are now found, for example, in East Africa, Pakistan, and India, and are headed by the Agha Khan.

A second faction chose to follow the man whom the sixth Imam designated after the death of Isma'il. This faction continued the line of succession down to the disappearance of the twelfth Imam in 873. Hence, they are now known as the "Twelvers." They constitute the vast majority of the population of Iran and about half that of Iraq. Shi'ism has been Iran's state religion since the sixteenth century. For both the Seveners and the Twelvers, religious experience has been decidedly millenialist. A strong messianic hope awaits the return of the last Imam (either the seventh or the twelfth), who will inaugurate a new age in which all believers will benefit from the Imam's redemptive suffering and that of the whole family of the Prophet. However, to say that Shiite spirituality is very much involved with the concept of redemptive suffering is not to say that Shiites are motivated by some sort of "martyr complex," as the news media have often alleged in recent years.

"Martyr complex" simply does not do justice to the willingness people have shown, in many ages and in many religious traditions, to die for what they believe in. What I have said thus far is but a superficial glance at some immensely intricate historical developments; but we must move on to consider the Quran. It is not fitting that God should speak to a human being except by inspiration [a technical term used for the revelation given to a prophet], or from behind a veil, or by the sending of a Messenger to reveal, by God's leave, what God wills.... And thus we have, by our command, sent an inspiration to you [Muhammad]. You knew neither what the Scripture was, nor what the Faith was. But we have made it [the Quran] a Light by which we guide such servants of ours as we will. And truly you [Muhammad] guide them to the Straight Way, the Way of God, to whom belongs whatever is in the heavens and whatever is on earth.... (Quran 52:51-53)

The light of the Quran's guidance is the primary touchstone against which Muslims must judge the authenticity of their faith and action. Some texts of the scripture provide explicit regulations regarding matters of personal and social morality as well as ritual. But the Quran is not primarily a legislative handbook. Very early in Islamic history, local communities faced issues on which the book gave no specific ruling. The most pressing problem for the community was then, as now, how to interpret the sacred text in such a way as to preserve its spirit and still respond to new needs. From about the late seventh century, the community as a whole began elaborating various interpretative principles and procedures. Schools of thought, each with its own peculiar emphasis on one or another aspect of legal reasoning, began to take shape.

All agreed that the Quran and the Prophetic Example (Sunnah) were fundamental; but the schools differed in the relative stress they placed on community or scholarly consensus, private opinion, and analogical reasoning. By the end of the ninth century several distinct and formally constituted legal methodologies had come into being. Today, Sunni Muslims consider the four extant schools - the Malikite, Hanifite, Hanbalite, and Shafi'ite - equally acceptable and "orthodox." More than one school may be found in a given Islamic country, but one generally predominates; for example, Morocco, Turkey, Saudi Arabia, and Indonesia are dominated, respectively, by the schools listed above. In cases for which no explicit solution can be found either in the Quran or in the Sayings of Muhammad (Hadith), the Sunni schools usually leave the final decision to scholarly or community consensus, rather than to the judgment of an individual legal authority.

Shiites, who do not recognize the Sunni schools of law, vest overriding legal competence in some individual whom they consider to be divinely sanctioned by reason of a spiritual-genealogical link to Muhammad, via the descendants of Ali. The point I want to make is that Islam is not now, and never has been, the monolithic religion many outsiders have thought it to be. For although, the historical revelation of the "straight way" demands an exclusive commitment to a single and unique community of faith, the meaning of the original call has for many centuries been variously interpreted. Hence, it is neither fair nor accurate to equate Khomeini's approach to Islam with that of Sadat, or that of Qaddafi with that of Pakistani President Ziya al-Haqq or Wallace D. Muhammad, a leading figure in the World Community of Islam in the West. All things consid-ered, we may say that the Islamic religious experience of God's signs in the historic scripture, revealed through the historic personage Muhammad, has been mediated through the community's ongoing experience of reinterpretation as required to keep the spirit of both the primordial revelation and the paradigmatic leader alive and growing.

Signs within the Individual

On the terrain of creation, God lays open the main road of the Muslim community's unique and exclusive history. Believers discover and set out on that road in the company of others. But Islamic tradition has not denied the individual person either the right and exhilaration or the requirement and risk of exploring and journeying alone before God. Community supports the individual's desire to acknowledge God's signs, for God has created an affection between the hearts of believers such as all the riches on earth could never effect (Quran 8:63); but the choice must be made and renewed in the solitary heart. The individual experiences the light of faith, which God casts into the core of his or her being, as a personalized gift, often articulated in mystical language and symbol-system.

The expression is "mystical" in the sense that it describes, in Hodgson's definition of mysticism, an "inward personal experience, more or less transitory as an event but enduring in relevance, which is felt to express or lead to a special authoritative and normative relation between individual and cosmos." The term includes much more than ecstatic experience, but it does not rule out experiences that are usually associated with the "great mystics" of any religious tradition. An important and sometimes controversial element in Islamic tradition has been the Sufi Path. Although Sufism has witnessed the development of a great variety of formally constituted religious orders, the Sufi Path is not itself an institution. It is the personal counterpart to the main road of the revealed law (called the Shariah) which circumscribes the Islamic community as a whole. Both in the more technical handbooks on Sufi doctrine and practice and in the intensely personal poetry of some of Islam's "great mystics," the individual appear as a wayfarer on a course designed uniquely for him or her.

It is the journey of a love relationship between servant and Master, creature and Creator. Authors of Sufi manuals elaborated a number of psycho-spiritual typologies to describe the various "stations" and "stages" along the path. But they all agree that intimate knowledge of God is the crucial ingredient in the experience. (I must point out here that I know of no clear connection between classical forms of Islamic Sufism and the "Sufi Numbers" or "Enneagrams" that have gained some popularity in recent years.) Guidance along the path comes ultimately from God, as does the community's guidance along the main road. Sometimes, however, the wayfarer needs counsel tailored to individual temperament and gifts. The theory and practice of spiritual direction in Islam are highly developed. That topic would require its own treatment elsewhere; but it is definitely a matter we Christians, and especially Catholic religious, could very profitably explore.

Muslims not formally affiliated with religious orders, as well as members of orders, have sought and received spiritual direction from a shaykh (spiritual guide) either in person or by letter. Some of the material needed for a thorough study of the subject is beginning to be made available, and there is much more still to be edited and translated. Sufism's emphasis on individual religious experience, on the ability to recognize and interpret the "signs within the self," has had considerable influence on the broader range of Islamic popular piety. Whether for good or ill, the growing popularity and esteem of certain early Sufi shaykhs soon transformed some of them into saints in the eyes of the people. A cult of the saints grew up, often encouraging pilgrimages to a holy person's tomb in the hope of receiving boons and miracles of all kinds.

Sunni Islam has never officially sanctioned the cult of the saints the way Shi'ite Islam has recognized popular reverence at the tombs of the Imams, but both devotional practices appear very much a part of popular piety and are probably here to stay for a long time. What I have proposed here is a synthetic model. Nowhere do the primary Islamic sources analyze Islamic religious experience precisely this way. This model is therefore a reconstruction; but the materials - the language and imagery of journey, sign, and light - are Islamic in inspiration. So long as one is aware of the limitations inherent in such models, they can be drafted appropriately into service as vehicles for cross-cultural understanding. Even so, the reader may as yet see no realistic way of setting out on the journey described in these pages. It may seem impossibly compromising, perhaps bordering on an outright betrayal of one's allegiance to Christianity.

Islam, the religion of peace, is constantly linked by the mass media with images of war, conflict and terrorism. On an almost daily basis we are told of 'Islamic fundamentalists', 'Muslim extremists' and even 'Islamo-fascists'. Islam is represented as monolithic, austere and conservative, even puritanical. This false and misleading picture of Islam, so vigorously promulgated in the West, is extremely one-dimensional, focusing exclusively as it does on the narrow exoteric side of the religion. Little or no attention is given to Islam's fluid and multifaceted mystical dimensions. For just as there is an inner side to Christianity and Judaism, so there is to Islam. This subterranean tradition has always acted to counterbalance the forces of dogmatism and dry formalism. Constituting the inner core of Islam, it has been celebrated by the greatest Muslim poets and sages from al-Hallaj and Ibn Arabi to Kermani, Rumi and Hafiz.

Do not attach yourself to any particular creed exclusively, so that you disbelieve all the rest; otherwise you will miss much that is good; indeed, you will fail to see the real Truth. God the omnipotent and omnipresent is not contained by any one creed, for He says in the Quran, 'Wherever you turn, there is the face of Allah.' – Sufi Grand Master Ibn Arabi

The mysticism or esotericism (called in Arabic *tasawwuf*)

of Islam is today identified with the Sufis (a word commonly thought to come from the Arabic *suf* meaning 'wool', after the rough woollen robe worn by early Muslim mystics). However, there are several Muslim communities, such as the Ismailis, Qarmatians, Alawis and Druze, who derive their doctrines and practices from Islamic esotericism. In the days of the Prophet Muhammad there was no sharp distinction between the esoteric and exoteric teachings of Islam. The Prophet instructed his inner circle, known as the Companions, in both the exoteric (*zahir*, the outer or apparent) and esoteric (*batin*, the inner or secret) meanings of the revelations he received from Allah. Although Prophet Muhammad, as the last of the Messengers of God, was the repository of a complete treasure of precepts, he proclaimed only some of them publicly, leaving the rest undeclared.

The Prophet is said to have privately entrusted the undeclared precepts to a select few of his Companions, foremost among them Ali, "so that they would progressively reveal them at appropriate junctures according to their wisdom, whether by inferring the particular from the absolute, or the concrete from the abstract." Soon after the death of the Prophet the Muslim community was riven with power struggles and a rising tide of legalism which sought to suppress the mystical side of Islam. In the decades following the Prophet's death, Sufi orders grew in secret as disciples (*murids*) gathered around an individual master (called *murshid*, *shaykh* or *pir*) to receive personal instruction in esotericism. Thus the inner teachings of Islam survived to become crystallised principally in Sufism.

No man can be said to have originated Sufism. No one knows who the first Sufi was. Sufism is not a religion, and ultimately exists above and beyond all labels. It is said Sufism is older than Islam and that it really had no beginning, being just the latest flowering – taking on the form of Islam – of the ancient secret tradition stretching back to Adam. A Sufi tradition relates how "the seeds of Sufism were sown in the time of Adam, fermented in the time of Noah, budded in the time of Abram, and began to develop in the time of Jesus, and produced pure wine in the time of Muhammad." Prophet Muhammad and Jesus are revered as the greatest Sufis. Sufi Masters like Ibn Arabi and Suhrawardi studied Plato and Pythagoras declaring the Pagan sages to be Sufis.

I looked for Him on the Christian cross, but he was not there. I went to Hindu temples and shrines – but nothing. I visited the Ka'aba in Mecca, I did not find Him. I questioned learned scholars, but He outstripped their understanding. Finally, when I peered into my own heart– there, and nowhere else, was His home –Jaluddin Rumi, Sufi Master and poet.

In the nineteenth and early twentieth centuries many of Europe's leading esotericists travelled to the Muslim East in search of ancient wisdom. As Joscelyn Godwin, a leading authority on the history of Western esotericism, explains:

The initiatic journey to Islamic soil has been a repeated theme of European esotericism, ever since the Templars settled in Jerusalem and the mythical Christian Rosenkreuz learnt his trade in "Damcar" (Damascus). We find it in the lives of Paracelsus and Cagliostro, then, as travel became easier, in a whole host that includes P.B. Randolph, H.P. Blavatsky, Max Theon, G.I. Gurdjieff, Aleister Crowley, Rene Guenon, R.A. Schwaller de Lubicz, and Henry Corbin. There was very likely some element of this in Napoleon's Egyptian campaign of 1797, when he announced to an astounded audience that he, too, was a Muslim; then returned to Paris to convene the Jewish Sanhedrin and to reinstate the Christian clergy.

In Egypt during the mid 1800s Madame Blavatsky studied Sufism, Coptic Christianity, and the Druze order which she described as "a last survival of archaic wisdom." Claiming to be a student of her Master "Serapis Bey," while in Cairo Madame Blavatsky met Jamal ad-Din al-Afghani, an outstanding Muslim thinker, radical political leader and Sufi teacher. She also travelled widely, often in Muslim dress, in the company of Albert Rawson, who would later write an account of his initiation by the Druze for Blavatsky's *book Isis Unveiled.* Rawson was one of the founders of the Nobles of the Mystic Shrine, a secret society incorporating principles and symbols drawn from Islamic mysticism. He also wrote favourably about Gnosticism and called for a new Church of Humanity that "should be broad and comprehensive, embracing many diverse elements, all working together for the common good [revealing] to ordinary people the extraordinary attributes of their own nature by exemplifying before them the transcendent heights and depths of the human soul."

Another influential spiritual teacher who journeyed through Muslim lands in search of hidden knowledge was George Ivanovitch Gurdjieff. He spent much of his life in Central Asia where he encountered Sufi brotherhoods and learnt of their texts, particularly 'The Walled Garden of the Truth' composed in the twelfth century by Sufi Master Hakim Sanai of Ghazna. According to the author of The Teachers of Gurdjieff, Hakim Sanai's book influenced Gurdjieff's own writings. One of Gurdjieff's prominent students, J.G. Bennett, believed the origin of Gurdjieff's system can be traced to the Sufis of Central Asia.

While many people are familiar with Madame H.P. Blavatsky and G.I. Gurdjieff, few are aware of the mystic teacher who is credited with laying the foundation for the spread of Islam among Black Americans. Early in the twentieth century, Noble Drew Ali (born Timothy Drew), the self-taught son of former Black slaves, took a job as a merchant seaman and found himself in Egypt. According to one legend, Noble Drew Ali traveled around the world before the age of twenty-seven, in an effort to discover all he could about the heritage of his people and the tenets of Islam. It is commonly believed he received a mandate from the king of Morocco to instruct Black Americans in Islam. At the Pyramid of Cheops he received initiation and took the Muslim name Sharif [Noble] Abdul Ali; in America he would be known as Noble Drew

Ali. On his return to the United States in 1913 he founded the Moorish Science Temple, "to uplift fallen humanity by returning the nationality, divine creed and culture to persons of Moorish descent in the Western Hemisphere."

A charismatic leader, Noble Drew Ali taught that the true origin of Black Americans was 'Asiatic', and Islam their original religion. "The fallen sons and daughters of the Asiatic Nation of North America," he wrote, "need to learn to love instead of hate; and to know of their higher self and lower self." Allah, the one true God, has been known by many names, "but everywhere His is the causeless cause, the rootless root from which all things have grown." Noble Drew Ali acknowledged Prophet Muhammad as "the founder of the reuniting of Islam" and the promised one foretold by Jesus. All prophets came with basically the same message, and Islam was the original divine faith to which Muhammad called people to return. Through his message thousands of Black Americans were exposed to Moorish history, culture, religion, as well as the Islamic principles of "Love, Truth, Peace, Freedom, and Justice." But his meteoric success brought disaster. Noble Drew Ali died in 1929, in the words of one commentator, "some say from severe police beatings, others say he was assassinated by his rivals in the movement. In his sincerity and undoubted innocence, Noble Drew Ali met a martyr's end."

One of the most intriguing and mysterious organisations to emerge from the Moorish Science Temple established by Noble Drew Ali is the Moorish Orthodox Church. Founded in the late 1950s by European Americans who had obtained Moorish Science Temple passports as "Celts" or "Persians," the Moorish Orthodox Church attracted a bohemian element. A Moorish Orthodox Church document posted on the internet states they're committed to the "universal spirit hidden anywhere, revealed in all cultures, always occult and dissident, an 'Invisible College' embracing East and West but rejecting all official stultifying Consensus Reality." Today the foremost spokesman for the Moorish Orthodox Church is Peter Lamborn Wilson. A gifted writer and expert on the mystical dimensions of Islam, he is known for his books The Drunken Universe, Scandal: Essays in Islamic Heresy, and Sacred Drift. Wilson writes from experience having spent many years living among Sufis and diverse Muslim communities in Asia and the Middle East.

In his quest for Gnosis, Burton never stopped searching...
– Edward Rice

Sir Richard Burton, a contemporary of Madame Blavatsky, was a British explorer and spy master who fell in love with Islam and with Moorish culture. He memorised huge portions of the Quran, and was so expert in abstruse points of Islamic theology that he could pass as a Muslim scholar. Remembered today for his incredible exploits and magnificent translations of the Arabian Nights and the Kama Sutra, Burton was also the first European to perform the pilgrimage to Mecca as a convert to Islam. His fellow British officers called him the "White Nigger" and "that Devil Burton," because of what they considered his 'odd beliefs' and 'strange practices'. The spiritual quest was central to Richard Burton's life. His biographer Edward Rice tells us:

Burton's adult life was passed in a ceaseless quest for the kind of secret knowledge he labelled broadly as "Gnosis," by which he hoped to uncover the very source of existence and the meaning of his role on earth. This search led him to investigate the Kabbalah, alchemy, Roman Catholicism, a Hindu snake caste of the most archaic type, and the erotic way called Tantra, after which he looked into Sikhism and passed through several forms of Islam before settling on Sufism, a mystical discipline that defies simple labels. He remained a more or less faithful practitioner of Sufi teachings the rest of his life, seeking the mystical heights denied all but the elect, what certain Muslims define as Insan-i Kamil, the Perfect Man, who has attained the most profound spiritual goals.

For Burton, Sufism was the most pure form of Gnosis, the secret knowledge passed down from the ancients, the Zoroastrians, the Hindu yogis, the Platonists, and the Essenes, the followers of the Secret Path having continued "up to the present time, under diverse mystical appellations, with tenets modified by the ages in which they live... They formed from the 'archetypes' of existence, a regular system of spiritual creation anterior to the material." Early in his military career Richard Burton learnt to keep certain opinions and interests to himself and became a master of the Shia Muslim practice known as *taqiya* – dissimulation or concealment – in which one's private religious practices are kept hidden. This practice can be traced back to the Prophet Muhammad and even further to the Gnostic communities of the early centuries of the Christian era. Many of Burton's biographers ignore or play down his spiritual pursuits, principally the several years he spent among the Ismailis (who derive from the medieval 'Assassins') and his initiation into the Qadiri order, a Sufi brotherhood.

Burton was the first European to publish accurate material about Sufism based on an insider's training and direct experience, gained under the guidance of Sufi Masters in India and the Middle East. Burton wrote:

> The merit of Tasawwuf [Sufism] is its beau ideal of goodness as connected with beauty, and universal charity and love as flowing from the source of all goodness.... The Quranic ideal of the human soul or spirit, for instance, is similar to [the Christian]; but the Sufi, deducing the doctrine of the soul's immortality from its immateriality... and convinced by reason that nothing can be at once self-existent, immaterial, and unbounded by time except the Deity, concludes that the spirit of man is nothing but the breath, the particle of the Divine soul lent to mankind, the noblest of God's works.

In the last two decades of his life Burton found other esoteric subjects to investigate: Theosophy, Spiritualism,

Hermeticism, and Extrasensory Perception (Burton was the first to use the term "ESP"). Despite his private studies, Islam (what he called "the Saving Faith") dominated his writings. In his essay "El Islam" Burton explained why he embraced Islam and Sufism:

> "The world is the Muslim's prison, the tomb his stronghold and Paradise his journey's end."... To the Muslim, time is but a point in illimitable eternity, life is but a step from the womb to the tomb.... He has no great secret to learn. The Valley of Death has no shadow for him; no darkness of uncertainty and doubt horrifies his fancy.... As in Christianity as in El Islam, eye hath not seen, nor hath ear heard, nor hath fancy conceived the spiritual joys of those who in mundane life have qualified themselves for heavenly futurity.

As for the Sufi Path, Burton says:

> The whole practice of the Sufi consists of seeking the Divinity, not as the "popular prudential and mercenary devotee," but from fervency of love to God and man. He "proclaims the invisible truth above visible comfort"; his entire resignation can face the horrors of eternal death inflicted by divine Will; "he has something higher even than everlasting gain."

Burton's spiritual quest often bewildered his family, friends, critics, and admirers. Indeed, his religious pursuits can only be understood in the light of his life-long commitment to Gnosis. In the words of Edward Rice: "He wanted Gnosis, the secret knowledge that unlocked the mysteries of the universe, and if it came in his teenage investigations of the Kabbalah or a Bombay cage or a Catholic chapel in primitive Baroda or the Arabian Desert, it did not matter."

> God brings upon those that love Him, a kind of sudden and supernatural madness, in which a man may speak and act against the directions of religion which He has revealed from Heaven. – Junayd (tenth century Sufi Master).

The Order of the Bektashi Dervishes is a Sufi movement

instituted in the fifteenth century by Haji Bektash Veli, a wandering holy man. From the beginning the Bektashi Sufis took a strong stand against hypocrisy and the literalist obsession with ancient texts and outward forms. After the manner of the greatest Sufi scholars, the Bektashi sought out wisdom wherever they could find it, recalling the admonition of the Prophet: "Seek knowledge even unto China" (the furthest ends of the Earth). They are said to have synthesised Shia Islam with shamanic elements along with Christianity, and other sources, including possibly Buddhism.

Some Sufis say that wherever Haji Bektash travelled he was accompanied by two angels, one hovering above his left shoulder and the other above his right. These, it is suggested, may be the spirits of Islam and Christianity. The Bektashi allowed women to participate in their rites and gave them a considerable degree of equality. All this made the Bektashi suspect to the so-called 'orthodox' religious leaders who were quick to accuse them of disregarding various precepts of Islam. Renowned for their love of justice and dislike of dogmatism, the Bektashi order quickly gained the respect of the Turkish people. An Ottoman Prince attributed many of his victories to the presence in his army of Haji Bektash. He built for him a monastery (*Tekke*) and college, and sought his approval and blessing on every undertaking. And when Sultan Murad formed the elite military units known as Janissaries from Christian children of the Balkans, Haji Bektash was asked to bestow his blessing upon them. Haji Bektash declared, "The troop which thou hast formed shall be called Janissary ("New Troops"). Their faces shall be white and shining, their right arms strong, their sabres keen, and their arrows sharp. They shall be fortunate in battle, and shall never leave the field save as victors."

True to the Master's blessing the Janissaries were destined to develop into the "strongest and fiercest instrument of imperial ambition ever devised upon earth." Bektashi *Babas* (celibate spiritual advisors) accompanied the Janissaries as chaplains. Following the decline of the Janissary Corps many Bektashi Sufis fled to the remote areas of the Balkans, gaining a sizeable presence in Albania. The Bektashi order resembles in many ways the Knights Templar, the once powerful order of Christian knights accused by the Roman church of antinomianism and heresy. Both the Bektashi and the Templars preserved occult teachings and served as a link between Islam and Christianity, East and West. And both orders met with persecution from the combined forces of church and state.

The purpose of this chapter is to present a simple introduction to a side of Islam rarely discussed and offer a little light to those readers sincerely seeking the Secret Path. At a time of growing religious intolerance and when certain forces are furthering a divide between Christians and Muslims, it is important to highlight the inner dimension of religion. In closing I would like to quote from a booklet issued by the secretive and elusive 'Darul Hikmet' over fifteen years ago. The student must grasp one very important point to do with the presentation of the Teachings of the Ancient Secret Tradition. We have no hesitation in utilising different and often times quite varied forms in setting forth certain concepts. Forms differ from people to people, faith to faith, culture to culture, but they are only different expressions of the same thing. One superficial reader may see in our writings an emphasis on Christian terms, while another sees in us a purely Islamic position, while a third person may see our arguments sacrilegious altogether.

One may see us the most conservative while another will declare us ultra radical and libertine. They have not seen the total picture. What we are aiming at is the presentation of the Truth beyond the form. Truth is one and is the same for all who have attained to its understanding by whatever way. At this table assemble the inner circle of humanity each having passed through the forms of all the celestial religions. "Words cannot be used in referring to religious truth, except as analogy" wrote Hakim Sanai. Whenever "Islam" is mentioned, we need to keep in mind that the word designates the religion of over one billion people, a religion that has been flourishing in much of Asia, Europe, and Africa for well over a thousand years and more recently in North America. We also need to remember that it is difficult to generalize about any religion. In this particular case, specialists have largely given up the old Orientalist habit of talking about Islam as if it were a single, clearly identifiable entity. They readily admit that we are in fact dealing with a multiplicity of phenomena, or, if you prefer, many Islam. In other words, to assert without qualification that "Islam believes this," or "Muslims do that," is misleading to say the least.

The fact that specialists are wary of generalizations in no way hinders the mistaken perception of most people in the West that there is a clearly defined something out there called "Islam." Politicians, ideologues, and the media constantly talk about Islam as if it were one, simple phenomenon, and it is obvious that they do so with their own agendas. If, however, we have any interest in understanding the relationship between current events and the Islamic tradition, we should never forget that Muslims have histories, cultural divergences, and differences in belief and practice every bit as complex as those of Christians. The fact that I am talking not about "Islam" but about "Islamic mysticism" does not make the task any easier. The first problem arises because of the English word mysticism.

Webster's Third provides three definitions. Most people nowadays, especially in the academic community, seem to understand the word in terms of the third of these, which is "vague speculation, belief without foundation." Mysticism commonly signifies mystification, madness, or mindless mush. The average hard-nosed American would likely agree with Bertrand Russell, who famously wrote a book called Mysticism and Logic. His point: You cannot be a mystic and a rational person at one and the same time. Webster's gives the first meaning as "the experience of mystical union or direct communion with ultimate reality." Putting aside "mystical union," which begs the question, we are left with "the experience of direct communion with ultimate reality." Surely those who have any sympathy with religion would agree that religion, without some sort of communion with ultimate reality, would have nothing to distinguish it from a merely human construction. It would be an ideology, or a political agenda, or an illusion.

If we do take mysticism in the first meaning of the word, then it points to the origin of religion, the founding moment that is often called "revelation." What is it that drives a prophet, an avatar, or a Buddha, if not the experience of direct communion with ultimate reality? The word mysticism in this sense also points to the goal of religion. Why does one engage in religious practice if one is not convinced that some sort of direct communion with ultimate reality is possible, if not in this life, then in the next? In short, "mysticism," as I would prefer to understand it, stresses the fact that many religious people have been seriously and intimately engaged with ultimate reality, or, at the very least, that they have been engaged with a quest for communion with that reality. In this sense, the word does not imply "vague speculation" or "belief without foundation" unless, of course, one takes the position- common enough these days-that there is no such thing as "ultimate reality."

If that is one's belief, then the quest to achieve communion with a nonexistent entity is certainly stupid and misguided. Indeed, the "enlightened" position of the modern intellectual is often that of Freud: religion is a neurosis or a delusion. If you are religious, you are in fact mad. So, unless we take our stand in atheism or agnosticism, we should agree that religion in any meaningful sense of the word has by definition something "mystical" about it. The experience of communion with ultimate reality lies at the foundation of religion, and the quest for such communion has always motivated the practice of religious people. Let me now turn to mysticism in the context of Islam. Anyone who surveys the literature on Islamic civilization will quickly discover that a great deal has been written on the topic. Scholars have defined and described Islamic mysticism in many ways.

Some of the earlier Orientalists went to great lengths in order to show that mysticism was alien to a harsh and sterile religion of the desert-that is, to Islam as they imagined it to be. They wanted to prove that any discussion of mystical topics in Islamic texts in fact derives from outside sources, such as Christianity, Zoroastrianism, Manichaeism, Buddhism, or Hinduism. It is worth noting that modern-day "Islamism"—that is, ideological posturing and political activism in the name of Islam —agrees with the early Orientalists on the origins of Islamic mysticism. Despite the fact that the Islamists are harshly critical of Western scholarship, they adopt many of its positions. They love Western technological expertise along with its guns and bombs, and they also love the various political theories that justify totalitarian control. By claiming that mysticism derives from outside sources, they embrace the Orientalist myth of a harsh and sterile Islam and ignore the spiritual and intellectual heritage of their religion. They have focused all their efforts on turning people away from the Islamic tradition and establishing authoritarian regimes.

In my own writings, I have always avoided the word "mysticism," partly because of its strong negative connotations. I prefer instead the word "Sufism," which has the advantage of deriving from Arabic and pertaining specifically to Islam. Nowadays, this word is rather well known in the West. In the United States, Rumi has recently been the best-selling poet, and every introduction to his poems points out his affiliation to the Sufi tradition. Health clubs and New Age centers teach "Sufi dancing" along with yoga and Zen meditation. At least the name is no longer strange in

English, even if, in contrast to "mysticism," few people have any real idea as to what it might mean. One of the problems with "mysticism" is that there is no corresponding word in the pre-modern Islamic languages.

The modern usage of the word has everything to do with the history of the Christian tradition, but we should not ignore the fact that there are many basic differences of outlook between Christianity and Islam, not least in the case of "mysticism." We have a similar problem with the word "theology," which designates a discipline that has always played a central role in Christianity. Many historians have assumed that the Islamic discipline known as kalâm—a word that might better be translated as "dogmatic theology"—plays an exactly analogous role. In fact, kalâm's role in Islam has been much more limited than that of theology in Christianity. In the same way, Sufism has had a much more pervasive presence in the Islamic tradition than has mysticism in Christian civilization. It is true that there are many parallels between Sufism and various teachings and practices associated with mysticism.

Nonetheless, much that happens under the name of Sufism in the Islamic world would not be placed in the category of mysticism in the West. For example, the vast majority of people who have engaged in the practice of Sufism would not be "mystics" in the current sense of this word. A mystic is typically understood as someone who undergoes supra-normal or perhaps "extrasensory" experiences. In contrast, most so-called "Sufis" are ordinary Muslims who happen to be more serious about the practice of their religion than others. What then is Sufism? There is no simple answer. It is certainly not a sect within Islam. It has nothing to do with the two major denominations, Sunnism and Shi'ism, since it has been found in both from earliest times. Both men and women and women engage in Sufi practice, and it is common for some members of a single family to be Sufis, and for others not to be.

A husband may be a Sufi, while his wife may not, or vice versa. Certainly, not every Muslim is a Sufi, but Sufism has been present wherever there have been sizable Muslim populations. This is especially obvious from about the 13th century, when clearly defined institutions associated with the word came to be established. It is, in short, extremely difficult if not impossible to draw a clear distinction between Sufis and other Muslims. Even if we take an anthropological perspective and say that a Sufi is someone who says that he is a Sufi, we may find that for historical or political reasons the word itself is not employed by people who would be called Sufis by most other definitions of the term. The original Arabic word, sûfî ("one who wears wool"), does not offer much help in clarifying the meaning, since it simply suggests that some early Muslims had an ascetic tendency. In fact the word has been controversial since it first came to be used in the eighth century (the second century of Islam).

Moreover, many other words have also been used to designate the same teachings and practices, such as "poverty" (faqr) and "gnosis" (ma`rifa). Historically, it is not at all clear why Sufism rather than some other word should have become the general designation. Instead of trying to provide an exact definition, it seems best simply to say that Sufism is a specific approach to Islamic learning and practice that has been found among Muslims everywhere. Having said that, few characteristics that differentiate the Sufi approach from other approaches. It should be kept in mind, however, that I am generalizing. I am talking about family resemblances in a host of phenomena. My remarks will not necessarily apply to any given historical or cultural situation.

We need to begin by looking in broad outline at the teachings established by the Quran (the book received from God by Muhammad) and the Sunnah (the practices and sayings of Muhammad). As soon as we do so, we can see that, like any great religion, Islam addresses three primary domains of human concern. These can be called body, mind, and spirit; or doing, knowing, and being. The body is the realm of activity, ritual observance, and social relationships. The mind is the realm of perceiving, believing, knowing, and understanding. The spirit is the realm of the deepest awareness of self and of direct communion with ultimate reality, which is God, or true and real being. The Quran is perhaps unique among the world's scriptures in the degree to which it stresses the importance of knowledge and understanding. Many sayings of Muhammad confirm the importance of knowing things correctly. Because of this stress on knowledge, Islamic civilization has been marked by a high level of learning and scholarship. From the beginning it was an enormously bookish culture.

This is one of the main points of the classic study by the great Orientalist Franz Rosenthal of Yale: Knowledge Triumphant: The Concept of Knowledge in Medieval Islam. As Islamic civilization developed, many Muslims devoted themselves to the pursuit of knowledge. These Muslims were not priests or ministers, since Islam has no priestly class. They were simply people who took seriously the various Quranic and prophetic injunctions to seek knowledge, such as Muhammad's saying, "The search for knowledge is incumbent upon every Muslim, male and female." Because of the devotion to knowledge and understanding, Muslims came to study and assimilate the sacred lore that was set down by the Quran and the Prophet with more and more attention to analysis, explanation, and systematization. Some people were interested in learning everything that there is to know about the proper way of dealing with the body—that is, personal, social, and ritual activities. What exactly does the Quran command people to do? How exactly did Muhammad put the Quranic commandments into practice? How does one perform the so-called "five pillars" of the religion—uttering the declaration of faith, performing the daily prayers, paying the alms-tax, fasting in the month of Ramadan, and making the pilgrimage to Mecca? What is the correct way to go to the toilet, to wash oneself, to eat one's meals? What are the proper rules for interpersonal activities, marriage, inheritance, trade?

The moment one takes seriously the Quranic revelation and its embodiment in the Prophet, all these questions need to be asked and answered. But, notice that all of them are connected with proper activity. They focus on what the body does. Other Muslims were much more concerned with how to understand the objects of faith, which the Quran designates as God, the angels, the scriptures, the prophets, the Last Day, and divine providence. Muslims who focused on understanding these objects held that a person's faith depends upon knowledge. The claim of an ignorant person to believe in God is simply ignorance. No one can believe in God without knowing who God is and what his reality entails. By the same token, no one can claim to believe in the other objects of faith without knowledge. What exactly are "angels" that Muslims should have faith in them? What exactly are prophets, scriptures, and the Last Day? Having faith in any of these depends upon knowledge, and achieving sound knowledge of such realities is not easy.

All those who want to achieve adequate understanding in Islamic terms must dedicate themselves to the study of God's self-revelation in both the Quran and in the words of the Prophet. Learning and knowledge are essential. Still other groups of Muslims focused their attention not primarily on activity or understanding, but on developing the love, generosity, nobility, justice, and sincerity that are commanded by the Quran and typified by Muhammad's relationship with God and with other people. For these Muslims, the basic question was this: "How can one become a good person?" How can one develop all the beautiful character traits and virtues that were found in Muhammad and the other prophets of God and in God's special friends? One might ask why most Muslim scholars became specialists in one of these domains rather than attempting to encompass all three.

First of all, generally they did try to encompass all three domains, but actually doing so was beyond the capacity of most, though there are many exceptions. Scholars usually ended up being a lot more informed about one of these domains than the other two. Specialization, after all, is a general characteristic of all those who want to know something completely and thoroughly. Each of the three domains of Islamic knowledge—proper human activity, correct understanding of God and the world, and the actualization of virtue and goodness—can be unpacked and analyzed without end. There is a second reason for specialization that is perhaps even more telling: People have natural aptitudes, personal inclinations, and mental limitations. The fact that someone may have a gift for football and this does not mean that he will necessarily be good at mathematics, or painting, or music.

The fact that someone may have a great aptitude for understanding religious law—for deriving proper rules and regulations from revealed injunctions and principles—does not in any way imply that he will also have an aptitude for theology, or that he will necessarily attempt to become a better and more virtuous person. What I am saying is that from the very beginning of Islam, being a Muslim meant recognizing that the Quran and Muhammad provided the basic guidelines for bringing the body, the soul, and the spirit into conformity with the divine purpose in creating the world. However, people differed among themselves as to which guidelines were the most important and how they should put into practice. Some Muslims were naturally inclined to place their first priority in the body, others felt that they should focus their attention on the mind and expand their understanding of God and his creation, and still others held that the whole point of human existence was to harness the body and the mind in order to strengthen the spirit and to achieve communion with ultimate reality.

Specialization in Islamic learning did not become obvious

until about the ninth century (the third Islamic century). Before that time, most scholars were interested more in transmitting all the lore received from God and Muhammad, often classified according to category. Little by little, however, scholars who dedicated most of their efforts to providing the guidelines for proper activity came to be known as "jurists" (fuqahâ'). They busied themselves with understanding the principles and rules of proper Islamic activity on the basis of the Quran, the sayings and activity of the Prophet, the opinions of the Prophet's companions, and the views of learned Muslims of earlier generations. Scholars who focused on understanding the objects of faith became differentiated into several schools of thought. The dogmatic theologians (the authorities in kalâm) said that the best way to understand God is by rational interpretation of the Quran. The philosophers (falâsifa) held that human reason is a sufficient guide to the truth of things and that divine revelation may not be indispensable for understanding that truth.

The Sufis maintained that the best and most reliable path to correct understanding was by direct communion with God. Scholars associated with Sufism developed a distinctive methodology. With good reason, their approach has often been called "mystical." Webster's second definition of mysticism tells us that it can mean "the doctrine or belief that direct knowledge of God, of spiritual truth, or ultimate reality. . . is attainable through immediate intuition, insight, or illumination and in a way differing from ordinary sense perception or ratiocination." This doctrine is certainly characteristic of the Sufi approach to understanding God and the world. However, they held that this direct knowledge —which they typically called "unveiling" (kashf)—must be rooted in the Quran and the Sunnah of Muhammad.

Many of them also had a good deal of respect for the various rational approaches to knowledge. They maintained, however, that despite the opinions of the philosophers, reason alone is not sufficient to attain knowledge of God, and despite the opinions of the theologians, a merely rational understanding of the Quran is also inadequate. In short, Muslim scholars who focused their energies on understanding the normative guidelines for the body came to be known as jurists, and those who held that the most important task was to train the mind in achieving correct understanding came to be divided into three main schools of thought-theology, philosophy, and Sufism. This leaves us with the third domain of human existence, the spirit. Most Muslims who devoted their major efforts to developing the spiritual dimensions of the human person came to be known as Sufis. They taught that people must attune their intentions, their love, and their sincerity to the divine will. Those who came to be recognized as having achieved this goal became the Sufi teachers.

In effect, they functioned as spiritual therapists and depth psychologists for the Muslim populations. But, unlike modern psychologists, they were not interested in pathology but rather in healthy and sound human souls who needed assistance in achieving communion with ultimate reality. One way to understand Sufism and the manner in which it has been differentiated from other approaches to Islamic learning is to look at the Sufi understanding of the human role in creation. Like Jews and Christians, Muslims in general believe that human beings were created in the image of God. Islam does not have a concept of original sin, but Muslims do maintain that Adam slipped and fell from the Garden because he was forgetful of God. Forgetfulness is the general failing of all of his children. It clouds the original brightness of the human soul, made in the divine image.

Nonetheless, human beings have the potential to become brilliant mirrors reflecting the divine reality. They can do so if they follow the guidance of a prophet, Muhammad in particular. The proper role of human beings in the universe is to actualize the divine image and become God's representatives on earth. People can do so by "submitting" and "surrendering" to God (Islam) and by acting as God's "servants" (abd). Once they become perfect servants, God may then choose to make them his "vicegerents" (khalîfa). The jurists defined service of God and submission to him in terms of proper activity. The theologians, philosophers, and Sufis held that proper activity depends upon right understanding of God and the world. The Sufis added, however, that proper activity and correct beliefs must be perfected and completed by direct communion with God. Only such communion can actualize the divine qualities latent in the soul and bring about the appropriate manifestation of these qualities in society and the world.

The qualities that define the human image of God are much discussed by Muslim scholars and theologians. They are commonly called the "most beautiful names of God" and are typically said to number ninety-nine. They include knowledge, awareness, power, speech, creativity, compassion, love, justice, forgiveness, generosity, and so on. According to the Sufi teachers, people must actualize these divine qualities in themselves by serving God with their bodies, knowing him with their minds, and loving him in their spirits. In the pursuit of knowledge, Muslim jurists wanted to discover the right way to perform every activity. Theologians tried to prove rationally the correctness of the Quranic teachings about God, the prophets, and the Last Day. Philosophers strove to develop their minds and actualize intelligence and virtue with the help of methods and tools largely derived from the Greek tradition.

Sufis maintained that the only reliable way to actualize the self, gain awareness of God, and become a good person was to subordinate rational thought to prophetic guidance and to find God's names and qualities within one's own spirit. The Sufis took Muhammad as their model. He gained knowledge and self-realization not by studying books or by going to school, but by devoting himself to God. Once he had done so, God taught him the Quran. Of course, the Sufis all agreed that Muhammad is the last prophet. They were not striving to receive new revealed books, but rather to actualize their understanding of what they considered the final and most perfect revealed book, that is, the Quran. The Sufis saw the Prophet's career as marked by two grand events: the descent of the Quran, and the ascent of Muhammad to God. Muhammad's career as a prophet began when God sent the Quran down upon him by means of the angel Gabriel. When Muhammad had fully submitted himself to the revealed message, Gabriel took him up to meet God in a journey known as al-mi'râj ("the ladder").

Muhammad's ascent to God is referred to allusively in two passages of the Quran (17:1, 53:1 ff.). The details come down to us through Muhammad's accounts told to his companions. In brief, Gabriel came to Muhammad one night and took him in a flash to Jerusalem. In Jerusalem, at the spot that is now marked by the Dome of the Rock, Muhammad met all 124,000 prophets from the time of Adam down to Jesus and led them in prayer. Gabriel then took Muhammad up through the celestial spheres, in each of which he visited one of the prophets and various angels. He was also given a tour of hell and paradise. Finally, Gabriel could lead him no further, so Muhammad had to ascend on his own to meet God. After coming back to Mecca, Muhammad told his companions about his journey. They asked him if he had brought them anything from God. He replied that he had, and then instructed them in the performance of the five daily prayers, which God had sent for the community.

Hence the daily prayers, which are the most basic of all Muslim rites, are closely associated with the journey to God. When the companions asked the Prophet if they also could travel to God, he replied, "The daily prayer is the ladder of the believer" (al-salât mi`râj al-mu'min). In other words, it is the daily prayer that establishes "direct communion with God," whether or not the believer is aware of God's presence.

The Quran says, after all, that God "is with you wherever you are" (57:4). It is through the prayer that people can come to experience and realize their intimate connection with the divine. It is obvious that the descent of the Quran to Muhammad is the founding event of Islam, but it is not so obvious that Muhammad's ascent to God is the culmination of the Quran's descent. By sending down the Quran, ultimate reality communicated with human beings, but the meaning of that communication does not become clear until we understand that its concrete fruit was Muhammad's ascent to God.

By taking the initiative and sending the Quran by means of Gabriel, God communicated with human beings and established the means of achieving communion with him. By ascending to God with Gabriel's guidance, Muhammad demonstrated the ultimate nature of that communion, which is accessible to all human beings in the depths of their spirit and after death. Just as the descent of the Quran from God demonstrates to Muslims the divine origin of the book and the truth of the message, so also Muhammad's ascent to God verifies the goal of the message and shows the fruit of putting its guidelines into practice. The Quran descended so that people can ascend. By submitting to the Quranic message and following Muhammad, people can achieve their proper status in creation, which is to be simultaneously God's servants and his vicegerents.

Among the various approaches that Muslims took to their religion, the Sufi approach was most concerned with imitating Muhammad by ascending to God in this life. Other Muslims maintained that the meeting with God promised in the Quran was reserved for the afterworld. In general, the Sufis criticized the juridical approach because of the all too common idea that correct bodily activity is sufficient to make someone a good Muslim. They criticized the theological and philosophical approaches whenever these implied that one can understand God and the world adequately by the mere exercise of the rational mind. They held that the best way to understand God, the world, and oneself was to search for God in one's own spirit. To do so, one had to empty oneself of illusions and to make room for God in the heart. Egotism, pride, and worldly ambition obscure the divine image. One must "polish the mirror of the heart" by overcoming one's own desires and making way for God's desires. One does so not by conforming to the expectations of family and society or by becoming learned, but by following the dictates of God and his Messenger with full sincerity and total love.

Sufis were differentiated from ordinary Muslims not so much by what they did, but rather by their single-minded dedication to actualizing their spirits and living in the presence of God. One of the most characteristic methods they employed in the attempt to keep God constantly in mind is known as "the remembrance of God" (dhikr Allâh). They held that anyone who can forget himself and remember God will overcome the forgetfulness inherited from Adam. Then one will be given access to spiritual reality and real being, just as Muhammad was given access to them. The actual practice of dhikr or "remembrance"—a word that also means "mention" —takes diverse forms. The Quran refers to itself as dhikr and it commands people to remember God by reciting its verses. Many Muslims, Sufis included, placed great emphasis on regular recitation of the holy book. The Quran also calls the daily prayer by the name dhikr, and this is another reason for the central importance of the prayer for all Muslims. Several Quranic verses specifically command the believers to remember and mention God's name.

Many formulae for remembering God's name are in fact employed on a daily basis in Islamic languages. For example, the phrase al-hamdu Lillâh, "Praise belongs to God," is typically recited to show gratitude after meals and on other occasions. The Sufi teachers made the remembrance of God a methodical practice. They had many Quranic verses and sayings of the Prophet to support their position. Among these is Muhammad's advice to a companion who asked him how he could worship God while working in the fields: "Keep your tongue moist with the remembrance of God." As the Islam tradition expanded and developed a variety of techniques and methods were employed to focus the mind and spirit on God. One of these was listening to the recitation of appropriate poetry, often accompanied by music. By the ninth century, music and various forms of rhythmic bodily movement were being employed to aid concentration on God's name. Many Sufi teachers, however, felt that the ecstatic states that music sometimes induced could become an end in themselves.

Too many people were concentrating on their own pleasure rather than on pleasing God. Such teachers forbade their disciples from listening to music. Other teachers felt that the advantages of listening to music outweighed the disadvantages. One form of listening to music was codified by the followers of Rumi. It is this that came to be known in the West as "the dance of the whirling dervishes." Even among Rumi's followers, however, this dance has played a relatively minor role. This then is an extremely brief account of the Sufi approach to Islamic teachings and practices. It needs to be kept in mind that in Islamic history, Sufism came to be associated with many thousands of teachers, numerous institutions, and a vast literature. On the level of historical actuality we find tremendous variety, local understandings, individual preferences, and a great deal of disagreement as to appropriate practices, beliefs, and methods of realization. Nonetheless, if we want to say that there is a common thread tying all of this together, we will not be far from the mark if we call it "the quest for direct communion with ultimate reality."

Islam is a great spiritual tradition that has much more in common with Judaism and Christianity than most Westerners realize. Among other things, Muslims worship the same God as Christians and Jews (Allah is Arabic for "the God") and revere many of the same patriarchs and prophets, including Abraham, Noah, Moses, Jacob, John the Baptist, and Jesus and his mother, Mary, whom Islam holds in special regard. Indeed, Islam counts Abraham as its patriarch, as well as the father of the Arab people, and so all three traditions are called "Abrahamic." Muslims view their religion accordingly as the third and final installment in the scriptural revelation that began with the Hebrew Bible and the Gospels of the New Testament. They believe that the Quran was sent by God to the Prophet Muhammad to correct misconceptions that had crept into the previous religions. Even the Muslim conception of God who is present in history, and who intervenes to shape the course of events is also at the heart of both Judaism and Christianity.

And yet few non-Muslims are aware of the close historical and theological ties among these three monotheistic traditions, or are conversant with even the most basic teachings and principles of Islam. As a result, misconceptions abound not only about Islam but also about the more than one billion Muslims throughout the world who practice this religion. As an example, Islam is no longer primarily the Middle Eastern religion it is perceived to be, since only about 20 percent of the world's Muslims live in the Middle East or are Arabs; the majority are found in Indonesia and South Asia. There are now about seven million Muslims living in the U.S.-roughly the same as the number of American Jews and somewhat more than either Presbyterians or Episcopalians. Because of the political conflict that has set the Middle East against Europe and America, and because of the militant actions of certain Muslim extremists, some Westerners view Islam as a warlike religion-a view that is completely at odds with the basic tenets of Islam, and even with the word "Islam" itself, which in Arabic can mean both "surrender" and "peace."

In the Quran, which Muslims believe consists entirely of the word of God, as revealed to the Prophet Muhammad by the angel Gabriel; Allah plainly announces the concept of a continuum of revelation. Speaking in Arabic, He uses both the first and third person, and sometimes, as in this passage, the royal plural:

> We have sent revelations to you (Muhammad) as we sent revelations to Noah and the prophets (who came) after him; and we sent revelations to Abraham and Ishmael and Isaac and Jacob, and their offspring... and to Jonah and Aaron and Solomon, and to David we gave the Book of Psalms... Then in their train we sent our apostles, and succeeding them Jesus, son of Mary, and gave him the Gospel, and put into the hearts of his followers compassion and kindness.

Muslims believe that God revealed the same message anew to successive prophets with the aim of reforming a wandering humanity, but that each message was gradually distorted by the people who received it. Muhammad saw himself in the tradition of the Hebrew prophets, and the revelation that he conveyed does include elements that would sound familiar to most Christians: the Last Day, the Resurrection of the Dead, Final Judgment, the rewards of Paradise and the punishments of Hell, and the Second Coming of Jesus. Muhammad himself proclaimed that the Virgin Mary, the Mother of Jesus, is "the highest of the women of the people of Paradise," and the Quran affirms the doctrine of the Virgin Birth of Jesus.

Islam was born in what is now Saudi Arabia about 600 years after the death of Jesus, in a culture that was lagging behind other parts of the world financially and socially. Tribal warfare, blood feuds, and vendettas made life unstable, especially for anyone who lacked the support of a powerful clan, or extended family. Because of the harsh desert climate, the Arabs had been unable to generate the agricultural abundance that could produce wealth and allow it to progress economically and culturally. When Muhammad was born, idolatry, drunkenness, and the harsh treatment of women, orphans, and the poor threatened to undermine

Arabian society.

The Quran was revealed to Muhammad over a period of 22 years, and apart from its already familiar doctrine of monotheism, it also laid the foundation for a religion that initiated important social reforms. Some scholars believe that Muhammad was as much a social reformer as a mystic and theologian, and perhaps more so. The Quran makes frequent reference to zakat, the requirement to give a fixed portion of one's annual income to the poor, and this became a cornerstone of Islam, along with a special concern for the unprotected, especially orphans and women, who would have difficulty surviving in a tribal society. Addressing the horrendous treatment of women in Arab culture at the time, Muhammad forbade female infanticide and the prostitution of slave-women, and introduced the right of women to inherit a half-share of their father's estate, whereas before they got nothing.

He insisted that married couples have reciprocal duties and rights, and that women should be educated, and limited the number of wives a man may lawfully have to four (although he himself had more). In practice, Muhammad gave something close to equal status to women in the first Muslim community and drew great strength from his first wife, Khadija, during the time he first began receiving his revelation and implementing the basic principles of Islam. (The fact that his treatment of women was not carried on with the same generosity by his followers makes Islam vulnerable to some of the same criticisms as Christianity, because Christ's followers have not always practiced his radical teachings on nonviolence and compassion for others.)

The Five Pillars of Islam

Among other things, Allah revealed to Muhammad what are now known as the Five Pillars of Islam, which every true Muslim must follow. They can be briefly summarized as:

Saying the profession of unity (tashahhud): "There is no god but God, and Muhammad is the Messenger of God." This is the keystone of Islamic belief.

The five-times-daily prayer (salat), performed just before dawn, just after noon, in midafternoon, just after sunset, and after nightfall.

The compulsory annual charity (zakat), traditionally one-fortieth of a person's income and distinct from the duty of giving alms on a spot basis to those in need. Muslim tradition insists that one should never refuse a beggar.

The fast kept from before sunrise to sunset each day for the full lunar month of Ramadan, the ninth month of the Muslim calendar (sawm). Because Muslims follow a lunar calendar, Ramadan moves by 11 days each year, and when it falls during the long summer days it can be a challenging spiritual practice.

The Hajj or pilgrimage to the Kaba in Mecca is expected of every healthy and solvent adult at least once in a lifetime.

Islam is a supremely practical religion that has never embraced celibacy or even a priestly class. The imams who lead Friday prayers at the mosque are generally drawn from the local population, although they are expected to have a thorough knowledge of Islamic law and tradition. Moreover, Islam has no central religious leader equivalent to the Pope or the Dalai Lama to give the definitive ruling on points of religious law or moral action. Those are defined by Muslim scholars based on the Quran and the example of Muhammad's life as contained in traditions known as hadith. Together these sources make up what is known as Sharia, the Holy Law of Islam, which is subject to interpretation by legal scholars. But as with Christianity and Judaism, scholars don't agree on every aspect of Islamic law. And like those other two faiths, interpretations range from extremely conservative (as with Saudi Arabia and the Taliban) to extremely secularized (as in Turkey).

The Life of the Prophet

Muslims revere Abraham as the father of the Arab people through Ishmael, the son born to him by his wife Sarah's Egyptian handmaiden, Hagar. According to the Hebrew Bible, Hagar and Ishmael were forced to leave Abraham after Sarah finally bore him a son of her own, although the Lord did promise Hagar that her son, too, would be the father of a great people. They settled in the Becca Valley, near Mecca in modern-day Saudi Arabia, and according to Muslim tradition Ishmael later rebuilt the Kaba, the black, cube-shaped monument that was a center of worship long before Muhammad was born. Today the Kaba is the focus of the annual Hajj, in which millions of Muslims participate from all over the world.

Muhammad is believed to have been born around the year 571. His father, AbdAllah, died before Muhammad was born, and his mother, Amina, died when he was only six. The boy was taken into the family of his grandfather Abd al-Muttalib, and when he, too, died; Muhammad's Uncle Abu Talib became his guardian. From then until the time of his first marriage at age 25, Muhammad worked the caravans and discussed spiritual beliefs with the Christian monks and gnostic Jewish practitioners who lived in desert caves and remote communities along the caravan routes. Unlettered but gifted with a retentive memory, he learned much about Jewish and Christian scripture and beliefs.

At 25, Muhammad married a wealthy 40-year-old merchant named Khadija, and for the next 15 years managed her caravans and estate. At that time in Arabia, monotheism was one of several belief systems, although not as popular with most desert Arabs as the worship of idols. The Kaba, decorated with hundreds of such idols, was also an important center of pilgrimage and commerce. Muhammad probably already believed in the one God when he began to have visions in his sleep and sought solitude in a cave in

Mount Hira. He was about 40 when, in the month of Ramadan, an angel appeared to him in human form in the cave and commanded, "Recite!" Muhammad replied, "I am not a reciter," perhaps meaning that he could not read, but the angel embraced him and repeated the command three times until he recited as told. As he fled the cave in awe, Muham-mad heard a voice telling him, "You are the Messenger of Allah, and I am Gabriel." As the revelations continued, the angel Gabriel showed Muhammad the ritual ablution with water before worship and the prayer postures that are now part of Muslim practice: standing, inclining, prostrating, and sitting.

Ramadan was already the traditional Arabic month of retreat, but with divine guidance Muhammad instituted the practice of fasting from before sunrise to sunset. Although the new beliefs caught on among Muhammad's immediate family and a circle of friends, many of the members of his own clan opposed his new teaching, fearing it would discourage other Arabs from visiting the Kaba and might reduce their wealth. Sentiments against Muhammad and his radical teachings ran so high that his life was in danger and he was forced to flee Mecca. He took refuge in an oasis to the north now known as Medina, where his teachings were accepted openly and he was able to gather his forces and repel the anti-Muslim Arabs. During the years of warfare ensued, many lives were lost on both sides, but Muhammad emerged victorious and returned to capture Mecca with virtually no bloodshed. Instead of following the Arab custom of slaughtering the defeated parties, Muhammad spared them, and this act of compassion led many to convert to Islam immediately. Following Muhammad's death in 632, Islam began to be spread beyond Arabia. During the seventh and eighth centuries, Muslim armies took the new religion and its culture west across North Africa as far as Spain, and east across Iran and Iraq to India, and, in later years, as far as the Malayan archipelago.

Islam in the Wider World

During the middle Ages, as Western and Northern Europe struggled to recover from the decline and fall of the Roman Empire, Islam often led the way in science and medicine, and Muslim scholars preserved and translated the works of Greek philosophers. Sufism blossomed as a profound mystical tradition within Islam, generating its own great mystics, including poets such as Rumi and Kabir. But after dominating much of the civilized world for more than a thousand years, Islam began to decline in military power, wealth, and cultural significance. The West was evolving a new technology and a new market system based on investment capital that would gradually replace the old agrarian way of life. Over a period of more than three centuries, these developments helped to create an ever greater reliance on democratic and increasingly secular government to help capitalism and industrialism grow.

Aided by advances in science and industrial technology, the West soon outstripped Muslim culture. By the middle of the 18th century, European cultural powers had begun to displace or colonize Muslim countries, beginning with the British in India and the Middle East and the French in North Africa. As the colonizers sought to develop only those aspects of these nations that would serve their own economic interests, they left the Muslim countries weakened and less able to develop the industrial and financial infrastructure of their own that they would need to compete in the modern marketplace. Muslim religious restrictions on lending money at interest have further complicated their ability to catch up with the West. Scholars such as Bernard Lewis have argued that the reversal of fortune of so many Middle Eastern nations-from being part of a dominant culture to being in the shadow of the Christian West-has left Muslims with a profound sense of shock and resentment. This feeling of exploitation, magnified by revulsion at the West's blatantly secular culture, has fueled Muslim rage.

The presence of autocratic rulers and a vast gulf between the oil-rich royal families of Saudi Arabia and the Gulf States and their impoverished populations have also fueled the growth of Muslim fundamentalism. Alongside the more visible war being waged by a network of extremists against the U.S. and other Western powers, Islam is also engaged in a struggle within itself over how to adapt to modern cultural realities without losing its spiritual identity. Many Muslim political leaders who were reluctant to support the American-led assault on Afghanistan, or to lump their condemnation of the Sept. 11 attacks with a condemnation of Palestinian violence, have to contend with large internal fundamentalist movements that could threaten the stability of their own governments.

Especially in the Middle East, Muslim governments vary from monarchy to republic to theocratic republic; apart from Turkey, none of the nations has anything resembling a Western democracy. Of course, a genuinely Western-style democracy might not fit precisely with the Muslim understanding of law, since for Islam; absolute authority must reside not in the public but in God. Yet Islam also was founded on the basis of respect for all individuals within society, including the disadvantaged, and Islamic law does admit some freedom of interpretation and consensus. There would seem to be a viable middle path between absolute theocratic rule-or monarchy or dictatorship—at one end of the spectrum, and all-out secular democracy at the other end. One positive result of this ongoing internal conflict has been the emergence of moderate voices within Islam pushing for long-overdue political and religious reforms.

This is especially true among Muslims living in the West, including many feminist Muslim women, who had previously been reluctant to publicly question the reactionary trend. Many orthodox Muslim authorities in the Middle East did speak out forcefully against the terrorist attacks of Sept. 11, pointing out that Muhammad, who won victory for Islam principally through non-violence, had explicitly forbidden the murder of civilians or even the destruction of property during war. They have emphasized the Quran's statement that in matters of religion, there can never be any compulsion. And yet the Arab street seems to have accepted the use of violence in preserving Islam against Western and Jewish interests, leaving opinion divided.

The Third Way

Solutions to this political-religious dilemma have been hard to come by, yet one of the most promising has been promoted by a Muslim scholar. Farid Esack, a prominent South African Muslim educated in Pakistan and Great Britain, has called for a return to what he labels "Islam's third way." Esack says that Muslims often look to the life of Muhammad to determine whether certain behaviors were sanctioned by the Prophet or by early Muslims. But, he acknowledges, Muslims face a problem in that they have only two theological precedents on which to base their lives: One is the paradigm of a community of oppressed people in Mecca, during the time that Muhammad and his followers were under attack by Arabs opposed to the new religion. And the other is of the Muslim community that took control in Medina, the city where Muhammad fled to build his following in relative safety. What Muslims today don't have, Esack admits, is a model for coexisting peacefully with other religions in a situation of true equality. But there is a third way, according to Esack, which he calls the "Abyssinian paradigm."

He refers to the time when Muhammad sent a group of his followers from Mecca to dwell in Abyssinia, a Christian kingdom to the south, where they lived peacefully for many years-and from which some did not return, even after Muslims were in power in Mecca. "They did not make any attempts to turn Abyssinia into an Islamic state," Esack concludes. "They sent good reports back about the king under whom they were living, and how happy they were living there. This is the third paradigm that Muslims today more than ever need to revive because it is crucial for the sake of human survival and coexistence. Until recently the notion of coexistence and cultural tolerance was pretty controversial for mainstream Islamic thinkers, but I was surprised at a recent Muslim conference to hear more and more people talking about the need to revive this Abyssinian paradigm."

Although, from a Muslim perspective, Islamic beliefs and customs do not need to be defended or explained, non-Muslims find much about the culture perplexing; Western women feel especially threatened by Islamic customs such as veiling and polygamy. And yet there is much to recommend Islam-moderate, tolerant Islam-to the forward-looking Western consciousness. For one thing, Islam is a full-time religion that requires one to focus explicitly on the Divine at least five different times during the day. Its prayer forms are physical-perhaps not as elaborate and health-conscious as yoga or qigong, but they do require standing, kneeling, and prostrating oneself in a way that involves the entire body in worship.

These attributes are similar to those that many Westerners, disenchanted with the relatively mechanistic, once-a-week worship of their birth religions, find attractive in, say, Buddhist mindfulness practice, Hindu mantra, or the Eastern Orthodox prayer of the heart. And the Sufi tradition-which bares much the same relationship to orthodox Islam as mystical Christianity does to mainstream Catholicism or Protestantism-offers even more profound levels of practice to deepen one's experience of Islam. Finally, Islam values compassion for the less fortunate, incorporated into Muslim law as well as custom and tradition, in a way that should recommend it to a Western sensibility. However Islam continues to be viewed by the West, and however successful Muslim moderates are in changing from within Islam's attitudes to the West, one thing is certain. As Islam continues to be the fastest growing religion in the world, non-Muslims will need to establish and maintain an ongoing dialogue with Muslims throughout the world.

The two meanings that its name conveys in Arabic: "surrender" (to God) and "peace." For although Islam was born in battle in the deserts of Arabia, it has a long tradition of peace and accommodation with Judaism and Christianity, the two religions with which Islam has the most in common. Indeed, in the Quran, Allah (whose name in Arabic means simply "the God") identifies Himself as the same divinity who revealed Himself to the Jews and the Christians, whom Muslims still refer to as the "people of the book," because they too had received scripture from God.

2

Sufism

Sufism has come to mean a wide range of beliefs that center on the quest for personal enlightenment in the union with God. Sufis are sometimes described as the mystics of Islam, but Sufism fits awkwardly in the categories of religions. Technically Sufism is a denomination of Islam, however there are many Sufis that are not Muslims and there are many Muslims that are reluctant to consider Sufism part of Islam. One of the few concepts that Sufis seem to agree on is that all religions offer a path to salvation or enlightenment and that true God realization, no matter how it is achieved, transcends the limitations and classification of any religion. Basically, a saint in any religion is equal to a saint in any other religion because they are inspired by the same Divine source. Initially the term Sufi referred only to those who had achieved God realization, but it has since come to be applied to anyone who follows that particular spiritual path. The name Sufi comes from "suf," the Arabic word for wool or "saf," the Persian word for pure. The dervishes or advanced students of Sufism wore inexpensive wool clothes as part of their life of renunciation.

Sufism and Islam

Sufism began as religious teachers in the Middle East came to learn the Truth of Islam directly from Mohammad. Masters who were "ordained" directly by Mohammad founded three major Sufi schools or orders. The most essential mystical knowledge was then passed down from each master to a disciple selected to follow as the leader of the school. Other disciples were sent out as masters to establish new schools. A Sufi school (ashram or convent) is often a community center that may include a residence for the students and master, a school, hospital, orphanage or any number of community services. Some of these services may be very modest and others may be very extensive, but they are often a vital part of the local community. Schools are sometimes set up near the tomb of a Sufi saint in order to maintain the shrine and provide services to pilgrims, including places to retreat and meditate.

While mainstream Islam promotes community service, mosques rarely umbrella such services beyond theological schools since mainstream Islam distinguishes the needs of the spirit from the needs of the body. There is no firm historical source for Sufism. Many of the early orders were considered an integrated part of Islam, but as teachings were codified and the elements of Shi'i and Sunni Islam became more distinct, Sufism emerged with an identity. One of the basic ideas of Sufism is to minimize the self or individual identity. Belonging to a particular group with a unique name is contradictory to this effort. It is said, "a Sufi is one who is not," and with a philosophy that seeks the destruction of self-identity it is thought that Sufi's received their name from outsiders. Initially the term Sufi referred only to those who had achieved God realization, but it has since come to be applied to anyone who follows that particular spiritual path. While Sufism did not exist prior to Islam, Sufi doctrine contains many elements that go beyond the teaching of Mohammad.

Islam is an external structure in which the individual exists while the internal quest for enlightenment belongs to a realm of Sufi knowledge. This knowledge integrates Islam and ancient doctrine that resembles elements of Greek Philosophy, Zoroastrianism and Hinduism that are part of the Sufi path to God-realization. The most sacred knowledge of the Sufi masters is not written and is passed to each generation orally, which makes it somewhat difficult to historically trace the evolution of Sufi doctrine. Nonetheless, it seems reasonable that the Sufi doctrine that differs most from the rest of Islam had its beginnings much earlier (although this is a very non-Muslim view of Sufism). For many years these extra qualities created a great deal of friction between mainstream Islam and the Muslim mystics. After centuries of falling in and out of favor, Sufis became integrated and an important central part of Islamic culture and society. A cornerstone of mysticism is that true knowledge of God is achieved directly and not through an intermediary like a prophet, saint or priest.

Over the centuries this has led to a great deal of political conflict between mystics and non-mystics. If a cleric or Priest behaves or commands something that seems in conflict with dogma, the individual is not in a position to disagree as long as there is no direct relationship between God and the individual. Many Sufi orders encourage honoring Saints and Prophets by visiting them if the are alive or their tombs if they have passed on. Pilgrims often will go to ask for favors in the form of miracles or prosperity. In many communities the pilgrims are people from other religions who come to the tombs in hopes of finding favor or receiving miracles.

The high status afforded saints in communities influenced by Sufism implies an alternative means to communicate with God other than through the Imam, the Islamic clerics. In a fundamentalist Islamic community the highest-ranking Imam is the supreme authority, both politically and religiously, and Sufism presents a potential conflict to this authority that has over the centuries led to persecution of Sufis in several Arab countries. Saudi Arabia and Iran are two countries where the tombs of Sufi saints have been destroyed. In some areas teachings of the Sufi masters are held in high regard practicing Sufism is discouraged or even criminalized.

Sufism Outside of Islam

The difference between Sufis and Islam is sometimes as extreme as the difference between Mormons and Catholics, depending on the particular order. Some Western Sufi orders have even completely divorced themselves from Islam altogether. Yet, Sufism is integrated in Islam. The mystical aspects of Sufism may have ancient influences, but these traditions center on what goes on within a individual. Islam stresses service, virtue, honesty and charity, the essence of Sufism and a foundation that is necessary for the inner spirituality of Sufism. It may seem that either Sufism influenced Islam or the other way around, but there is little surviving recorded history that sheds light on this.

Even when an order does not incorporate Islam for the laws and practice of daily life, there are disciplines and doctrine to the place of Islam. Islam recognizes Abraham, Moses and Jesus, but they credit Mohammad for reintroducing the true religion without contamination. Sufis extend this, believing that all prophets and saints of all religions are inspired by the same source and the rejection of any one is a rejection of the essential Truth behind them all - the one God. That one God is absolute, extending beyond time or space, and all that is within the universe is of God, including good and evil.

Tenants of Sufism

The basic Sufi tenants are slightly different from order to order with some variations, additions and/or subtractions, but generally they include the following.

There is only one God, and that God possesses everything. In some orders God is everything and nothing; all that we can perceive and all that we cannot.

Since God is in your Heart, God is always very close even when humanity is very far from God. Some Sufis believe that since God is in all of us. To truly love God we must love every human and every component of creation, which are considered to be aspects of God.

There are four Holy Scriptures including the Torah, the Psalms of David, the Gospels of Jesus and the Quran (this is aligned with Islam so it may differ in some orders). There are also hundreds of other works revealed by prophets including books by Sufi saints.

Nothing happens without God's will, and Human will is very critical, but it exists within the context of Divine will.

Because of God's will, all things, good and bad, are from God.

Life as we know it is an illusion, and the true life revealed when we reach in the hereafter. Some orders go as far as to describe this process of reality beyond illusion as reincarnation, which is a distinct departure from mainstream Islam.

The Sufi Way

The Sufi Way consists of four stages. The first stage involves learning the morality and ethics of all religion, which is accomplished by studying Islam. Non-Islamic Sufis rely on other religions or the writings of Sufi saints to establish the foundation of morals and ethics. The second stage is the path of Sufism, which is a focus on internal practices in the same way that Islam offers the external practices of law and worship. The first two stages are accomplished through practice and imitation, basically surrendering blindly to rituals.

The third stage is where the aspirant begins to understand the meaning behind the teaching and practices, experiencing God within and the mystical states of Sufism. The fourth stage is *ma'rifah* or gnosis. This is where the knowledge of God is realized and is only achieved by prophets, great masters and saints. The goal of following the Sufi way (or to be devoted to any other religion) is not to become a saint, but rather to align your life with the will of God and to do all that you can to accept and live by God's Grace. Indeed, if your goal *is* to become a saint, it is all but assured that because of your own desires you will never become one.

Sufism in the West

Sufism is much more complex than this description, but each order or school has its own unique departure from the most general concept of Sufism outlined here. There are dozens of Sufi orders in the West. Many represent orders in the East and adhere to Islam. Other Western orders allow non-Muslims to study the path, although the Master is usually a teacher in the direct line that goes back to those who were ordained by Mohammad. There are also a growing number of orders with teachers that are not in that direct line and have broken with Islam altogether. Meher Baba's teachings are non-denominational and most of his followers are not Sufi. Sufism Re-oriented is a group that has embraced Meher Baba's teachings and has published some of his most important books.

The organization has roots with Hazrat Inayat Khan, a Master that came to this country soon after the turn of the century. It should be said that Sufism Reoriented is not considered to be within the mainstream Islamic Sufism movement in the West. Meher Baba's teachings are intended to free Sufism so that those from other religions may embrace it. Meher Baba described all religions like rivers flowing to the ocean. Only the rivers are all dry now as the water is misdirected from the main stream, and the ocean must flood the rivers. In his meditative work Meher Baba may have reoriented all religions towards the ocean of one God, although Sufism is the one in which he offered the most direct guidance through his writing. No matter how it is explained, Sufism and any related movement is a spiritual force that is spreading.

Jesus stated that loving God with all of your heart, soul and mind is the greatest commandment and that the second is loving your neighbor as yourself. In no religion is this held to be more absolute and uncompromising than in Sufism. Every minuscule detail of Sufi doctrine, in virtually all denominations, holds these commandments to be all-important. If in your own heart, through your own beliefs, you can also embrace and live by these commandments of Christ, then your salvation and your union with God are in progress. For those that do not find the alignment and continuity in your own religion to follow these commandments, Sufism may be a place to learn more.

Sufism in Life

Remember, to be a Sufi is to be no more than a student of a school. The Sufi way is one that is accepting (not just tolerant) of all other religions, and some orders welcome non-Muslims while encouraging continued participation in one's own faith. For others, the extraordinary discipline and focus of Islamic life may be an essential component of a new spiritual path. Yet, to be a student is to choose your own commitment to study. Your encounter with Sufism may be no more than reading the works of Sufi Saints and the study of Sufi Philosophy to serve as simple spiritual inspiration. For anyone interested in mysticism, the study of Sufism is an area of riches. Mysticism in many ways provides a bridge between individual religions by exploring the experiences of personal spirituality. A good first encounter with Sufism would be through reading the works of the ancient Sufi poet Rumi, who is currently the best selling poet in this country. Certainly anyone with spiritual interests of any religion will find rewards in an exploration and further understanding of Sufism.

The word, 'Sufi' has been ascribed various origins, among them words meaning 'purity' and 'wisdom.' The Sufi, therefore, is one who has discarded all that does not belong to his innermost self, and who has cultivated the garden of the heart, for there is no other place where wisdom grows. The Sufi sees the Divine Presence reflected in all names and forms, and is limited by none. Knowing that no man-made distinction can contain the One Being, the Sufi offers sincere respect to all forms of worship, while ever striving to be free of dogmatic limitation. The Sufi is one who has two points of view: his own, and that of the other.

The subject of Sufism has been interpreted in various ways in India, Arabia, and other Middle Eastern countries over hundreds of years. This subject is also found in numerous historical documents as well as in contemporary publications, and yet to the question, 'what is Sufism?' there seems to be no precise definition which could satisfy the curiosity of those who, in the disguise of seekers on the spiritual path, are searching only for the key to performing wonders. Sufism is neither a religion nor a cult nor a sect, nor is it only from the East or from the West. Sufism, which means wisdom, has always been and shall always be an open door to Truth; the wise feel sympathy towards all beliefs, while at the same time avoiding speculation upon abstract concepts. Sufism believes in the Divine origin of every form of worship in which the unity of religious ideals is respected.

Sufism, which is without any religious obligations, regards spirituality as the religion of the heart. That religion is one wherein the unity of religious ideals is followed unconditionally in search of truth, without going astray in following the followers of the followers of the great religious reformers, whose messages have been altered beyond recognition through the centuries by those who confuse mysticism with fanaticism. In Sufism there is no place for comparisons or preferences. All Messengers are regarded with the same respect and their messages are worshiped with the same veneration, knowing that Buddha was not a Buddhist, Christ was not a Christian, and Mohammed was not a Mohammedan. They were bringers of new impulses of the Divine Message, which the multitude uses as toys to play with, and impostors use for power games.

Sufism is an attitude of inner sympathy towards all beliefs. All religions are Sufi religions as long as they recognize the limits inherent in any speculative interpretation of Truth. One might say that Sufism is a process leading to the widening of the horizon of the heart, so that Truth may shine within as a brilliant sun, illuminating all that is receptive of its rays of light. Through the ages there has been one religion after another, but each one came as a confirmation of the previous one. Now, in our century and with the development of science and communication, it has become clear that each religion had a special purpose to fulfill at a particular period of human evolution. For the wise, one can only be really attuned to any religion if one's heart is open to all religious beliefs with the same love and understanding for each.

If one took six or seven different glasses, each one of a different colour, and poured water in each glass, the water would appear red in one glass, blue in another, green in a third, and so on, although it were the same water in each. In the same way, all religions are in their origin of divine inspiration, but, like the image of water poured into different coloured glasses, as soon as divine inspiration is crystallized in human thought, it acquires the colour of that thinking. We then call the one colour Hinduism, another colour Buddhism, another Islam and still other colours are called Judaism, Christianity, or by any other religious denomination.

Therefore, since the origin of all religions is of divine nature, these can only be understood inasmuch as one is prepared to recognize the unity of all religious ideals, at which level all religions are so many derivations of one and the same impulse, the cry of the heart, the longing of the soul for God. Wisdom might reveal itself in the guise of a recognizable form, although wisdom is not tangible, nor does it have a form of its own. Examples of wisdom might perhaps be described, although wisdom cannot be defined in words. Furthermore, there are just as many expressions of wisdom as there are seekers of wisdom. Yet, for the one who is really wise, there is only one wisdom but many different ways of understanding that one wisdom, and different forms of expression through which the one and only wisdom is recognized by the wise.

Wisdom takes it for granted that some very specific dogmas must have made much sense at the time that they were preached, but these don't necessarily apply any more in our world today, where science has taken over the responsibility of such subjects as health and education, which were originally once part of the basic structures of ancient religion. The word Sufi means wisdom, but that does not mean that when pursuing the Sufi path one is necessarily wise. Sufism is a test with which one is constantly confronted, when expected to show an example of how well one understands what spirituality truly is.

Spirituality does not mean drifting away upon the clouds of illusion; it means having the feet firmly on the ground of reality, proving thereby, without pretence to have acquired discipline over the physical and mental energies. It is only then that one can possibly inspire others on the path where honesty in spirituality is the watchword. A Sufi is a religious soul whose nature is to refuse to submit to imposed beliefs, and who is conscious that life is not necessarily just what one might think it to be, nor what one is told it to be. Life is not only lived at the level of physical experience, nor only at the level of thought, nor only at the level of feeling, but also, and most importantly, at a still higher level of consciousness, where the self is no more the barrier separating reality from illusion.

On the path of spirituality, one ventures to vanquish one's own faults rather than to judge others, whose faults are not very different to one's own. One tries to master one's own feelings rather than misinterpreting those of others, and one treasures even the smallest sign of appreciation coming from those who are dependant upon one's sympathy. At this level of consciousness, there are neither limitations nor opposites, nor is there any relationship with pre-conceived ideas, such as those expressed in all dogmatic religious interpretations of Truth. When trying to explain God one only fashions an individual concept, limited to the size of ones thoughts. Perhaps one might discover someday what it really means to have inner security, when seeing that all things only have just as much importance as one attaches to them.

Nothing is important and yet everything is important, but that which seems so important to oneself does not always seem important to others. The Sufi will always remain free from judging others and from specifying what is good and what is bad. For the Sufi, good and bad are concepts that can only be discerned within one's own conscience. As soon as one attempts to define abstract concepts, one is taken away into the labyrinth of one's own thoughts that soon break down into speculative descriptions from which one constructs dogmatic ideas; these are then added to the many preconceived ideas picked up through one's education, together with the numerous impressions and influences which constitute our mind world. Then, when one tries to express one's beliefs and understandings, the words tend to deviate from the original ideas, which were themselves only arbitrary concepts, and the result of all this is so often presented as being the one and only truth.

The Sufi Message is a message of, 'Spiritual Liberty,' revealing in its essence, the true nature of spirituality as being the liberation from dogmas and preconceived ideas. And in its call for "Unity of spiritual Ideals, the Sufi message offers a source of inspiration, reaching far beyond such feelings as 'my religion' as opposed to 'your religion,' because there is only one religion and several interpretations of the one Truth. Let us unite as brothers and sisters without any pretension, with the great ideal of bringing happiness to a world where illusion reigns regrettably in full authority, over the freedom of spiritual awakening. The religion of our time is destined to be the religion of the heart, and since there are many hearts, there are obviously many religions, although all religions spring forth from one and the same heart, the temple of God, wherein, when wisdom prevails, love harmony and beauty together constitute the living altar.

The Origin and Essence of Man

Man is the mystery of God. For a mysterious purpose, man was outwardly created of clay and God breathed life into him, and all of the angels were commanded to prostrate themselves before him. As the Quran, which we believe is the highest form of revelation, declares:

"And remember when thy Lord said unto the angels: Lo I am creating a mortal out of potter's clay. So when I have made him and shaped him and have breathed into him of My Spirit, do ye fall down prostrating yourself unto him."

It is this Divine Spirit which is the essence of man. The body is merely the outward physical form which contains the Divine spark. The body is made of the material elements fire, earth, air and water, and has five external senses - sight, hearing, smell, taste and touch; and five internal faculties - discursive thinking, imagination, doubting, memory and longing. All these powers, that is, both the external senses and the internal faculties, serve the heart. By the 'heart' we do not mean the physical organ which pumps the blood, and which is possessed by both man and animals. Rather by 'heart' we mean the Divine spark which distinguishes man from the animals. And unlike the physical heart which dies and decomposes with the rest of the physical body, the Divine spark or heart is indivisible and transcends death because its origin is in the spiritual world.

The position of man in the universe is most important. Man is the microcosm, that is, a miniature universe. As such, he comprises in his outward or physical aspect all the elements found in the universe. In his inner aspect, he contains the potential qualities of all creation from the lowest to the highest, that is, animal, satanic and angelic. He shares the qualities of lust and selfishness with the pigs; the qualities of jealousy and anger with the dogs; his cunning and deceit with Satan; his power and his spiritual light with the angels. But, what is more important, through love and devotion to God he can rise even higher than the angels, for he is the mystery of God before whom the angels were commanded to fall in prostration. He was given command over the whole universe.

The Quran declares:

"It is God who created the heavens and the earth and sent down out of heaven water, wherewith He brought forth fruits to be your sustenance, and He subjected to you the ships to run upon the sea at His commandment, and He subjected to you the rivers, and He subjected to you the sun and moon constant upon their courses, and He subjected to you the night and the day and gave you all you asked Him." But although the universe was created for the service of man, man was created for the service of God and *for that purpose alone*. To the extent that he deviates from that purpose, he becomes unworthy of Divine guidance and favour. Consequently, he is left to his own devices with all his enormous powers, which, under the influence of his animal and satanic qualities, are capable of dragging him to the lowest of the low.

Sufism helps man to be increasingly aware of his purpose of life - namely, unfailing service to his Lord and Creator. It is a path travelled under the guidance of a Sufi master, who is able to deliver man from the narrow confines of the material world into the limitless reality of a spiritual life, wherein he can experience the Divine spark which eternally shines within him. It is most important to understand that material man acquires his knowledge generally through the five external senses and five inner faculties of which we spoke earlier. The spiritual man, on the other hand, has, in addition to these, a number of other means of acquiring knowledge, such as prophetic dreams and inspirations from beyond the material world. To the extent that a man adheres to the truth in his waking state, his dreams too disclose a similar degree of certainty. The Prophet (pbuh) expressed this in the saying: "The more truthful a man, the more prophetic his dreams." Although knowledge through dreams comes in a state of sleep, insights through inspirations are gained in a state of wakefulness. The shaykh, or the Sufi teacher, interprets the dreams of a disciple, helps him to understand his inspirations, and resolves his doubts and uncertainties.

The Spiritual Mentor (Shaykh)

The disciple's need to have a shaykh is inevitable. If a man does not have a shaykh, Satan becomes his shaykh and lures him back into the temptation of his ego and finally destroys him in confusion and error. A disciple keeps unwavering faith in the words of his shaykh and receives infinite love and care from him. The relationship is strictly based on the pattern of the Prophet's (pbuh) relations with his companions which enjoyed Divine support. To quote the Quran:

"Now there has come to you a messenger from among yourselves. Grievous to him is your suffering; anxious is he over you, gentle to the believers, compassionate."

The Quranic Roots of Sufism

Sufism really has its roots in the Quran itself and in the religious experience of the Prophet Muhammad (pbuh). The preliminary signs of revelation were given to the Prophet (pbuh) in the form of visions and the Prophet (pbuh) deliberately sought solitude until the book of his heart, which was pure and unspoiled by schoolmen, was opened and the Divine Pen engraved upon it the revelation, the Quran. The Sufi's knowledge of God comes from the Quran directly. And in spite of the Sufi's proximity to God, the undisputed basis of their direct experience of God has always been the Quran. The Quran contains instructions suitable to man with varying levels of spirituality. It satisfies those who are content with merely exoteric practices, but also contains the deepest and most profound esoteric meaning for those who desire a closer, more mystical relationship with God.

The Quranic verses which are the favourites of the Sufis include:

"We [God] are closer to him [man] than his jugular vein."

"Say, surely we belong to God and to Him do we return."

"He is the First and the Last and the Manifest and the Hidden."

"God is the light of the heavens and the earth."

Such verses are limitless in their depth, scope and

meaning, and man may draw from them as much mystical meaning as he has the capacity to understand. God says in the Quran that God sent His Prophet Muhammad (pbuh) first and foremost as a Mercy unto all peoples. And men of different levels of spiritual understanding may avail themselves of this Mercy according to their various capacities. The Prophet (pbuh) and his close associates never stopped at merely observing the minimum requirement in regard to prayer and devotional practices. All through his life, the Prophet (pbuh) kept long night vigils and practised voluntary fasts during most days. He never ate barley bread (the staple food of his day) on three consecutive days, and he never even touched a loaf of wheat bread - which was a luxury. One of his favourite sayings was "Poverty is my pride," and this saying came to be quoted in every manual of Sufi doctrine, making the rule of poverty a basic characteristic of Sufi life.

Significance of Remembrance

The Sufis live with an ever increasing awareness of God. One aspect of this awareness is the practice of *zikr*. It means 'remembering God' usually by pronouncing His name or by uttering a number of recognized formulae. The Quran repeatedly admonishes believers to celebrate the praises of God and to do this often. For remembering the name of God brings satisfaction and comfort to man's heart. The following verse of the Quran reveals the significance of *zikr*:

"Recite that which has been revealed to you of the scripture, and observe prayer. For prayer restrains one from lewdness and iniquity, but remembrance of God is the greatest virtue."

In one passage of the Quran, the importance of *zikr* is enhanced to such an extent that a response to it from God Himself is assured:

"Therefore remember Me, and I will remember you."

The Quran warns those who neglect *zikr*: "Whoso blinds himself to the remembrance of the All Merciful, to him we assign Satan for a comrade and debar them from the way, and yet they think they are guided." Again, "Be not as those who forgot God, and so He caused them to forget their own souls. Those, they are ungodly." The key to human happiness lies in the remembrance of God, as in the Quranic verse: "Verily, in the remembrance of God do hearts find peace."

Some orientalists who considered themselves experts on Islam invented the myth that the history of Sufism began with the appearance of certain introductory treatises on the Sufi tradition in the ninth and tenth centuries. In their assessment of the Sufi writings, they failed to give due consideration to the esoteric aspect of the Quran and the enormous literature on the sayings and deeds of the Prophet (pbuh), which has inspired the Sufis of all generations.

The Methodology of Sufism

Sufism is an esoteric doctrine transmitted by word of mouth, and sometimes without even a spoken or written word, by an authorized teacher to a disciple, and from disciple to another disciple, in confidence. These secret instructions are acted upon by a disciple with perfect faith in the teacher. The disciple gives a report of his condition and experience in confidence to his teacher and receives another set of instructions most suitable to his state. It is only the writings of the Sufi teachers, who speak from within the tradition, that allow an outsider a glimpse of the inner beauty of Sufism. One of the greatest scholars of all times was al-Ghazzali. He lived in the later eleventh and early twelfth centuries. He wrote his famous work *The Revival of the Sciences of Religion* in Arabic, with an abridged form, *The Alchemy of Happiness,* in Persian. These works were followed by the other writings and poetry by such Sufi teachers as Abdul-Karim al-Jili, Ibn Arabi, Suhrawardi, the famous Chishti saints, Hafiz, Sadi, Rumi and so many other Sufi poets.

At the same time there was an immense upsurge of open Sufi activity under the auspices of different Sufi orders in all parts of the Islamic world. Each Sufi order constituted a focal point of activity, from which Sufi teachings were carried to the mass of the population by the representatives of the head of the order. The Sufi organizations constituted the social cement of the society in which they lived. Because of the strength of this social cement, Islamic civilization was able not only to withstand the many political upheavals of this period, but it also acted as a civilizing influence on the powers that were responsible for these upheavals.

Suluk

This brings us to say something about the Sufi discipline. The first and foremost requirement is the purification of the soul. The process is generally a long and difficult one. It consists of the three stages. In the first stage, one struggles against the carnal soul or *nafs al-ammara* as it is called by the Sufis. *Nafs al-ammara* is the tendency in man to disobey God, and to take pleasure in evil deed and thought. This inclines man towards gossip, backbiting, vain talk, pride, selfishness, lust, hatred and jealousy. The struggle to overcome *nafs al-ammara* involves the purifying of the body, tongue, mind and heart.

a. The body is purified by keeping it free from dirt, by preserving its members from harm and by not indulging in sexual license.
b. The tongue must be purified by restraining it from backbiting, malicious gossip and vain talk, or from using it to alter the truth.
c. The mind must be purified by abstaining from suspicion, plotting and thinking ill of others.
d. The heart must be purified by keeping it free from lust, jealousy, greed, selfishness, hatred and pride.
e. In this stage, a Sufi constantly examines the motives of his likes and dislikes.

The Reproaching Soul

When he has subjugated the carnal soul, *nafs al-ammara*, the Sufi enters upon the second stage of purification in which he is able to respond readily to the call of the reproaching soul which is called *nafs al-lawwama*. It is the *nafs al-lawwama* which reproaches man for his evil deeds and impels him to acts of mercy and generosity.

The Contented Soul

After this stage has become firmly established in him, the Sufi enters the third stage which is known as the station of the contented soul, *nafs al-mutma'inna*. In this stage, the Sufi develops to the fullest the tendency to obey God and to act in perfect harmony with His commandments. Here the soul is reconciled with all other stations of the path, such as poverty, patience, gratitude and trust in God. Here the soul finds perfect satisfaction in being governed by the heart, the Divine spark in man. Here the Sufi becomes truly free from fear and grief. As God said in the Quran, "*Lo, indeed, the friends of God have neither fear nor are they grieved.*" Fear and grief are qualities of man, and friends of God are relieved of the burden of these qualities. Fearlessly, and with the strength of faith, they invite man to God, the source of man's creation and the goal of his life.

Here lies the difference between a true teacher and a false one - the true teacher invites man to God, and the pretender invites man to himself. In this stage, a Sufi is filled with love, mercy, kindness, and a burning zeal to help others. In order to reach this high station, a Sufi must constantly strive to control his ego, to curb his anger and impatience. He must eat less, sleep less, talk less, and deny himself the pleasure of other people's company. Sometimes he withdraws completely from the worldly activities and occupies himself entirely with the remembrance of God and meditation. As he makes progress spiritually, he is able to extend the length of his periods of seclusion, culminating in retreats of forty days' duration and in this seclusion, the Sufi fasts during the day, breaking his fast after sunset with only a small piece of bread and some water. During the nights, he keeps constant vigil and chants a selected verse from the Quran 125,000 times.

The verse usually chanted is: "There is no God but Thou, the Holy Lord. I am indeed one of the evil doers." Or, "Say, He, Allah is one. Allah is Sufficient unto Himself."

Meditation, Ecstasy, States, Stations and Ascension

The various stages on the mystical path are known as *maqamat*, or the 'stations', which can be reached by any Sufi by means of prayer, fasting, meditation, and the *hal* or 'mystical state', which may be vouchsafed to the Sufi by the Grace of God but is not attainable by the mystic's own efforts. A Sufi may be blessed by an experience which reveals to his soul the reality of the whole universe, from the lowest layer of earth to the highest heaven. This experience is called *mi'raj* or the 'ascension.' In this, a Sufi is generally accompanied by the spirit of his shaykh, and comes in contact with the spirits of other shaykhs and prophets. Various stations are also revealed to him with different colours and lights.

Extinction (fana) and subsistence (baqa)

One of the important phases of mystical experience which is attained by the Grace of God by a traveller on the mystical path is the state of *fana fi Allah*, 'extinction of the self in God', which is the transition to the state of *baqa billah* or the 'eternal life in union with God.' By passing away from self, the individual does not cease to exist, but is permitted to enjoy the supreme mystical experience in union with God. He is fully absorbed into the Love of God which gives him an everlasting awareness of the all-pervading presence of God. This doctrine is further explained in an authentic tradition of the Prophet (pbuh) which states that God said:

Nothing is more pleasing to Me as a means for My slave to draw near unto Me than the worship I have made binding upon him. And My slave does not cease to draw near unto Me with added devotions of his free will until I Love him. And when I Love him, I am the Hearing wherewith he hears, and the Sight wherewith he sees, and the Hand wherewith he smites, and the Foot whereon he walks.

Most Sufis who have gone through this experience have preferred to live eternally in the greatest depth of silence which transcends all forms and sounds. Yet a few others have produced works of unsurpassed glory, especially in the fields of literature and music, which have crowned the culture of the entire Islamic world. Their works have inspired Sufis and non-Sufis for generations. As the great Persian Sufi poet, Hafiz of Shiraz, who is fondly remembered as the 'tongue of the unseen', said centuries ago for all times: "He whose heart is alive with love, never dies."

The Pseudo-Sufis

Over the centuries, as the Sufi orders grew, the Sufi masters were generally recognized as sages and men of wisdom and grace, enjoying the esteem of the general populace. The growing social prestige of the Sufis attracted self-seekers who posed as Sufis and dervishes and embarked upon exploiting the goodwill of the people. These pretenders indulged in superstitious practices, neglected moral order and religious ordinances, and boasted of their ignorance and lack of learning. In order to cover their own lack of discipline and dedication to the goal, some of these charlatans even tried to cut Sufism from its very roots-namely, the Quran and the practice of the Prophet (pbuh).

The acts of these pseudo-Sufis never altered the true course of Sufism. The heart of Sufism remained pure, well guarded by the traditional practice of the initiation of a seeker into a Sufi order by a Sufi master. The master's authority had properly been passed upon him by a previous master through the investiture of the traditional mantle of authority, symbolized by the presentation of a patched cloth. This initiation is supported by the tree of lineage going back through all the previous masters to the Prophet (pbuh) from whom the authority to instruct in the esoteric doctrine originated. Even today, this is the general practice of all the recognized Sufi orders. It is Sufi masters such as *al-Junayd, al-Ghazzali, Ibn Arabi, Shaykh Abdul-Karim al-Jili, Khwaja Muinuddin Chishti,* and *Jalaluddin Rumi,* among many others, who devoted their lives to spreading the light and grace among all men, irrespective of man's geographical, social, religious and racial origin. They left for all men a rich tradition of love and peace for all times. Even today, their example is a source of light and guidance to the seekers of truth everywhere. Indeed, only through total surrender to the Will of God can man hope to attain freedom and peace.

Development of Sufi Thought

Sufism is a blend of various thoughts and philosophies and by intermingling a few traces of Islamic teachings with it, the Sufi thinkers attempted to sanctify their doctrines and demonstrate its conformity to Islam. Greek philosophy, and in particular the teachings of Neo-Platonists, have left an indelible mark on many aspects of Sufism. This came about as a result of the translation of Greek philosophical works into Arabic during the third Islamic century. Greek pantheism became an integral part of Sufi doctrine. Manicheanism is also one of the mainstreams of Sufism. N. Fatemi observed:

"It is interesting how near to Manichean ideas the Sufis are, remembering that both Manicheanism and Sufism were nurtured in Persia."

Vedanta, the chief Hindu philosophy, which is an example of pantheism in its metaphysical strictness, also had a great impact on Sufism following the conquest of Sindh by Muhammad b. Qasim in the second century A.H. Sufi occultism, with its host of philosophical and theosophical doctrines, is beyond doubt antithetical to Islam. Islam proclaims that the matchless entity and essence of Allah is totally different from that of His slaves, i.e., man. Sufis, on the contrary, subscribe to the belief that matter, man and God form in effect one single entity and essence.

Ibn Arabi's doctrine of pantheism was a combination of

Manichean, Gnostic, Neo-Platonic, Vedantic and Christian philosophies and speculations, which he tried vainly to give an Islamic sanction by relating it to Prophetic traditions. "Of his main theme," R.W.J. Austin wrote, "the one that predominates over the rest and to which they are subordinate in the oneness of being (wihdat al-wujood). The concept of the Oneness of Being is all-embracing one, in that all Ibn al-Arabi's other concepts are but facets of it, just as he would say that all distinction, difference and conflict are but apparent of a single and unique reality, the 'seamless garment' of Being, whose reality underlies all derivatives being and its experience."

Ahlu al-Sunnah wa al-Jama'ah, on the other hand, are agreed that Allah is One Alone, qualified with all the attributes wherewith He has qualified Himself and named with all names whereby He has named Himself, without resembling creation in any respect; that His essence does not resemble the essences of His creatures nor His attributes resemble theirs.

"There is nothing like unto Him; He is the Al-Hearing, the All-Seeing."(42.11)

Muhiyddin Ibn Arabi, one of the leading authorities on Sufi mysticism, who captured the imagination and the adulation of Sufis around the world, was born in the year 560 A.H. (1165 A.D.), and pursued the study of the occult and the metaphysical doctrines of the Sufis.

"Such learning and accompanying practices," R.J. Austin wrote, "often led Ibn Arabi, even while he was still young man in Seville, to spend long hours in the cemeteries communing with the spirits of the dead."(!)

He talked about his "cemetery revelations" as matters of fact, and managed to compile a massive compendium on Sufism entitled Al-Futoohat Al-Mekkiyyah (the Meccan Revelations). Of this, Ibn Arabi wrote, "Some works I wrote at the command of God sent to me in sleep, or through mystical revelations."

The other striking impression that Ibn Arabi wanted to leave on the readers of his Meccan Revelation is that he, too, as a spiritual and mystical figure, experienced the heaviness of revelation, resembling that of the Prophet. He noted that sometimes the pressure of mystical revelation was so strong that he felt compelled to finish a work before taking a rest.

"And who is more disbelieving than he who forges a lie against Allah, or says, 'It has been revealed to me,' when nothing has been revealed to him, or who says, 'I will send down the like of which Allah has sent down.'"(6.93)

According to the Quran, revelation is of two kinds. The first is the revelation that came from Allah to His Prophets and Messenger through an angel, such as Jibreel (Gabriel). This came to an end with the death of the Prophet Muhammad. Muslims believe that the Prophet is the last of the Prophets, with whom the line of Prophet hood is closed. Therefore, anyone who claims to be a prophet or a recipient of Divine revelation is an imposter and a heretic.

In order to substantiate his theosophical and pantheistic doctrine and make it appear Islamic, Ibn Arabi resorted to ta'weel, which is giving far-fetched interpretations to selected verses of the Quran or Prophetic traditions from the Sunnah, changing their apparent meaning to one which falls in line with his beliefs, a technique which was used before him by all the 'Batini' or secretive sects that strayed away from the path of Islam. He referred to Almighty Allah as "Creator-Creature," and took pains to present the Divine Being in a theosophical context and to convince his readers that Allah's creation springs from nothing other than His "fundamental being."

Thus, the god that Ibn Arabi believed in is, in reality, all the elements that constitute the universe: human, animal and every other existing thing. As an example he depicted his own master, as a divine reality. And to make sure his readers did not misconstrue his heresy, he further emphasized: "In relation to existence, He (God) is the very essence of existing things. Thus in a certain sense, relative beings are elevated in themselves, since in truth they are none other than He who bears the name Abu Said al-Kharraz."

From this heretical concept of Allah, one may deduce without limit, principles which contradict the prescripts and fundamental tenets and creeds evident in the Quran and the Sunnah. For example, man, as alleged by "Son of Plato," is nothing less than God Himself, and since Fir'awn (Pharaoh) was a man, his declaration of being a god would have been true according to Ibn Arabi's pantheistic doctrine. Furthermore, if nothing exists in reality but God, then every animal, regardless of its family, is in reality god also. And since all existing things have one essence, wine is nothing but water, and every forbidden (haram) thing is lawful or (halal). There can never be more abhorent heretical belief than pantheism. Allah the Exalted is far removed from what Ibn Arabi and his followers ascribe to Him.

And it does not befit believers to make far-fetched interpretations of the essence of Allah or His attributes. True Muslims accept them as they are given in the Quran or in the authentic traditions of the Prophet. The above verse is an informative statement which connotes a command from Allah to the believers not to impute to Him any attributes or names other than those given to Him by Himself or by His Messenger Muhammad in authentic traditions. Nor are they allowed to subject Allah to similitudes or examples.

The Sufis, like their masters, would have us believe that their doctrines originated in the Quranic verses. They interpret certain verses freely, both linguistically and theologically, to corroborate their beliefs and give them Quranic sanction. Besides giving Quranic verses different interpretations, they also reduce them to symbols and codes and juxtapose them in a metaphysical perspective. From these straightforward words, one can easily understand that Allah created Adam first, and, according to numerous verses, He fashioned him from earthly matter, and subsequently he created Eve from one of Adam's ribs, as stated in the authentic traditions. In an attempt to substantiate his pantheistic beliefs, Ibn Arabi gave the above verse the following meaning: "From him (Adam) came forth the mate and child, who all came from the 'Universal Nature,' that is, God, Who is manifested in her (Nature's) many forms in the form of Adam, in the form of Eve and in the form of the progeny."

The Divine element, according to him, inhabits every being. "Glory be to God," Ibn Arabi exclaimed, "Who created things, being Himself their essence."

Origins of Sufism

Like many other Sufi doctrines, pantheism is adopted from man-made religions and philosophies, as confirmed by S. R. Sharda in his book, *Sufi Thought:*

"Sufi literature of the post-Timur period shows a significant change in thought content. It is pantheistic. After the fall of Muslim orthodoxy from power at the centre of India for about a century, due to the invasion of Timur, the Sufi became free from the control of the Muslim orthodoxy and consorted with Hindu saints, who influenced them to an amazing extent. The Sufi adopted Monism and wifely devotion from the Vaishnava Vedantic School and Bhakti and Yogic practices from the Vaishnava Vedantic School. By that time, the popularity of the Vedantic pantheism among the Sufis had reached its zenith."

It is quite obvious that the Sufis did not develop their thoughts independently. Christianity and the worldly religions had their impact on Sufi doctrines. "At the beginning of the ninth century," N. Fatemi elaborates, "the Sufis developed an ecumenical doctrine based on the idea of Zoroastrianism, Buddhism, Judaism, Christianity, Neo-Platonism and Islam".

Sufism regards all religions as more or less perfect shadowing forth of the great central truth which they seek fully to comprehend, and consequently it recognizes them as good, in proportion to the matter of truth they contain. Ibn Arabi, the most infamous Sufi philosopher, including most of his heretical ideas in his book, the Bezels of Wisdom, which he alleged was given to him by the Prophet Muhammad. He wrote:

"I saw the Prophet in a visitation granted to me in the latter part of Muharram in the year 627 A.H. in the city of Damascus. He had in his hand a book, and he said to me, 'This is the book of Bezels of Wisdom; take it and bring it to men that they might benefit from it.'"

Suffice it to say that the Prophet has been in his grave since the moment his honourable body was laid in it, a fact agrees upon by the entire Muslim nation, and that it was never reported that he made any visitation to any of his companions, let alone those who came six centuries after him.

Abu Hurairah reported that the Prophet said:

"I am the most eminent of the children of Adam on the Day of Judgment, and the first from over whom the grave will cleave asunder, and the first intercessor, and the first whose intercession will be accepted (by Allah)."

In the Bezels of Wisdom, Ibn Arabi presents certain aspects of what he terms "Divine wisdom," as he conceives it, in the lives and persons of 27 prophets mentioned in the Quran. The contents of this book are best described by its translator, R.W. Austin. He says in his introductory note to chapter III:

"This chapter is the most difficult and controversial of all the chapters in the book, by reason of the unusual and extraordinary interpretation of the Quran that feature in it. Certainly, from the standpoint of the exoteric theology, Ibn Arabi's approach to the Quranic material in this chapter is at best reckless, and at worst flagrantly heretical."

This chapter deals with the surat Noah, one of the five Apostles who were endowed with earnestness, constancy and patience. He made sincere efforts for 950 years to persuade his people to abandon worshipping idols and to worship Allah alone, to no avail. Finally, the Messenger of Allah, Noah, peace be upon him, prayed to Allah to punish his stubborn and heedless people. Allah responded by drowning Noah's people in the flood in this world, and condemning them to Hell-Fire in the next, a punishment fitting their crime. But Ibn al-Arabi interprets the relevant verses of Surat Noah in the most outrageous fashion, since he suggests meanings diametrically opposed to those accepted by all Muslim scholars.

He interprets the "wrongdoers," "infidels," and "sinners" in Surat Noah as 'saints and gnostics' drowning and burning not in the torment of Hell, but rather in the flames and water of knowledge of God. Ibn Arabi regarded the idols worshipped by Noah's people as divine deities.

On which Ibn Arabi commented:

"If they (Noah's people) had abandoned them, they would have become ignorant of the Reality to the extent that they themselves for in every object of worship there is a reflection of Reality, whether it be recognized or not."

The "Reality" to which Ibn Arabi refers is nothing but the divinity of his pantheistic beliefs. Yet his disciples, the Sufis, still argue that their doctrines are based on the teachings of Islam. However, the fact remains that their cardinal doctrines are not far from the Christian doctrine of incarnation, promoted by Mansoor el-Hallaj, one of the infamous Sufi leaders, who was crucified for claiming identity with God.

"I am He Whom I love," he exclaimed, "He Whom I love is I; we are two souls co-inhabiting one body. If you see me you see Him and if you see Him you see me."

Fundamentals of Sufism

Sufism is a schism developed during the fourth century of Hijrah, exploited by the deviationist sects, the Batini (clandestine) sects and the rest of the enemies of Islam, such as the Jews, the Magians and the Crusaders, to undermine Islamic aqeedah (dogma) and Muslim unity.

"Sufism," states the renowned Shaikh Abu Bakr al-Djaza'iri, "is a shameful deception which begins with dhikr (chanting the name of Allah) and ends with disbelief. Its outward manifestation appears to be piety, but its inward reality forsakes the commands of Allah." In order to explore Sufism in depth, its fundamentals must first be scrutinized; the better to caution the Muslim ummah against falling into the snares of this innovation, since the number of promoters and advocates of Sufism is increasing. Freemasonary is a likely advocate of Sufims today, in an attempt to counter the feared awakening of interest among Muslim youth in pure Islam, based on the Book of Allah and the Sunnah of the His Messenger Muhammad. The enemies of Islam dread the wide consequences of such revival, because it affects the entire Muslim world and diminishes their influence.

The following are the most important fundamentals of Sufism judged by the Quran and Sunnah, so that Muslims can tell for themselves how devastating it is to the Muslim ummah:

Structure of Sufi Orders

The Certified Shaikh

Al-'Ahd (The Covenant of Allegiance)

The Ritual of Sufi Wird

Al-Khalwah (Seclusion)

Al-Kashf (Unveiling)

Al-Fanaa' (Annihilation)

Manifest and Hidden Knowledge

Al-Aqtaab

Al-Awliyaa'

Structure of Sufi Orders

Sufism presumes a fundamental link between the shaikh, head of the Sufi tareeqah (order), and the murid (novice), extending throughout their lifetime and continuing after their death. The murid takes an 'ahd (oath) of loyalty and swears obedience to the shaikh, who in turn promises to solve the murid's problems and deliver him from every dilema whenever he calls on his shaikh for help. The shaikh also promises to interced for him with Allah so that he may be admitted to Jannah. The murid pledges to be conscientious in practicing the set of dthikr (chants) assigned to him by his shaikh, to adhere to the rules of the order and to accept its claim on his loyalty for life over a wide range of behaviour affecting the well-being of the order. The quality and extent of the shaikh's hold over the murid is therefore almost total.

The murid's behavior even outside the order's group setting is expected to conform to rules laid down by the order. And where conflict with outside obligations arises, the murid must resolve it by acting as a Sufi and following his order's rules. The Tijaniyyeh Order makes every candidate for initiation pledge not to visit the grave of pious personality or visit any living scholar. This is one of the major factors in widening the rift between one order and another, causing an order to enter into conflict against his others in an attempt to convert, conquer or annihilate them.

The mechanism of the order structure in Sufism leads to many evil results:

Division of the Muslim ummah into fractions and orders ruled by deviant and ignorant shaikhs, thus making the ummah an easy prey for conquest by non-Muslims.

Enmity among the adherents of different orders, to the point that they will not marry into one another's families or cooperate with one another.

Deception on the part of the shaikh, who falsely claims the ability to deliver the murid from difficulties and deadly problems the befall him. The shaikh even claims he will be present at the murid's death, regardless of time or place, and ridiculously enough, will instrut him in his grave on what to tell the two angels of the grave, and will argue with them on his behalf.

Finally, the shaikh promises to intercede for him with Allah on the Day of Judgment, and to help cross over as-Siraat (the bridge over Hell) on that Day, and accompany him to Jannah.

This kind of deception, offering security in the grave as well as in the Hereafter, is a flagrant lie, not permissible under any circumstance. Sufi shaikhs lead simple-minded Muslims to believe in such claims, and the result is shirk (polytheism). Deceiving Muslims is one of the major sins.

Insulating the murid as far as possible from the world outside the order as to exploit and manipulate him.

The Certified Shaikh

Another fundamental of the Sufi order's structure is the certified shaikh, necessary to give the murid his wird. This can also be given by the shaikh's deputy. But the shaikh himself is the supreme authority, the one from whom the khulafa' (officials of the order) derive their positions. When a murid takes an oath it is really to the shaikh, although most will do it through the medium of their local deputy.

In the shaikh's hands ultimately lies the invocation of formal sanctions for the murid. The main two laws pertaining to such a right are:

The murid must not argue with his shaikh nor ask from him any proof for what he orders the murid to do.

Whoever opposes his shaikh has broken the 'ahd, and is cut off from the shaikh. Even if he stays bodily close to the shaikh, the door of meddad (assistance) is closed to him.

The Sunni Muslims believe that any single act of worship must be substantiated by the Quran and Sunnah only.

It has been reported that Ali bin Abi Taalib, may Allah be pleased with him, said:

"Were religion to be subject to opinion, then wiping the sole of a boot (in ablution) would be better than wiping its upper."

The sufi believe that the shaikh is needed, for he links them with Allah. They feel that the shaikh of the tareeqah is "the inspired man to whose eyes the mysteries of the hidden are unveiled, because, according to Sufis, they see with the light of God and know what thoughts and confusions are in man's hearts. Nothing can be concealed from them."

The knowledge of the unseen and unknown, and whatever man's breasts conceal, is restricted to Allah alone; anyone else who claims such knowledge is contending with Allah and assuming His attributes. The shaikhs, the leaders of chiefs of the Sufi orders, are regarded by their members as superhuman or divine, and paid more awe and reverence than was paid to the Prophet by his companions. M. Gilsenan describes how Sufis show their feelings of reverence to their shaikh at a hadhreh (Sufi worship session):

At the hadhreh, he (the shaikh) leaves the ranks of participants first, while they are still seated on the floor, wrapped in his father's robe, the symbol of authority, he walks out through the gap in the outer line made for him by the nuqaba' with one hand raised to his breast in humble acknowledgment of the cries that echo around him: "ya sidi Salamah, ya sidi Ibrahim! meddad! meddad!" (Help! help!), while the brothers sitting in the centre brush the carpet where he has trodden with their hands wash their faces and bodies with barakeh (blessings). Not only does he not let anyone kiss his hand, but no one is even allowed to approach him to touch him as he leaves. In order to maintain the awe and reverence according to him, the shaikh has to reinforce the concept of barakeh by increasing institutional space between himself and his muridin (disciples). By with-holding himself from them, he makes the so-called blessing more difficult to obtain, therefore more sought after. Scarcity brings value. When the muridin try to reach him, his official keeps them away. All blame devolves on them, while the shaikh remains above reproach, and the mystery is preserved, and all loyalty is concentrated and focused on him as "the living dramatic symbol and embodiment of the order and the way."

Doubtlessly, to take a learned shaikh as an exemplary and a teacher is praiseworthy and to be encouraged. It is not possible for anyone to know Allah, nor the things that please Him and the things that displease Him, and know how to worship Him, without receiving relevant instructions from a knowledgeable shaikh. But the dangerous part of this institution is that it often deputizes an illiterate who lacks the proper Islamic knowledge to instruct others in religion. It is a fact that most order's shaikhs, who are usually self-appointed, have little or no religious knowledge. The most important qualification for a Sufi shaikh, besides his social influence or status, is the length of service he has extended, to his superior, the shaikh of the order, who has himself inherited the title in a chain of succession which Sufis falsely claim to trace back to the Prophet's company.

Some shaikhs are bold enough to allege that they have no need of this imaginary chain, because their order derives directly (!) from the Prophet, not merely in vision but in reality. Shaikh Muhammad at-Tijari asserts in his book, *Jawahir al-Ma'ani* :

In respect of the chain of authority to which Muhammadiyyed Tijaniyyeh Order is traced, he informed me, "We have acquired our knowledge from a variety of shaikhs, but Allah did not ordain that we be limited to such. Verily, our authority and teaching mission in this order has been acquired from the Master of the Universe Muhammad; indeed, Allah has ordained that we acquire the knowledge and that we reach Him by His agency. Therefore, no shaikh other htan at-Tijani is is entitled to act according to His judgment in the disposal of our affairs. As for the merits of the followers of at-Tijani, the Master of the Univers (i.e. Muhammad s.a.w) has told him (at-Tijani) that anyone who loves him is loved by the Prophet, and shall not die before he is an absolute waliy or a favourite of Allah."

The thoughtful Muslim can see how gross these lies are that they forge against Allah the Exalted and His Messenger, and against the believers, with no shame or fear. Oddly enough, Abdul-Qadir Eisa, head of the Shadthiliyyeh Order in Syria, has related that Shaikh Muhammad al-Djaza'iri, from whom he inherited the order, named the chair of the order's leaders back to the Prophet, among whom are many Sufi imposters and Batini zealots (deviant clandestine sectarians). The chain is claimed jointly by four Sufi orders: Qadiriyyeh, Shadthiliyyeh, Darqawiyyeh and Ulaiwiyyeh.

All the Muslim ummah is agreed that the Prophet did not conceal any knowledge from his ummah, nor did he distinguish any of his companions with any particular knowledge. He conveyed the Divine Message as Allah commanded him in the best manner, for which he deserves to be the best of all the Prophets and Messengers of Allah.

The Prophet has severely warned those who forge lies against him, saying:

"Do not forge lies against me, because he who does so enters the Fire."

And he also said:

"He, who willfully or intentionally forges a lie against me, let him occupy his seat in the Fire."

Al-'Ahd (The Covenant of Allegiance)

The covenant is one of the cardinal principles of Sufism, upheld by all Sufi orders. It is taken during a ceremony in which the shaikh and murid hold hands, fingers interlaced and eyes closed. Then the shaikh or deputy administers the oath to the murid that he takes the shaikh as his leader and his guide before Allah the Most High, according to the way and the tareeqah (order) of the shaikh, that he shall adhere to this order throughout his life, never converting to another, and that he pledges loyalty and obedience to the shaikh.

The Quranic verse quoted above, from Surat al-Fath (#48), has a serious connotation. Allah revealed this verse when 1500 companions of the Prophet swore allegiance to him in al-Hudaybiah, and swore to support him and fight in the way of Allah. But to use such a verse to trap simple-minded Muslims into taking an irrelevant oath is sheer deception. Sufis also base the principle of 'ahd on fabricated hadeeth (tradition) telling of a similar 'ahd which they allege that Ali, may Allah be pleased with him, made to the Prophet. The oath of allegiance made to the Prophet by his companions to obey him and to fight in the way of Allah was made later on by the Muslims to the Khalifah, the head of the Muslim ummah.

The practice of taking 'ahd to a shaikh and the ceremony surrounding it, were unknown at the time of the Prophet and also during the time of the best three generations of the Prophet's companions and their followers. The Sufi order system and the rituals associated with it are no more than bid'ah (innovation) originated by subsequent generations. The Prophet repeatedly warned his ummah against every form of innovation. He was very particular about that, to the point of prefacing all his speeches with the warning:

"Verily, the best of speech is the Book of Allah, and the best of guidance is the guidance of Muhammad, and the evil of all religious matters is their innovations. Every innovation is a bid'ah, and every bid'ah is misguidance, and every misguidance is in the Fire."

'Ahd or Bai'ah in Light of Quran and Sunnah

In order to make Muslims aware of the seriousness of the Sufi bai'ah, it must be defined linguistically and judicially. Linguistically it signifies bartering or exchanging commodities. It also signifies making a covenant, a compact, an agreement or the like, as though each of the two parties sold what he had to the other, and gave his own special property and his obedience, and that pertains to the case. And judicially it signifies making pledge to the Khalifah, or the Muslim ruler to promise or swear allegiance to him, making a covenant to him to submit to him the judgment of his own case and the cases of Muslims in general, not to dispute with him, but to obey him in whatever command he might impose upon him, pleasing or displeasing. In doing so, it was usual for the person making this covenant to place his hand in the hand of the Khalifah, or the ruler of the Muslims, in confirmation of the covenant, as is done by the seller and the buyer; hence the act is termed bai'ah (or bargain).

The Prophet said,

"If two califs were given the covenant of allegiance, then kill the second of them."

The great Imam Ahmad bin Hanbal was asked about the above hadith. He said:

"Do you know who the Imam is? It is the one upon whom all the Muslims agree; of whom every one of the Muslims says, 'This is the Imam.'"

Imam al-Qurtubi said,

"As for appointing two imams or three at one time, in one country, it is a practice which is unanimously held as impermissible."

Based on the above, every bai'ah which is made to other than the Khalifah of the Muslims or the Muslim ruler who is invested with authority to declare wars or ratify peace treaties and execute religious castigations, or hudood is null and void. In his book Al-Bai'ah, Ali Hassan Abdul-Hameed refutes the proofs presented by Sufis and certain Islamic parties who hold bai'ah as a central religious rite. They claim, "There is no text which prohibits the rite of bai'ah." The author refutes this saying:

"All of the statements of the preceding scholars pertaining to bai'ah refer to the bai'ah as an exclusive right which belonged to the Khalifah or the ruler of the Muslims. No one of them made reference to an exceptional bai'ah.

If we approve, for the sake of discussion, of the innovated type of bai'ah (Sufi or otherwise) then we pose to them the questions, is it (the bai'ah) restricted to one particular group of people, or are all the Muslims entitled to it?

If their answer to the first question is 'yes' then by approving such bai'ah, they initiated an act of worship which is sanctioned by neither the Book nor the Sunnah, because Allah never distinguished one particular group of Muslims from the other with any act of worship. And if their answer to the second question is positive too, they accordingly approve the disunity of the ummah, and deem lawful dividing it into orders, sects and parties, and give the excuse to every group to follow its desires and devise its own bai'ah.

And if they claim that this exceptional type of bai'ah is legal, then is it possible that the pious predecessors whom Allah praised in His Book were unaware of such an act of worship?"

Abu Na'eem al Asbahani reported in his book Hilyatul Awliyaa that Mutarrif al-Shikh-khir said,

"Once I visited Zaid b. Soohan while he was with a group of people circulating a sheet of paper on which were written statements such as, 'Allah is our Lord, Muhammad is our Prophet, and al-Quran is our imam. He who is with us we are with him, and he who is against us we are against him etc.' the paper was shown to every man present, every one of whom was then asked, 'Do you acknowledge this covenant? Thereupon, the head of the group interjected saying to his men, 'Do not take a hasty action against the youth. Then he turned to me and enquired, 'What do you say, young man?' I said, 'Allah has already taken a covenant from me in His Book, after which I shall never give a covenant to anyone.' Thereupon, every single man relinquished his previous acknowledgment of the covenant. I asked Mutarrif, 'How many of you were there?' He said, 'We were about 30 men.'"

Now compare those truthful and sincere predecessors, who rejected any act of worship, regardless how good it sounded, once they realized it was not practiced by the Prophet or his companions, may Allah be pleased with them all, with the Sufi Shaikhs and party leaders of today, who not only make imperative that their followers give bai'ah to them, but also consider bai'ah as an indispensable religious rite.

Ritual of Sufi Wird

The wird is another central principle of the Sufi orders, which literally means a set portion of the Quran, or any other specific act of worship, which the worshipper commits himself to recite or perform, either at a particular time or occasion or on a regular basis. But according to Sufism, the wird, or dthikr, is a practice of repeating the name of Allah, and a set of invocations assigned to the murid by his shaikh or deputy as a liturgy of communion. They involve beseeching the dead, and seeking help from sources other than Allah.

The Sufi dthikr is of two forms, the dthikr al-khafiy or hidden dthikr wiht the repetition being in the mind or muttered in a low voice; and the dthikr al-jaliy, the open recitation, in which the Sufi murid recites aloud. Sufis distinguis three types of dthikr: the dthikr of the common people (al-awaam), which involves uttering repeatedly the Kalimah, meaning, "There is no God but Allah, Muhammad is the Messenger of Allah;" the dthikr of the upper class, which involves uttering repeatedly the single name of God, "Allah," or the word "haiy" (the living); and the dthikr of the elite, which involves uttering repeatedly the divine pronoun "hu" (He).

The last two types of dthikr have never been uniue to Islam. Sufi dthikr, however, is not limited to the above three types: In many cases it includes litanies and hymns, or as the Sufis prefer to call them, "twassulaat" (supplications or petitions), to the Prophet and his family.

Supplicating beings other than Allah entails associating partners with Him, a practice which is not only condemned by Allah and His Messenger but it renders a worshipper's good deeds null and void. The type of dthikr practiced communally by Sufis is not merely recited; it is rather performed in their hadhrah. Sufi dthikr ranges from quietism to ecstatic and hysterical behaviour. In many orders, the ritual has a section called samaa' in which singing, dancing and playing musical instruments, such as the flute and the drum, are highly important.

The dthikr which the Prophet enjoined should be recited individually, and only according to the manner prescribed by him. Making dthikr in a different manner, or communally, is an innovation leading to misguidance.

The prominant companions of the Prophet confirmed that the "idle talk" referred to in the above verse means singing and music. The Prophet verified this fact in the hadeeth which says, "There will be some people who will consider legal fornication, and the wearing of silk, the consumption of intoxicant drinks and the use of musical instruments."

It is a must for all Muslims to adhere to the two Divine sources of Islam, the Quran and the Sunnah, the Prophet's companions, may Allah be pleased with them all, developed great understanding of these two fundamental sources as required and necessitated by the profession of the faith: ("There is no God worthy of being worshipped but Allah; Muhammad is the Messenger of Allah.") They were very critical of the slightest sign of deviation among Muslims. Whenever they noticed one, they vehemently objected to it and tried their best to rectify the situation or eliminate it. Abdullah b. Mas'ood, may Allah be pleased with him, who was governor of al-Koofeh, Iraq, at a time, happened to enter the mosque one day, and saw some people sitting in circles. In the middle of each circle was a heap of pebbles and in every circle was a man instructing the people: "Say, Sub-han-Allah (Allah is far removed from every imperfection) a hundred times. Say, Al-hamd-du-lillah (praise be to Allah) a hundred times. Say, Allahu-Akbar (Allah is the Greatest) a hundred times." Whereupon Abdullah b. Mas'ood said to them,

"O people, you are either following a religion which is

better than that of the Messenger of Allah, or you are entering through a door of deviation without consideration." They responded,"Abu Abdur-Rahman! (his nickname), by Allah, we intend to do a good thing." He exclaimed, "How often one intends to do good but never attains his purpose."

The above quotation clearly shows that sincerity and good intentions alone are not sufficient to render acts of worship acceptable to Allah. The acts must first conform to the Book of Allah and the Sunnah of His Messenger. Originating new methods or concepts of such acts only incurs Allah's anger. The religion of Islam has already been completed by Allah. It needs no one to tamper with it for the purpose of mundane gain. Thus it follows by necessity that any religious opinion or practice must be judged by and referred to the Book of Allah and the Sunnah of His Messenger to decide its validity.

3

Historical Outlines of Classical Sufism

"Islamic mysticism is the attempt to reach individual salvation through attaining the true *tauîd,*" says one of the leading Western orientalists. In fact, the quintessence of the long history of Sufism is to express anew, in different formulations, the overwhelming truth that "there is no deity but Allah" and to realize that He alone can be the object of worship. The history of Sufism is a chart showing some of the stations on this path of interpretation, some of the forms in which this one reality was expressed, some of the different ways in which the mystics Imam Quli signifying "the servant of God" in the Turkish language, is native of the village of *Dizbad* in the Khorasan. This village now flourishing, is situated in the mountains and hangs on the highest flank, the *Kuh-e-Binalud* 10535 feet), at half way between *Nishapur and Mashad.*

He is known under the name of Khaki Khorasani but as a writer he uses the pen name of Khaki (that belongs to the soil). Unfortunately we have very little information about his life in order to give a complete biography. We will, therefore, content ourselves with the elements that the author is giving us indirectly in his works and of folklore. We will be able to reconstitute broadly the surrounding in which the Imam Quli lived and grew.

According to the date of his books, it can be affirmed that he lived under the reign of the Safawid Kings, probably under Shah Safi (1037-1052/1628-1642) and under Shah Abbas II (1052-1077/ 1622-1667). The Safawids, as it is known, were a dynasty of Sufi origin and Shi'a belief. They imposed *Shiaism* as state religion while they were patronizing the growth and the propagation of Sufi ideas. To the Ismailis, this policy brought a certain relief and a greater freedom in their religious practice and the expression of their ideology. Violently persecuted after the fall of Alamut, it is understood that Sufism served them as alibi and as convenient refuge. The Ismailis continued to practise and propagate their faith in using the cloak of Sufism upto the dawn of the nineteenth century. Thus a quite important Sufi-lsmailite literature was born. This junction of Ismailism and Sufism would have been unthinkable if both did not have a common source.

In fact, the theology of Sufism revives nearly in its entirety, the metaphysical doctrine of Ismailism (Haqa'iq). However, while using the vocabulary of Sufism and professing the same theosophical metaphysic, the gnostic Ismailis as well as Khaki Khorasani was hostile to sufi practice and beliefs. Since the massacre of the last Imam of Alamut, Imam Ruknud-Din Kurshah by the Mongols (1257), his descendants established themselves in the south of Caucasus. They lived there hidden under the garb of Shaikhs and of venerable land-owners (vide W. lvanow, Brief survey of Ismailism, No. 7, Leidan, 1952. p.18). Later in the IX/XVth century they settled down in *Anjudan* (about twenty miles from Arak). Khaki Khorasani was the contemporary of two Imams residing at *Anjudan,* whose names he cites in his poems: Imam Shah Dhulfikar Ali (920-922/1514-1516) and Imam Shah Nur-ad-Dhar (i.e. Shah Nurd-Din Ali) (922-957/1516-1550). For the latter, Khaki cites a later date: 1056/1646.

However, in spite of this comfortable situation for the Ismailis, the faithfuls had to be very careful and observe the *taqiyya,* the secret to avoid reviving the fanatism and the hostility which during centuries had impregnated the mind of certain less educated religious group. That fanatism resulted, as historv showed it, in acts of violence and in considerable loss of human lives in the lsmaili community. This lack of understanding still existed at the time of Khaki. The folklore has preserved the painful souvenirs of the tortures that the Imam Quli endured by the authorities of his villages he outlived, it is said, by divine blessings. It was the exact opposite for his predecessor Qasim *Amiri of Shiraz,* a star in the pleiade of Ismaili poets of the post-Alamut period. In fact, in spite of the precautions he took to conceal his faith, he was accused of heresy in 973/1565 and was rendered blind under the orders of the King Tahmasp (930-984/1525-1576); he was later on executed by Abbas the First (999/1591).

Life of the Poet

The few historical points related, we will now try to recall broadly the childhood of Imam Quli and the events that provoked the spiritual crisis and which marked the starting point of his poetical career and of his mission. His parents, as most of the inhabitants of Dizbad, were small land-owners who cultivated orchards and vegetables. They probably possessed some flock of goats, sheep and some cows: thus they enjoyed a modest but comfortable life. His family was impregnated with a religious mind and with a very great devotion. An atmosphere of piety surrounded the childhood of Imam Quli. These fortunate circumstances allowed the child to receive a traditional religious education. This education contained through the reading of classical works on Sufism, Shiaism and Ismailism books which he obtained from religious schools or which he took from his family library.

Childhood

The Ismailis of Khorasan and particularly the descendants of the Khaki Khorasani family kept a living image of their ancestors. They conjure up with emotion the few facts that ruled the childhood of the poet. It is related that the parents of Imam Quli were used to going out late at night to meet their friends, after ensuring that their children were sleeping well. The daily absence of the parents aroused the curiosity of the child. Where could they go so late? His mother had told him one day that they were going to a place (Ja'i). This reply did not satisfy the seven-year old child but increased his anxiety and perplexity. He said nothing but decided to act. The next night his parents left, closing the door discreetly after them; the Imam Quii left his mat and followed them in the night without their knowledge, up to the secret place. (Today we can see the ruins of this place at l, 3 miles from Dizbad and at 546 yards from the village of Qasimabad).

Imam Quli did not enter the place. He stayed outside, concealed behind the door. He could see inside the room the members of his family and the elders who came from the village of Dizbad and from Qasimabad. He did not understand the sense of the religious ceremonies that were going on but his heart palpitated with a secret joy because he just saw the Imam sitting before the congregation. After the service, the food offerings that the faithful had brought, were shared. The Imam Dhulfikar Ali recommended to the voluntary waiter to give a share to each one. When he finished, he was asked to see outside if someone else was left out. Imam Quli was found out and could obtain his share. Since then Imam Quli cultivated greater love and devotion towards the Imam and he longed to see him again. The occasion presented itself later on.

One day the ladies were assembled in a room to weave cotton with Imam Quli when the Imam Nurud-Dhar entered then went out and mounted his horse. Imam Quli begged him to take him along. The Imam replied: "When you will be able to pass a comb through your beard then I will take you with me". The child made the gesture to touch his beardless face and was surprised, his fingers felt his beard. The Imam took him along. They rode together towards the end of the village up to the place where today from a rock, gushes the miraculous spring of *Nohesar* (each year, the Dizbadis arrive in pilgrimage to piously drink the water of the spring and to spend the day there). They had an intimate conversation in the course of which the Imam advised his young disciple to work on the path of God if he would like to achieve his goal and realise his salvation. This event marked the beginning of the poetical and missionary career of Imam Quli. He was aware of the difficult conditions which he will have to face and of the obstacles which he will have to overcome in order to fulfill his task. But to defend and to live according to his faith, he was ready to struggle during all his life time and to bear with patience all the sufferings. Allusions which bear evidence to this firm decision are to be found in his poems.

His Works

The works he left are:

a. The Diwan or selection of poems.
b. A long religious poem in the form of "matha navi" entitled "Tulu'as-shams" (The rising of the sun).
c. Two short religious treaties written in verse in the form of *qasida* entitled *"Nigarestan"* and *"Baharestan"*. These have been published by W. lvanow with an introduction in "An abbreviated version of the Diwan of Khaki Khorasani".

Style

His poetry has a tinge of deep piety and a sincere aspiration towards justice, truth and peace. Apart from the praises and prayers he addresses to Mowla, to Sahibuz-zaman, to the Lord of the century, he calls upon the Ismailis to practise charity, to cultivate virtue and to remain steadfast in their faith. He insists that they pursue ceaselessly their endeavours in the quest of God, that they acknowledge the Imam of their century in order to attain salvation and to obtain deliverance of all human limitations. His poetry is a popular poetry, rustic, accessible to all. It is deprived of artifice and the splendour of the court at the time of the Safawid sovereign. Khaki calls himself a common man *(ammi)* with a modest knowledge: "I am unfit to deliver sermons for I am imperfect and a sinner. I am a common man and I speak and teach as a common man" (Verse 1 331).

His frequent quotations from the *Quran* and the *Hadith* point to his knowledge of religious sciences. His references to Nizami, Hafez, Sa'di, Attar, Sana'i, Maghribi and Qasim Anwari as well as to the classical accounts of Laila and Majnun, of Khurasaw and Shirin, of Mahmud and Ayaz indicate his interest in esoterism and the mystical pathway. Not less deep is his knowledge of the lsmailian doctrine. W. lvanow rightly observes that his teachings borrow in its essence and even in its terminology from another Ismaili Da'i, Khary Khah Herati (svi) of." On the recognition of the Imam (Fasl dar bayan-e Shenakht-e Imam). Bombay, 1949 especially as far as the concept of the Imam and the Hujjat are concerned. Unquestionably, Khaki possesses a poetical talent although sometimes he lacks originality and a creative spirit. Nevertheless, he lives in the heart of many Ismailis who admire his will, his fortitude, and his militant spirit and praise his sincere and firm faith.

Viewed in this context, Khaki can be considered as the true mystical knight who during his entire lifetime fought with the sword of truth, virtue and loyalty thereby doing credit to the principles of his "order", the Ismaili *Da'wat.* His only aim was to serve God by championing the cause of his Lord, of Mowlana Murtaza Ali. The fond nostalgic be experienced from his first meeting with the Imam overcame him and dominated his whole life. The following *Qasida* reveals under the symbolic language a very personal expression:

"I have run during my whole life in search of the Lord, In spite of my eagerness, I have not attained what I was searching for. From the start to the end (of my life) the Khidr (the Imam) of the time was as a father to me. I was thus able to drench myself with the 'purifying' drink from the jar of the Lord. O brother, do not think this path to be easy, I have gone through many roads in the desert of Love; it is not a valley of repose, it is a place of ordeals and of sufferings. The misfortunes, torments and the pains I have to endure there were many. I have forsaken my reason, my work and my knowledge, taking for real what I was told.

The child and the young man, from the beginning to eternity, must follow the direction of the Pir, of whom I acknowledge to be the disciple. Every patience I showed was a key opening on intimacy. It is the means to glory and a key for those who are searching. Day and night, I feel the nostalgia (to contemplate) the Face of the Beloved (Imam). I am disturbed and I am the martyr of the face which has delighted my heart. Because of the injustice (committed) by the rivals, I suffer of being separated from my Friend; I aspire to rejoin him, for a violent rupture has separated us (from each other)."

Death

The tomb of Khaki Khorasani which stands in white amidst the green orchards of Dizbad, bears no inscription. The death of Khaki is established around 1056/1646. He left a son, "Ali Quli", poet as himself, but of lesser talent, and is better known under the pen name of *Raqqami'*.

During this term we will attempt to understand how Sufism - the tendency in Islamic religion that recognizes emotion and experience as a source of knowledge-complements the better-known aspects of Islam, the Islam of personal rigor and moral action. Sufis emphasized the immanent, knowable, and cherishing aspect of God, while other Muslims understood God to be the transcendent Judge and utterly other. In contrast to the universalistic emphasis of the better-known Islam (which we will call "orthoprax Islam"), Sufism often stressed the local and the specific; the orthoprax stressed the absolute equality of all the faithful before God, while Sufis saw themselves as God's Friends and Intimates, qualified to a higher degree for God's friendship because of their greater knowledge and self-cultivation. In this course we will begin, as all courses on Islam ought to begin, with the Quran.

We will then consider some of those whose lives later Sufis looked back upon as decisive. We will then consider the formative history and doctrines of Sufism, particularly in 9th-13th-century Iraq, Iran, and Central Asia. Next we will consider the crucial doctrines of Sufism: that life is a journey, that this world is an illusion, that being is other than it appears to be. This theosophical unit will give us a chance to read a classic of Sufism, The Path of God's Bondsman, and to discuss it at length. We will then turn to the praxis of Sufism: the rituals and institutions characteristic of it. In this section we will consider the Sufi orders, and the rituals designed to induce ecstatic apprehension of divinity. We will end the course with a consideration of Sufism in the Modern world, both in Islamdom, and in the West. Sufi studies: a particular branch of comparative studies that uses a.o. the technical lexicon of the Islamic mystics, the Sufis, to exemplify the nature of its ideas; hence the frequent reference to Sufi Orders. It may be divided into two main branches, the orientalist/ academic and the spiritual.

Early Sufi studies in France

The earliest Europeans to study Sufism were French, associated (rightly or wrongly) with the Quietist movement. They were Barthélemy d'Herbelot de Molainville (1625-1695), a professor at the Collège de France who worked from texts available in Europe, François Bernier (1625–1688), the physician of the Mughal emperor Aurangzeb who spent 1655-69 in the Islamic world (mostly with Aurangzeb), and François Pétis de la Croix (1653–1713), a diplomat who spent 1674-1676 in Isfahan, where he studied Rumi's *Masnavi-ye Manavi* and visited the Bektashi order. D'Herbelot's great work, the *Bibliothèque orientale* (published posthumously in 1697), included an entry on Sufism (as *tasawwuf*) and detailed entries on Al-Hallaj, Najmeddin Kubra, and Abd-al-karim Jili. There were a number of references to the *Masnavi* and to Rumi (as

Gellaledin Mohammed al Balkhi), and there may also have been entries on them.

Bernier published an article on Sufism entitled "Mémoire sur le quïetisme des Indes" in the periodical *Histoire des Ouvrages des Savans* in September 1688. Following this chapter, there is said to have developed in France a view that the French expression of the creed of Pure Love (Pur Amour/ Quietism) was in fact a disguised form of Islam. The debate over Quietism between the bishops Fénelon and Bossuet was remembered as the "Querelle du Pur Amour". Many Quietists (including Jeanne Marie Bouvier de la Motte Guyon) were imprisoned. Others exercised caution and self-censorship. Pétis de la Croix did not publish himself, but his son (writing later under a pseudonym) gave reasons why he thought "the Mevlevi are perfect Quïetists" (Ahmed Frangui, *Lettres critiques de Hadgi Effendi à la Marquise de G... au sujet des mémoires de M. le Chevalier d'Arvieux*, Paris, 1735). D'Herbelot de Molainville's *Bibliothèque orientale* went through several editions, one of the last of which was the 1777 edition printed in the Hague. It has been suggested that some entries on Sufi topics that were present in the 1697 edition were absent from the 1777 edition. The word "Sufi" appears.

Early Translations

In 1671, Edward Pococke (1648-1727), the son of Oxford professor Edward Pococke (1604-1691), published a Latin translation of the *Hayy Ibn Yakhthan* of Ibn Tufayl. This led to a number of other translations, including the English translations of 1674 (by George Keith) and 1686 (by George Ashwell), and a Dutch translation of 1701. The anonymous Dutch translator, "S.D.B.," gave a concise biographical review of the philosophers related to the text: Al Farabi, Avicenna, Al Ghazali, Ibn Bajjah, Ibn Rushd, Junayd, and Mansur Al-Hallaj (with a description of his death and a reference to his famous "Ana al-Haqq"). *Hayy Ibn Yakhthan* may have partly inspired Robinson Crusoe. In 1812, Joseph von Hammer-Purgstall published a translation of the *divan* of Hafez, which was received with delight by Goethe, who was inspired by it to publish in 1819 his *Westöstlicher Diwan*. A Sufi appears in Gotthold Ephraim Lessing's play *Nathan der Weise*, first produced in 1779, though it is not clear from where Lessing learned of Sufism, perhaps through his association with Johann Jakob Reiske. In 1821, F.A.G. Thölluck published *Ssufismus sive Theosophia persarum pantheistica* in Berlin (in Latin).

One of the earliest sociological treatments of Sufism is to be found in Sir John Malcolm's 1825 work, *The History of Persia, From the Most Early Period to the Present Time, Containing an Account of the Religion, Government, Usages and Character of the Inhabitants of that Kingdom*. Malcolm's treatment, though interesting, is not well informed. In *An Account of the Manners and Customs of the Modern Egyptians written in Egypt during the years 1833-1835* (1836) Edward William Lane noted, and illustrated with his own woodcuts, his close observations of the Rifa'i while living in Cairo "in disguise". The success of his work also introduced the success of the "disguise". Sir Richard Burton's *Personal Narrative of a Pilgrimage to El-Medinah and Meccah* (3 vol.1855-1856) was undertaken while travelling as a Qadiri, and Armin Vambéry reached Baveddin near Bokhara to visit the shrine of Baha-ud-Din Naqshband Bukhari in 1863 in the guise of a murid. *Voyage dans l'Asie Centrale, de Téhéran a Khiva, Bokhara et Samarkand, par Arminius Vambéry, savant Hongrois déguisé en derviche* was the subject of four instalments of the popular and copiously illustrated "Le Tour Du Monde, Nouveau Journal Des Voyages (Edouard Charton)" Paris, Londres, Leipzig 1865, deuxième semestre -Hachette et Cie ed.

The "disguise" was by no means superficial and necessitated a variety of resources in linguistics and social integration that left marks far beyond the mere popular success of travelogues. Towards the end of the nineteenth century, the resistance to the European conquest of North Africa was often led by Sufis, notably Abd al-Qadir and later the Sanusi order. This drew further attention to Sufis and Sufism, and a number of studies were performed and published. These generally suffered from their authors' preoccupations with security.

Aguéli to Guénon

One line of 20th century Sufi studies that came to fruition in the West appears to have been born from many colours in a painter's workshop. It was the Swedish painter Ivan Aguéli who -inspired by the quasi occult tradition (Symbolist painters, Les Nabis) developing *en marge* of the great workshops of Paul Gauguin and Emile Bernard- took his intellectual search into the realm of Sufism proper. This culminated into his initiation, in Egypt, by Sheikh Rahman Elish Kabir into the Shadhili tariqa. When he returned to Paris from his travels in the East in 1909, he found a mind receptive to his own spiritual affiliation in the person of René Guénon whom in turn he initiated into the Shadhili Order (1912).René Guénon -who finally settled in Cairo where he died (1951) a convert to Islam under his adopted name of Abdel Wahid Yahia- had an enormous influence on a circle of friends centered around the periodical "La Gnose", that he had started in 1909. This circle pooled the resources of a.o. Frithjof Schuon, Titus Burckhardt, Marco Pallis, Ananda Coomaraswamy, and Martin Lings e.a., each with his own focus on Islam, Buddhism, and Hinduism...

René Guénon focused on a measure of criticism towards what he called "solidified" (petrified) forms of initiation in the West; Freemasonry in particular which he sought to revive in reference to Emir Abd Al-Qadir whose name was widely respected among Masons. If one looks at the aspect of Sufi initiation proper the following background to René Guénon's brand of "Perennial Tradition" emerges. Through his affiliation with the Shadhili Order he was branched to the Akbari chain, going back to the "Greatest Sheikh" -Shaykh Al-Akbar- Ibn Arabi.

Abd Al-Qadir and al-Tijani

The Akbari already had a history of initiation in Western Europe in the person of Emir Abd Al-Qadir, the noble opponent of the French in their colonial struggle over Algeria, who they had held sequestered at the Château d'Amboise (1848-1853). In 1858 the Imprimerie Nationale (Paris) had printed his "Rappel à l'Intelligent; avis à l'Ignorant", an essay he had sent to the Société Asiatique in 1855. The Emir Abd Al-Qadir had been initiated into the Naqshbandi by Sheikh Diya al-Din Khalid Al-Sharazuri and into the Qadiri by his own father Sidi Muhiuddin who led a North African branch of the Qadiri Order. In 1863, during his Hajj, he met with Muhammed al-Fasi al-Shadili, who became his last living teacher, in Mekka. Muhammad al-Fasi al-Shadili's proper teacher had been initiated into the Shadhili by al-Arabi ad-Darqawi, some of whose letters were translated by Martin Lings (1961); they form the background to Martin Lings' outline of the autobiographical writings of Ahmad al-Alawi, who was linked to the Shadhili through ad-Darqawi. Sheikh Ahmad al-Alawi died in 1932.

An approach from a different angle may be traced to Sheikh Ahmad al-Tijani who died in Fez in 1815 and was said to be the inheritor of the "paths" of his time, a.o. Qadiri and Shadili. Sheikh Hammalah ben Mohammed ben Sidna Omar, who died in forced exile to France, lies buried in Montluçon, France. He was the former Qutub al Zaman of the Tijaniyyah. A moving account of the circumstances of his death is given by the great African traditionalist and cultural ambassador Amadou Hampâté Bâ, himself a Tijani, in the biography of his own sheikh, Tierno Bokar.

Massignon to Nasr

Thus the current into which the friends of the Traditionalist School had tapped proved to be a lively one. René Guénon's wish to edit a series of Sufi translations was frustrated, but in the meantime Louis Massignon had prepared himself for the task. By 1922, his introduction to the technical lexicon of Sufism and the Passion of Al-Hallaj initiated the first line of textual study, translation and publication of sources that developed into the watershed of which the chief engineers were Henry Corbin and Seyyed Hossein Nasr. Since the observation is pertinent that thus far the watershed is fed from a distinct French sphere of influence, a mental exercise is needed to broaden the view. It is clear that Seyyed Hossein Nasr's participation in the collaboration with Henry Corbin infused this field with a genuine consideration for some of the finer aspects (Irfan) of Islamic culture as seen from a proper native source – Iran – and adding a distinct contemporary sting to ecology.

It may be interesting to compare two contributions to Sufi studies from this same angle -1) Seyyed Hossein Nasr "Revelation, Intellect and Reason in the Quran" in "Sufi Essays" -London and Albany, New York 1972. -2) Reza Arasteh:"Psychology of the Sufi Way to Individuation." in "Sufi Studies East and West" Rushbrook Williams ed. New York 1973. Both describe the control over the "nafs", the spiritual "breaths" that color man's essential character; a study comparing intelligence in its western and eastern traditional form. Pr. Arasteh had already introduced this "Sufi Way" in his academicals work on psychiatric theory ("Final Integration in Adult Personality" Brill Leiden 1965).

Idries Shah

Professor Reza Arasteh M.D. (remembered for his correspondence with Thomas Merton) wrote in honour of Sayyid Idries Shah, whose stature as a scholar was as fiercely disputed as his communication to a general public was successful. Nevertheless Sayyid Idries Shah caused the English feed of the watershed to be explored – through his own accessible style of writing, by providing affordable publications of great classical texts, and rebelliously askew on the niceties of an Oxford/Cambridge kind of rivalry over Pr. Nicholson and Pr. Arberry – and to exactly what extent can now easily be verified by the student willing to compare for himself the 11 naqshbandi Rules/Exercise-aims listed by

Sayyid Idries Shah in "Oriental Magic"(chapter VII) in 1957(!) with those presently divulged through the proper channel. They are indeed the same.

Margaret Smith

Special note could be taken of the little cited but brilliant academic Margaret Smith who wrote (1925-1935) on the history of mysticism in the Near and Middle East from a woman's perspective leading to classic pages on early Christian mysticism, women in the early Christian Church, Christianity and Islam at the beginning of the Islamic era, the rise of Sufism and the early ascetic ideal. Two exemplaries of her subject matter she studied in closer detail: Rabi'a al-'Adawiyya and Harith al-Muhasibi.

The summary of her work reposes in her:

"Studies in Early Mysticism in the Near and Middle East. Being an account of the rise and development of Christian mysticism up to the seventh century of the subsequent development of mysticism in Islam, known as Sufism, and of the relationship between Christian and Islamic Mysticism with references, a bibliography and two indexes."

Later Academics

By the end of the twentieth century, the academic study of Sufism was well established in university departments of religious studies. The perspectives of these later scholars varied. Some were purely scientific, while some followed in the line of Massignon, or (sometimes privately) in the line of Guénon and the Traditionalists, modified somewhat for an academic environment.

The major formal elements of Western modernism, the haptic image and abstract line, arrived to the West in considerable part through the influence of Islamic art. The occurrence of these tendencies in the nineteenth century accompanied a new understanding of perception as subjective and performative—an understanding that was long at work in Islamic aesthetics and philosophy. Theories of perception from Islamic thinkers such as Al Kindi and Ibn Al Haytham, as early as the ninth century, influenced European early modern optics, were eclipsed by Renaissance conceptions of visuality, and were revived—with their origins obscured-in the late nineteenth century in the new discipline of psychology the thought of Bergson, Riegl, and others. Abstract line and haptic space in European modern arts appeal to this embodied and subjective perception. What I call the haptic transfer and the travels of the abstract line facilitated the spread of Islamic aesthetics to the West in a time of genuine intercultural hunger, deeply altering the recipient society.

In European art from the mid-nineteenth century, painting began to let go of figuration in two ways. Color and texture began to lift off the forms they described, allowing haptic images to raise to the surface of the painting. Line unfurled from the figures it demarcated and leapt into abstract life. Abstraction in painting reached out to the senses of a perceiver, who had to consult her inner faculties in order to respond in a subjective and, often, embodied way. The haptic image and abstract line, the major formal elements of Western modernism, arrived to the West in considerable part through the influence of Islamic art. What I call the haptic transfer and the travels of the abstract line facilitated the spread of Islamic aesthetics to the West in a time of genuine intercultural hunger, deeply altering the recipient society. The occurrence of these tendencies in the nineteenth century accompanied a new understanding of perception –new, that is, in Europe; it had been developed by Islamic thinkers as early as the ninth century. Thus we can say that the haptic image and abstract line ushered a new form of perception into the West (for I contend that form it gives hints to the perceiver as to how it may best be perceived).

The haptic transfer and the travels of the abstract line, as in the well-known geometric and vegetal ornament of Islamic religious architecture, facilitated the spread of Islamic aesthetics to the West in a time of genuine intercultural hunger, deeply altering the recipient society. Developed by Islamic thinkers as early as the ninth century, the haptic image and abstract line ushered a new form of perception into the West. The occurrence of these tendencies in the nineteenth century accompanied a new understanding of perception – new, that is, in Europe– as subjective and performative.

Islamic Traditions of Embodied Perception

Writings by Arab classical philosophers, theologians, scientists, and literary critics establish again and again a perceptual position that is embodied, multisensory, contemplative, and subjective. These writings often coexist with and make sense of the arts—ceramics, textiles, painting, poetry, music, and more—that flourished in and beyond the caliphates of ninth-century Baghdad, tenth-century Cairo, and eleventh-century Cordoba. Two tendencies in Islamic classical thought especially support and require some notion of perception as embodied. To begin with, embodied experience is part of being a good Muslim. Islamic philosophy generally adopted the Aristotelian conception that the body is integral to human happiness, and not, as in the Platonic and Christian traditions, the cage of the soul.

Islam actively discourages asceticism. Ultimately, especially in mystical strands of Islam, body and world must be transcended, but meanwhile, Islam understands humans to be God's regents on earth. Sensuous experience, properly regulated, is part of the appreciation of the beauty engendered by God so material experience is a route to the transcendental, to the appreciation of (the ineffable) God. Indeed, poetry, architecture, music and wine are often praised in the courtly society of classical Islam as refined pleasures in their own right. These writings also indicate a multisensory aesthetics, as courtly literature frequently refers to the participation of fragrances, gustatory delicacies, fountains, music, and visual splendor, in aesthetic experience. Al-Kindi's (d. 866) books on music, adopting Greek doctrines that related elements and humours to notes and rhythms, recommended a multisensory therapy combining music, colors, and perfumes—a sort of proto-aromatherapy *gesamtkunstwerk*. The perceiver in classical Islamic thought is not only embodied but also subjective.

At the same time, Islam in principle permits fewer mediators to the transcendental experience than does Christianity, especially Catholicism. Without figural representations of the divinity, let alone its incarnation, the believer in Islam is confronted with a steep route toward spiritual knowledge. Images do not mediate or prop this experience so easily. Instead they assume the abstraction, ineffability, and unknowability—but also beauty and goodness—of God. I must note that there are many variations in Islamic use of figurative mediators. Unlike the more severe Sunni Islam, Shi'a Islam (with the mediating figure of the *imam*) and Sufism permit saints, shrines, and figurative images that mediate religious experience. Sunni Islam, while rejecting anthropomorphism, permits a conception of a personal God, which is in turn a mediator with the inconceivable divine. The result of these two qualities is that Islamic art has a tendency to be both embodied and abstract. The attention invited by Islamic art tends to be embodied, subjective, and performative.

Islamic aesthetics offers many ideas about the power of abstract pattern for spiritual contemplation, as well as disincentives to realism. Figurative images are not eschewed altogether, but their dependence on a higher order is emphasized. The radical abstraction of Islamic art is the result of the view, carried down from radical Mu'tazili atomistic philosophers of 9th century Iraq, that God, being indivisible, has no attributes. Thus any attempt to identify the properties of God in art risks blasphemy. It is impossible to conceive of God. Even less radical strains of Islam enjoin an imaginative engagement with the infinite in religious contemplation. Abstraction is thus a way not to represent but to *perform* the engagement with the infinite that is the act of worship.

As Gülrü Necipoglu has demonstrated, Islamic rationalist philosophy in the classical period placed great importance on the "internal faculties" that mediate between perception and intellect. Ya'qub Ibn Ishaq Al-Kindi (801-66), Al-Farabi (d. 950), and later Ibn Sina enumerated inner faculties such as imagination, memory, and estimation or judgment. These views were greatly expanded in the work, both philosophical and experimental, of Ibn Al-Haytham, known in the West as Alhazen. Al-Haytham introduced the intromission theory of vision in his *Kitab al-Manazir* or Treatise on Optics. Translated into Latin by Gerard of Cremona in 1572 and published in Basel by Reisner, it remained the major work on optics until Kepler in the seventeenth century. This great polymath's writings on perceptual psychology and aesthetics, synthesizing Neoplatonic and Islamic perspectives, explicate a conception of subjective, embodied, and multisensory perception. Perception for Al-Haytham consists of a compound of sensations that are mentally compared—for example, the sight, sound, and smell experienced by a man sitting on a riverbank listening to music and admiring lovely women.

In the Optics, Al-Haytham posited that there are two modes of perception, immediate and contemplative. The former is accomplished by the senses alone, the latter requires the internal faculty of judgment. He argued that contemplation is necessary for the recognition of form, for it requires memory and comparison, carried out in what he called the faculty of judgment. Form is thus a psychological concept, not a given in nature; and ascertainment can only be relative, to the limits of sense perception Sabra 1994, 170-171. Al-Haytham's understanding of perception is time-based, deductive, and subjective. He listed 22 visible properties (e.g. light, color, distance, solidity) that singly or in combination determine the appearance of things. However, each of these is determined by inference, by mental comparison. So in Al-

Haytham's Optics, almost all of perception takes place internally. Because of its emphasis on judgment, this theory of perception implies a subject who is educable and capable of introspection.

Al Haytham, born in Basra, spent some years working for the Fatimid court in Cairo (when he was not feigning insanity in order to avoid imprisonment by the mad caliph al-Hakim II). Necipoglu suggests that he was thinking of the arabesque and geometric patterns proliferating in the architecture of this city when he came up with his theory of subjective perception, as these vertiginous patterns, she writes, "presuppose a private way of looking". Oleg Grabar (1992) similarly remarks upon the relativism of Haytham's criteria for beauty: "He assumes that qualitative decisions of beauty are based on what would be called today the users or the observer's context, not on intrinsic properties of artifacts". Art historians thus agree that Al-Haytham's perceptual psychology was in tune with the abstract art of his time.

Rise and Fall of Embodied Perception in Europe

As religious conservatism waxed across the Islamic world, the rationalist philosophy and experimental science that produced these understandings of subjectivity and perception waned. They traveled westward, however, in the great movements of translation of Arabic manuscripts into Latin in medieval Europe. It is now generally acknowledged that the European intellectual renaissance was largely fueled by this intercultural movement. What's interesting to note is that a "European" concept of perception did not arise until some centuries later, with the rise of experimentation in visuality and perspective. During the medieval period of translation, Arab-Islamic notions of embodied, multi-sensory, and subjective perception echo in the aesthetics of Europe.

For example Doris Behrens-Abouseif (1999), citing De Bruyne's 1947 treatise, *L'Esthétique du Moyen Age,* suggests that Roger Bacon's statement that full aesthetic pleasure is simultaneous satisfaction of all the senses may have been Arab influenced, and that Thomas of York "used Arabic sources to emphasize the psychological and subjective character of beauty". As A.I. Sabra (1994) notes, the extreme subjectivity of Al-Haytham's theory of perception was due to an error (85-118). Although his theory of vision arose from experiment, he did not take account of the activity of the lens in focusing light rays in the eye. Such a perceptual experience would certainly have required mental judgment on the part of the perceiver to distinguish among all the resulting images: hence his emphasis on subjective judgment, which was taken up by European medieval theories of vision. Byzantine and medieval art, eliciting an embodied and multisensory response, might be said to combine Christian iconography with an Islamic visuality.

It was to be corrected by Johannes Kepler with his theory of the retinal image based on a comparison of the eye to a camera obscura. Kepler's intervention, though still grounded in the medieval tradition prepared the way for a more objectivist model of the eye's role in perception. In the late nineteenth century, as biologists were beginning to recognize the highly subjective nature of vision, Henri Bergson was one of the major philosophers to try to redefine the subject of perception as an alert and flexible "center of indetermination". In his *Matière et mémoire* of 1896, Bergson establishes his model of embodied perception, an ever-widening, quasi-hermeneutic circuit in which perception calls up memory and memory enriches and refines perception. But as Jonathan Crary (1992) points out, Bergson's theory of perception was an ideal of perception, posited with a certain anxiety for a subject that is already slipping away.

Industrial and urbanized Europe was increasingly to be producing perceptual situations that dazzled, overwhelmed, or crushed the perceiver, or simply left no time for the deliberate dialectic between perception and internal faculties.

Like Al Haytham and other Islamic philosophers, Bergson describes an ideal subject suspended somewhere between an internal point and the external world, between memory and perception, between interiority and dispersal. Their worries about the dissolution of communicability in their newly industrialized cities inform a certain urgency to define perception as a subjective foray into an objectively knowable world. In the Islamic ideal of subjective contemplation, the interior journey aided by one's internal faculties could intersubjectively confirm the existence of the empirical world, but ultimately confirmed the existence of an objective, *abstract* order: that of divine creation. Evidently this solution would not work for the late-nineteenth century European philosophers.

It is all too well agreed that the arts and sciences of the European Renaissance established a model of visual perception as relatively disembodied and objective, which lasted into the nineteenth century. Only then did experimental optics newly reveal visuality to be embodied, subjective, and subject to external and internal conditions. And then, in a revisionist history that is itself now well known, perception was newly understood to take place in a subject permeable to bodily, psychic, and social experience. Thus we may say with a *soupçon* of chauvinism that it took European optics four centuries (after Kepler) to first improve upon, then return to, the subjective perception Al Haytham delineated in the eleventh century.

It is interesting that around the same time, the mid- to late nineteenth century, Western art entered a period of abstraction that newly elicited a subjective, synaesthetic, embodied, and temporal approach on the part of its spectator—an approach we may call performative. Characterized both by haptic space and abstract line, the new art of nineteenth-century Europe had many formal commonalities with Islamic art, while the psychology inaugurated by Bergson and others has much in common with

Islamic theories of perception.

Performative Aesthetics in Islamic Art

Abstract line and haptic space are performative, rather than representational. They require the imaginative and subjective participation of the beholder to bring their effects into being, beckoning each pair of eyes to follow in their own fashion. Like the haptic image, with its lively interaction between figure and ground, the abstract line draws the beholder out of her. In favoring movement, the ego is thus disentangled. Repeating infinitely, as in the well-known geometric and vegetal ornament of Islamic religious architecture, the abstract line invites the beholder to try to feel the ungraspable infinity of God. Thus Ernst Gombrich (1979) thoughtfully reverses an Orientalist cliché, calling Islamic overall patterns an expression not of *horror vacui* but of "*amor infinity*".

Yet as Sayyed Hossain Nasr (1987) insists, this infinity is in a constant play with the void. "There is an aspect of nothingness or void which lies in the very nature of the whole created order and which is a direct consequence of the fact that, in an absolute sense, only God is real. The arabesque enables the void to enter into the very heart of matter". Nasr, as more sober art historians have grumbled, takes a romantic and historical view of the mystical effects of Islamic art. His description of an ecstatic loss of self in the contemplation of the abstract line echoes Sufi mysticism. And indeed many Westerners are drawn to Islam's mystical variant in search of a loss of self, as Sufism describes the love for God as a moth's love for the flame. But other figures in the history of Islamic aesthetics suggest a more guarded play of subjectivity in the contemplation of abstract pattern.

The principles established by Al Haytham, accepted and elaborated upon by later rationalist philosophers such as Ibn Rushd, demonstrate that in Islamic aesthetics the active engagement of the beholder is the subject of the work. Rushd, for example, emphasizes that a viewer constructs a series of subjective virtual worlds: "the principle of [the viewer's] cogitation about things indeed consists in rendering present all the different kind of images of the imagined possibilities concerning the thing on which he is cogitating, as if he were seeing what he is cogitating on". Rushd's aesthetics, as developed here in his commentary on Aristotle's *De anima*, emphasizes the subjective actualization of virtual states. This aesthetic describes artwork that has nothing to "say"—that does not require interpretation per se—but holds out an invitation to the beholder. Thus we can think of abstraction and ornament as *performative*.

Ornament obtains a certain license from Islamic theology. The Quran cautions artists not to compete with God, who is the only creator. In accordance with the conservative Asharite doctrine that came to dominate Sunni Islam, the world is finite, created by God out of nothing, and to which nothing can be added. In such a world, originality consists not in invention but in skilful new variations on a theme. Humans can only embellish the excellence of already existing creation. This is one of the reasons that ornament flourished in Islamic art: rather than creating from nothing, it reveals new connections. A conservative tendency in theology yields a lively engagement on the part of the viewer of art or hearer of music or poetry.

Baghdadi literary theorist 'Abd al-Qahir al-Jurjani (d. 1078) exemplified this tendency of Islamic aesthetics when he wrote that in all arts and crafts, "the more widely differed the shape and appearance of their parts are and then the more perfect the harmony achieved between these parts is," the more "fascinating" and praiseworthy the resulting work will be. The power of poetic imagery, Al-Jurjani wrote, is its "ability to penetrate hidden meanings and thus reveal invisible things". Veiled poetic speech "invites the recipient to search or the hidden pearl"; it's thus more precious than direct rational speech. Value is placed on works of art that beguile the viewer or listener to imaginatively explore them.

Ornament, according to Oleg Grabar (1992), may have a lucid or a liturgical function: "Both have prescribed rules of behavior and of utterance from which one should not deviate, but in a liturgy the outcome is always known in advance, whereas in a game it is not". Iconography is liturgical; "evocative manipulation" is a game: "It recalls meanings without compelling them. It transfers the decision of how to understand a work of art to its viewer or user". Ornament provides not an anarchic field for the play of perception, but the rules of the game, the abstract structure in which subjective perception acts.

"Ornaments are recursions that keep going by recalling previous and anticipating further forms," so Niklas Luhmann writes. Luhmann captures here the algorithmic qualities of ornament, whereby one theme, for example a geometric form, can be varied endlessly by simple iteration and change. It also indicates the performative way in which ornament is perceived: looking at a single form, we can anticipate its variations, where it came from and where it is going, as it were. As such, looking at ornament (or indeed listening to music or poetry with an ornamental structure) is a personal exercise in unfolding its possibilities in time. While meaning does not lie in the object alone, I think that we can analyze an object in terms of the kinds of reception it might afford. Islamic art implies certain forms of drawn-out attention and subjective contemplation, which in turn are in a certain way suggested by the work.

This is why non-figurative Islamic art often yields unsatisfying conclusions for those who like Eva Baer (1998), deploy iconographic interpretations and are more amenable to phenomenological approaches. Valerie Gonzales' (2001) interpretation of the Hall of Kings at the Alhambra shows how Islamic architecture lends itself to existential, embodied, and performative experiences more than to iconic analysis. While other art historians have interpreted the Comares Hall of the Alhambra as a literalization of its inscriptions about seven heavens, Gonzales "experiences" the hall phenomenologically: decoration leads the eyes up to the star-studded dome, the dome as a body of potential metaphors, to be explicated subjectively. Such a work invites a performative, embodied approach.

Westward Travels of Islamic Aesthetics

By the mid-nineteenth century, the path to Granada and beyond was heavily trodden by Orientalist pilgrims. In 1856, the British design reformer Owen Jones published his pattern book *The Grammar of Ornament*, which included 454 Islamic motifs, including a chapter on the Alhambra. This and other pattern books were read avidly by artists, architects, and designers (both professional and amateur) and their motifs were applied widely, together with Jones' propositions on ornament derived from his study of "Moresque" patterns. Jones noted, for example, the patterns' equilibrium whereby "the tendency of the eye to run in any one direction is countered by lines going in another, so that 'wherever the eye strikes ... it is inclined to dwell". Jones' description of aesthetic pleasure strongly echo Al-Jurjani's, and Jones' pattern books made it easy for artists to adapt the playful and fascinating patterns of Islamic art to their own projects.

Both art nouveau and straightforwardly Orientalist architecture dealt with modernization by seeking inspiration from beyond Europe. As John Sweetman (1987) details, world's fairs, train stations, and the architectural follies of rich clients featured 'Alhambresque' ornament. The life force of the abstract line twined into the biomorphic forms of *Jugendstil* and *art nouveau* architecture and design. Architects turned to Islamic models for the new iron and glass buildings of the industrial age, the train station and the shopping arcade. William Morris, leader of the British Arts and Crafts movement, incorporated these and other Islamic patterns into his designs for textiles and wallpaper. Morris supported the South Kensington Museum in its acquisition of the famous carpet from the shrine of Sheikh Safi at Ardabil.

This museum, which became the Victoria and Albert Museum, would be the model for the Vienna Museum of Art and Industry where Alois Riegl, art historian and curator of textiles, developed his theory of the intercultural transfer of plastic qualities. A complex carpet of Eastern Iranian or Indian origin appears in several of the paintings of John Singer Sargent, literally underlying the tendency toward abstraction in this painter's work. Sargent loved this carpet, calling it "more beautiful than any painting". He often tried to imitate its complexity in his paintings and lamented having to obscure it with his model: "Whenever I put my model on it, she covered something infinitely more beautiful than herself, so I gave up [trying to incorporate the pattern of the rug] and merely did a sort of map of the carpet for the pattern".

Islamic art was one of the levers that European artists applied to naturalism in order to release abstraction. The development of the internal faculties in Islamic aesthetics proved influential to another current of late 19th century art. Paul Gauguin lent Georges Seurat a so-called "Turkish painter's manual" by the Turkish poet Sünbülzade Vehbi. This manual advised to paint from memory, rather than from what is visibly present, invoking the authority of the Islamic visual tradition that appeals to the imagination. Vehbi's writings enjoin the poet to draw inspiration from the form's artifice: "First he should be skilled in signification's art that he might know the delicate, hidden point of poetry's meaning. Metaphor and metonymy, the real and the figurative flow endlessly through the riverbed of poetry. Without knowing the most lovely form of a simile's aspect, to what shall the heart-adorning face of poetry be compared?"

Henri Matisse, Paul Klee, and other modern painters incorporated the abstract line of the arabesque into the surfaces of their canvases, liberating the abstract line from its subservient role to figural representation. And thus the abstract line moved from Baghdad to Paris, a stowaway in rugs and a discreet mimic in figurative canvases, until it could move freely again. A tension between embodiment and transcendence describes the modern painting of the late nineteenth and early twentieth centuries, as well as the art of Islam with its embodied subject contemplating the infinite. They hold in common a *light* conception of the subject, as something that is meant to be dissolved and unwound, much as haptic surfaces dissolve our eyes' focus and the process of following abstract lines unravel our subjectivity like a ball of yarn. Like figure and ground alternating into each other, they play with the tension of immanence and transcendence in the fabric of an embodied subjectivity.

4

The Rose and the Nightingale Persian and Turkish Mystical Poetry

Turkish literature is the collection of written and oral texts composed in the Turkish language, either in its Ottoman form or in less exclusively literary forms, such as that spoken in the Republic of Turkey today. The Ottoman Turkish language, which forms the basis of much of the written corpus, was influenced by Persian and Arabic and used a variant of the Perso-Arabic script. The history of Turkish literature spans a period of nearly 1,500 years. The oldest extant records of written Turkic are the Orhon inscriptions, found in the Orhon River valley in central Mongolia and dating to the 8th century. Subsequent to this period, between the 9th and 11th centuries, there arose among the nomadic Turkic peoples of Central Asia a tradition of oral epics, such as the *Book of Dede Korkut* of the Oghuz Turks—the linguistic and cultural ancestors of the modern Turkish people—and the Manas epic of the Kyrgyz people.

Beginning with the victory of the Seljuks at the Battle of Manzikert in the late 11th century, the Oghuz Turks began to settle in Anatolia, and in addition to the earlier oral traditions there arose a written literary tradition issuing largely—in terms of themes, genres, and styles—from Arabic and Persian literature. For the next 900 years, until shortly before the fall of the Ottoman Empire in 1922, the oral and written traditions would remain largely separate from one another. With the founding of the Republic of Turkey in 1923, the two traditions came together for the first time.

Two Traditions of Turkish Literature

Throughout most of its history, Turkish literature has been rather sharply divided into two rather different traditions, neither of which exercised much influence upon the other until the 19th century. The first of these two traditions is Turkish folk literature, and the second is Turkish written literature. For most of the history of Turkish literature, the salient difference between the folk and the written traditions has been the variety of language employed. The folk tradition, by and large, was oral and remained free of the influence of Persian and Arabic literature, and consequently of those literatures' respective languages. In folk poetry—which is by far the tradition's dominant genre—this basic fact led to two major consequences in terms of poetic style:

The poetic meters employed in the folk poetic tradition were different, being quantitative (i.e., syllabic) verse, as opposed to the qualitative verse employed in the written poetic tradition; the basic structural unit of folk poetry became the quatrain (Turkish: *dörtlük*) rather than the couplets (Turkish: *beyit*) more commonly employed in written poetry.

Furthermore, Turkish folk poetry has always had an intimate connection with song—most of the poetry was, in fact, expressly composed so as to be sung—and so became to a great extent inseparable from the tradition of Turkish folk music. In contrast to the tradition of Turkish folk literature, Turkish written literature—prior to the founding of the Republic of Turkey in 1923—tended to embrace the influence of Persian and Arabic literature. To some extent, this can be seen as far back as the Seljuk period in the late 11th to early 14th centuries, where official business was conducted in the Persian language, rather than in Turkish, and where a court poet such as Dehhanî—who served under the 13th century sultan Ala ad-Din Kay Qubadh I—wrote in a language highly inflected with Persian.

When the Ottoman Empire arose early in the 14th century, in northwestern Anatolia, it continued this tradition. The standard poetic forms—for poetry was as much the dominant genre in the written tradition as in the folk tradition—were derived either directly from the Persian literary tradition, or indirectly through Persian from the Arabic (the *kasîde*). However, the decision to adopt these poetic forms wholesale led to two important further consequences:

The poetic meters (Turkish: *aruz*) of Persian poetry were adopted; Persian- and Arabic-based words were brought into the Turkish language in great numbers, as Turkish words rarely worked well within the system of Persian poetic meter.

Out of this confluence of choices, the Ottoman Turkish language—which was always highly distinct from standard Turkish—was effectively born? This style of writing under Persian and Arabic influence came to be known as "Divan literature" (Turkish: *divan edebiyatý*), *dîvân* being the Ottoman Turkish word referring to the collected works of a poet. Just as Turkish folk poetry was intimately bound up with Turkish folk music, so did Ottoman Divan poetry develop a strong connection with Turkish classical music, with the poems of the Divan poets often being taken up to serve as song lyrics.

Turkish folk literature is an oral tradition deeply rooted, in its form, in Central Asian nomadic traditions. However, in its themes, Turkish folk literature reflects the problems peculiar to a settling (or settled) people who have abandoned the nomadic lifestyle. One example of this is the series of folktales surrounding the figure of Keloðlan, a young boy beset with the difficulties of finding a wife, helping his mother to keep the family house intact, and dealing with the problems caused by his neighbors. Another example is the rather mysterious figure of Nasreddin, a trickster who often plays jokes, of a sort, on his neighbors. Nasreddin also reflects another significant change that had occurred between the days when the Turkish people were nomadic and the days when they had largely become settled in Anatolia; namely, Nasreddin is a Muslim imam.

The Turkic peoples had first become an Islamic people sometime around the 9th or 10th century, as is evidenced from the clear Islamic influence on the 11th century Karakhanid work the *Kutadgu Bilig* (*"Wisdom of Royal Glory"*), written by Yusuf Has Hajib. The religion henceforth came to exercise an enormous influence on Turkish society and literature, particularly the heavily mystically oriented Sufi and Shi'a varieties of Islam. The Sufi influence, for instance, can be seen clearly not only in the tales concerning Nasreddin but also in the works of Yunus Emre, a towering figure in Turkish literature and a poet who lived at the end of the 13th and beginning of the 14th century, probably in the Karamanid state in south-central Anatolia. The Shi'a influence, on the other hand, can be seen extensively in the tradition of the *aþýk*s, or *ozan*s, who are roughly akin to medieval European minstrels and who traditionally have had a strong connection with the Alevi faith, which can be seen as something of a homegrown Turkish variety of Shi'a Islam.

It is, however, important to note that in Turkish culture, such a neat division into Sufi and Shi'a is scarcely possible: for instance, Yunus Emre is considered by some to have been an Alevi, while the entire Turkish *aþýk/ozan* tradition is permeated with the thought of the Bektashi Sufi order, which is itself a blending of Shi'a and Sufi concepts. The word *aþýk* (literally, "lover") is in fact the term used for first-level members of the Bektashi order. Because the Turkish folk literature tradition extends in a more or less unbroken line from about the 10th or 11th century to today, it is perhaps best to consider the tradition from the perspective of genre. There are three basic genres in the tradition: epic; folk poetry; and folklore.

The Epic Tradition

The Turkish epic has its roots in the Central Asian epic tradition that gave rise to the *Book of Dede Korkut*, which is in a language recognizably similar to modern Turkish and which developed from the oral traditions of the Oghuz Turks, that branch of the Turkic peoples which migrated towards western Asia and eastern Europe through Transoxiana beginning in the 9th century. The *Book of Dede Korkut* continued to survive in the oral tradition after the Oghuz Turks had, by and large, settled in Anatolia. The *Book of Dede Korkut* was the primary element of the Turkish epic tradition in Anatolia for several centuries. Another epic circulating at the same time, however, was the so-called *Epic of Köroðlu*, which concerns the adventures of Rüþen Ali ("Köroðlu", or "son of the blind man") to exact revenge for the blinding of his father.

The origins of this epic are somewhat more mysterious than those of the *Book of Dede Korkut*: many believe it to have arisen in Anatolia sometime between the 15th and 17th centuries; more reliable testimony, though, seems to indicate that the story is nearly as old as that of the *Book of Dede Korkut*, dating from around the dawn of the 11th century. Complicating matters somewhat is the fact that Köroðlu is also the name of a poet of the *aþýk/ozan* tradition.

That the epic tradition in Turkish literature may not have died out entirely can be seen from the *Epic of Shaykh Bedreddin* (*Þeyh Bedreddin Destaný*), published in 1936 by the poet Nâzým Hikmet Ran (1901–1963). This long poem—which concerns an Anatolian shaykh's rebellion against the Ottoman Sultan Mehmed I—is a sort of modern, written epic that nevertheless draws upon the same independent-minded traditions of the Anatolian people that can be seen in the *Epic of Köroðlu*. Also, many of the works of the 20th-century novelist Yaºar Kemal (1923–), such as his long 1955 novel *Memed, My Hawk* (*Ýnce Memed*), can be considered modern prose epics.

Folk Poetry

The folk poetry tradition in Turkish literature, as indicated above, was strongly influenced by the Islamic Sufi and Shi'a traditions. Furthermore, as partly evidenced by the prevalence of the still existent *aþýk/ozan* tradition, the dominant element in Turkish folk poetry has always been song. The development of folk poetry in Turkish—which began to emerge in the 13th century with such important writers as Yunus Emre, Sultan Veled, and Þeyyâd Hamza—was given a great boost when, on 13 May 1277, Karamanoðlu Mehmet Bey declared Turkish the official state language of Anatolia's powerful Karamanid state; subsequently, many of the tradition's greatest poets would continue to emerge from this region.

There are, broadly speaking, two traditions of Turkish folk poetry:

The *aþýk/ozan* tradition, which—although much influenced by religion, as mentioned above—was for the most part a secular tradition; the explicitly religious tradition, which emerged from the gathering places (*tekke*s) of the Sufi religious orders and Shi'a groups.

Much of the poetry and song of the *aþýk/ozan* tradition, being almost exclusively oral until the 19th century, remains anonymous. There are, however, a few well-known *aþýk*s from before that time whose names have survived together with their works: the aforementioned Köroðlu (16th century); Karacaoðlan (1606?–1689?), who may be the best-known of the pre-19th century *aþýk*s; Dadaloðlu (1785?–1868?), who was one of the last of the great *aþýk*s before the tradition began to dwindle somewhat in the late 19th century; and several others. The *aþýk*s were essentially minstrels who travelled through Anatolia performing their songs on the *baðlama*, a mandolin-like instrument whose paired strings are considered to have a symbolic religious significance in Alevi/Bektashi culture.

Despite the decline of the *aþýk/ozan* tradition in the 19th century, it experienced a significant revival in the 20th century thanks to such outstanding figures as Aþýk Veysel Þatýroðlu (1894–1973), Aþýk Mahzuni Þerif (1938–2002), Neþet Ertaþ (1943–), and many others. The explicitly religious folk tradition of *tekke* literature shared a similar basis with the *aþýk/ozan* tradition in that the poems were generally intended to be sung, generally in religious gatherings, making them somewhat akin to Western hymns (Turkish *ilahi*). One major difference from the *aþýk/ozan* tradition, however, is that—from the very beginning—the poems of the *tekke* tradition were written down.

This was because they were produced by revered religious figures in the literate environment of the *tekke*, as opposed to the milieu of the *aþýk/ozan* tradition, where the majority could not read or write. The major figures in the tradition of *tekke* literature are: Yunus Emre (1240?–1320?), who is one of the most important figures in all of Turkish literature; Süleyman Çelebi (?–1422), who wrote a highly popular long poem called *Vesîletü'n-Necât* ("The Means of Salvation", but more commonly known as the *Mevlid*), concerning the birth of the Islamic prophet Muhammad; Kaygusuz Abdal (1397–?), who is widely considered the founder of Alevi/Bektashi literature; and Pir Sultan Abdal (?–1560), whom many consider to be the pinnacle of that literature.

The tradition of folklore—folktales, jokes, legends, and the like—in the Turkish language is very rich. Perhaps the most popular figure in the tradition is the aforementioned Nasreddin (known as *Nasreddin Hoca*, or "teacher Nasreddin", in Turkish), who is the central character of thou-sands of jokes. He generally appears as a person who, though seeming somewhat stupid to those who must deal with him actually proves to have a special wisdom all his own:

One day, Nasreddin's neighbor asked him, "Teacher, do you have any forty-year-old vinegar?"—"Yes, I do," answered Nasreddin.—"Can I have some?" asked the neighbor. "I need some to make an ointment with."—"No, you can't have any," answered Nasreddin. "If I gave my forty-year-old vinegar to whoever wanted some, I wouldn't have had it for forty years, would I?"

Similar to the Nasreddin jokes, and arising from a similar religious milieu, are the Bektashi jokes, in which the members of the Bektashi religious order—represented through a character simply named *Bektaºi*—are depicted as having an unusual and unorthodox wisdom, one that often challenges the values of Islam and of society. Another popular element of Turkish folklore is the shadow theater centered on the two characters of Karagöz and Hacivat, who both represent stock characters: Karagöz—who hails from a small village—is something of a country bumpkin, while Hacivat is a more sophisticated city-dweller.

Popular legend has it that the two characters are actually based on two real persons who worked either for Osman I—the founder of the Ottoman dynasty—or for his successor Orhan I, in the construction of a palace or possibly a mosque at Bursa in the early 14th century. The two workers supposedly spent much of their time entertaining the other workers, and were so funny and popular that they interfered with work on the palace, and were subsequently beheaded. Supposedly, however, their bodies then picked up their severed heads and walked away.

Ottoman Literature

The two primary streams of Ottoman written literature are poetry and prose. Of the two, poetry—specifically, Divan poetry—was by far the dominant stream. Moreover, it should be noted that, until the 19th century, Ottoman prose did not contain any examples of fiction; that is, there were no counterparts to, for instance, the European romance, short story, or novel (though analogous genres did, to some extent, exist in both the Turkish folk tradition and in Divan poetry).

Divan Poetry

Ottoman Divan poetry was a highly ritualized and symbolic art form. From the Persian poetry that largely inspired it, it inherited a wealth of symbols whose meanings and interrelationships—both of similitude and opposition—were more or less prescribed. Examples of prevalent symbols that, to some extent, oppose one another include, among others:

The nightingale — the rose

The world — the rose garden

The ascetic — the dervish

As the opposition of "the ascetic" and "the dervish" suggests, Divan poetry—much like Turkish folk poetry—was heavily influenced by Sufi thought. One of the primary characteristics of Divan poetry, however—as of the Persian poetry before it—was its mingling of the mystical Sufi element with a profane and even erotic element. Thus, the pairing of "the nightingale" and "the rose" simultaneously suggests two different relationships:

The relationship between the fervent lover ("the nightingale") and the inconstant beloved ("the rose"). The relationship between the individual Sufi practitioner (who is often characterized in Sufism as a lover) and God (who is considered the ultimate source and object of love)

Similarly, "the world" refers simultaneously to the physical world and to this physical world considered as the abode of sorrow and impermanence, while "the rose garden" refers simultaneously to a literal garden and to the garden of Paradise. "The nightingale", or suffering lover, is often seen as situated—both literally and figuratively—in "the world", while "the rose", or beloved, is seen as being in "the rose garden". Divan poetry was composed through the constant juxtaposition of many such images within a strict metrical framework, thus allowing numerous potential meanings to emerge. A brief example is the following line of verse, or *mýsra*, by the 18th-century judge and poet Hayatî

Efendi:

Bir gül mü var bu gülþen-i 'âlemde hârsýz

("Does any rose, in this rose garden world, lack thorns?")

Here, the nightingale is only implied (as being the poet/ lover), while the rose, or beloved, is shown to be capable of inflicting pain with its thorns. The world, as a result, is seen as having both positive aspects (it is a rose garden, and thus analogous to the garden of Paradise) and negative aspects (it is a rose garden full of thorns and thus different to the garden of Paradise). As for the development of Divan poetry over the more than 500 years of its existence, that is—as the Ottomanist Walter G. Andrews points out—a study still in its infancy; clearly defined movements and periods have not yet been decided upon. Early in the history of the tradition, the Persian influence was very strong, but this was mitigated somewhat through the influence of poets such as the Azerbaijani Nesîmî (?–1417?) and the Uyghur Ali ªîr Nevâî (1441–1501), both of whom offered strong arguments for the poetic status of the Turkic languages as against the much-venerated Persian.

Partly as a result of such arguments, Divan poetry in its strongest period—from the 16th to the 18th centuries—came to display a unique balance of Persian and Turkish elements, until the Persian influence began to predominate again in the early 19th century. Despite the lack of certainty regarding the stylistic movements and periods of Divan poetry, however, certain highly different styles are clear enough, and can perhaps be seen as exemplified by certain poets:

Fuzûlî (1483?–1556), a Divan poet of Turkmen origin

Fuzûlî (1483?–1556); a unique poet who wrote with equal skill in Ottoman Turkish, Persian, and Arabic, and who came to be as influential in Persian as in Divan poetry.

Bâkî (1526–1600); a poet of great rhetorical power and linguistic subtlety whose skill in using the pre-established tropes of the Divan tradition is quite representative of the poetry in the time of Süleyman the Magnificent.

Nef'î (1570?–1635); a poet considered the master of the *kasîde* (a kind of panegyric), as well as being known for his harshly satirical poems, which led to his execution.

Nâbî (1642–1712); a poet who wrote a number of socially oriented poems critical of the stagnation period of Ottoman history.

Nedîm (1681?–1730); a revolutionary poet of the Tulip Era of Ottoman history, who infused the rather élite and abstruse language of Divan poetry with numerous simpler, populist elements.

ªeyh Gâlib (1757–1799); a poet of the Mevlevî Sufi order whose work is considered the culmination of the highly complex so-called "Indian style".

The vast majority of Divan poetry was lyric in nature: either *gazel*s (which make up the greatest part of the repertoire of the tradition), or *kasîde*s. There were, however, other common genres, most particularly the *mesnevî*, a kind of verse romance and thus a variety of narrative poetry; the two most notable examples of this form are the *Leylî vü Mecnun* of Fuzûlî and the *Hüsn ü Aºk* ("Beauty and Love") of ªeyh Gâlib.

Early Ottoman Prose

Until the 19th century, Ottoman prose never managed to develop to the extent that contemporary Divan poetry did. A large part of the reason for this was that much prose was expected to adhere to the rules of *sec'*, or rhymed prose, a type of writing descended from the Arabic *saj'* and which prescribed that between each adjective and noun in a sentence, there must be a rhyme.

Nevertheless, there was a tradition of prose in the literature of the time. This tradition was exclusively non-functional in nature—the fiction tradition was limited to narrative poetry. A number of such non-fictional prose genres developed:

Evliya Çelebi (1611–1682?), an Ottoman travel writer.

The *târih,* or history, a tradition in which there are many notable writers, including the 15th-century historian Aþýkpaþazâde and the 17th-century historians Kâtib Çelebi and Naîmâ.

The *seyâhatnâme,* or travelogue, of which the outstanding example is the 17th-century *Seyahâtnâme* of Evliya Çelebi.

The *sefâretnâme,* a related genre specific to the journeys and experiences of an Ottoman ambassador, and which is best exemplified by the 1718–1720 *Paris Sefâretnâmesi* of Yirmisekiz Mehmed Çelebi, ambassador to the court of Louis XV of France.

The *siyâsetnâme,* a kind of political treatise describing the functionings of state and offering advice for rulers, an early Seljuk example of which is the 11th-century *Siyâsatnâma,* written in Persian by Nizam al-Mulk, vizier to the Seljuk rulers Alp Arslan and Malik Shah I.

The *tezkîre,* a collection of short biographies of notable figures, some of the most notable of which were the 16th-century *tezkiretü'º-ºuarâ*s, or biographies of poets, by Latîfî and Aþýk Çelebi.

The *münºeât,* a collection of writings and letters similar to the Western tradition of *belles-lettres.*

The *münâzara,* a collection of debates of either a religious or a philosophical nature.

The 19th Century and Western Influence

By the early 19th century, the Ottoman Empire had become moribund. Attempts to right this situation had begun during the reign of Sultan Selim III, from 1789 to 1807, but were continuously thwarted by the powerful Janissary corps. As a result, only after Sultan Mahmud II had abolished the Janissary corps in 1826 was the way paved for truly effective reforms. These reforms finally came to the empire during the Tanzimat period of 1839–1876, when much of the Ottoman system was reorganized along largely French lines. The Tanzimat reforms "were designed both to modernize the empire and to forestall foreign intervention".

Along with reforms to the Ottoman system, serious reforms were also undertaken in the literature, which had become nearly as moribund as the empire itself. Broadly, these literary reforms can be grouped into two areas:

Changes brought to the language of Ottoman written literature; the introduction into Ottoman literature of previously unknown genres.

The reforms to the literary language were undertaken because the Ottoman Turkish language was thought by the reformists to have effectively lost its way. It had become more divorced than ever from its original basis in Turkish, with writers using more and more words and even grammatical structures derived from Persian and Arabic, rather than Turkish. Meanwhile, however, the Turkish folk literature tradition of Anatolia, away from the capital Constantinople, came to be seen as an ideal. Accordingly, many of the reformists called for written literature to turn away from the Divan tradition and towards the folk tradition; this call for change can be seen, for example, in a famous statement by the poet and reformist Ziya Pasha (1829–1880):

> Our language is not Ottoman; it is Turkish. What makes up our poetic canon is not gazels and kasîdes, but rather kayabaþýs, üçlemes, and çöðürs, which some of our poets dislike, thinking them crude. But just let those with the ability exert the effort on this road [of change], and what powerful personalities will soon be born!

At the same time as this call—which reveals something of a burgeoning national consciousness—was being made, new literary genres were being introduced into Ottoman literature, primarily the novel and the short story. This trend began in 1861, with the translation into Ottoman Turkish of François Fénelon's 1699 novel *Les aventures de Télémaque*, by Yusuf Kâmil

Pasha, Grand Vizier to Sultan Abdülaziz. What is widely recognized as the first Turkish novel, *Taaºuk-u Tal'at ve Fitnat* ("Tal'at and Fitnat in Love") by ªemsettin Sami (1850–1904), was published just ten years later, in 1872. The introduction of such new genres into Turkish literature can be seen as part of a trend towards Westernization that continues to be felt in Turkey to this day.

Due to historically close ties with France—strengthened during the Crimean War of 1854–1856—it was French literature that came to constitute the major Western influence on Turkish literature throughout the latter half of the 19th century. As a result, many of the same movements prevalent in France during this period also had their equivalents in the Ottoman Empire: in the developing Ottoman prose tradition, for instance, the influence of Romanticism can be seen during the Tanzimat period, and that of the Realist and Naturalist movements in subsequent periods; in the poetic tradition, on the other hand, it was the influence of the Symbolist and Parnassian movements that became paramount. Many of the writers in the Tanzimat period wrote in several different genres simultaneously: for instance, the poet Nâmýk Kemal (1840–1888) also wrote the important 1876 novel *Ýntibâh* ("Awakening"), while the journalist ªinasi (1826–1871) is noted for writing, in 1860, the first modern Turkish play, the one-act comedy *"ªair Evlenmesi"* ("The Poet's Marriage").

In a similar vein, the novelist Ahmed Midhat Efendi (1844–1912) wrote important novels in each of the major movements: Romanticism (*Hasan Mellâh yâhud Sýrr Ýçinde Esrâr*, 1873; *"Hasan the Sailor, or The Mystery Within the Mystery"*), Realism (*Henüz On Yedi Yaþýnda*, 1881; *"Just Seventeen Years Old"*), and Naturalism (*Müºâhedât*, 1891; *"Observations"*). This diversity was, in part, due to the Tanzimat writers' wish to disseminate as much of the new literature as possible, in the hopes that it would contribute to a revitalization of Ottoman social structures.

Early 20th Century Turkish Literature

Most of the roots of modern Turkish literature were formed between the years 1896—when the first collective literary movement arose—and 1923, when the Republic of Turkey was officially founded. Broadly, there were three primary literary movements during this period:

1. The *Edebiyyât-ý Cedîde* ("New Literature") movement
2. The *Fecr-i Âtî* ("Dawn of the Future") movement
3. The *Millî Edebiyyât* ("National Literature") movement

The New Literature Movement

The *Edebiyyât-ý Cedîde*, or "New Literature", movement began with the founding in 1891 of the magazine *Servet-i Fünûn* ("Scientific Wealth"), which was largely devoted to progress—both intellectual and scientific—along the Western model. Accordingly, the magazine's literary ventures, under the direction of the poet Tevfik Fikret (1867–1915), were geared towards creating a Western-style "high art" in Turkey. The poetry of the group—of which Tevfik Fikret and Cenâb ªehâbeddîn (1870–1934) were the most influential proponents—was heavily influenced by the French Parnassian movement and the so-called "Decadent" poets.

The group's prose writers, on the other hand—particularly Halit Ziya Uþaklýgil (1867–1945)—were primarily influenced by Realism, although the writer Mehmed Rauf (1875–1931) did write the first Turkish example of a psychological novel, 1901's *Eylül* ("September"). The language of the *Edebiyyât-ý Cedîde* movement remained strongly influenced by Ottoman Turkish. In 1901, as a result of the article "*Edebiyyât ve Hukuk*" ("Literature and Law"), translated from French and published in *Servet-i Fünûn*, the pressure of censorship was brought to bear and the magazine was closed down by the government of the Ottoman sultan Abdülhamid II. Though it was closed for only six months, the group's writers each went their own way in the meantime, and the *Edebiyyât-ý Cedîde* movement came to an end.

Dawn of the Future Movement

In the 24 February 1909 edition of the *Servet-i Fünûn* magazine, a gathering of young writers—soon to be known as the *Fecr-i Âtî* ("Dawn of the Future") group—released a manifesto in which they declared their opposition to the *Edebiyyât-ý Cedîde* movement and their adherence to the credo, "*Sanat ºahsî ve muhteremdir*" ("Art is personal and sacred"). Though this credo was little more than a variation of the French writer Théophile Gautier's doctrine of "*l'art pour l'art*", or "art for art's sake", the group was nonetheless opposed to the blanket importation of Western forms and styles, and essentially sought to create a recognizably Turkish literature. The *Fecr-i Âtî* group, however, never made a clear and unequivocal declaration of its goals and principles, and so lasted only a few years before its adherents each went their own individual way. The two outstanding figures to emerge from the movement were, in poetry, Ahmed Hâþim (1884–1933), and in prose, Yakup Kadri Karaosmanoðlu (1889–1974).

The National Literature Movement

In 1908, Sultan Abdülhamid II had instituted a constitutional government, and the parliament subsequently elected was composed almost entirely of members of the Committee of Union and Progress (also known as the "Young Turks"). The Young Turks had opposed themselves to the increasingly authoritarian Ottoman government, and soon came to identify themselves with a specifically Turkish national identity. Along with this notion developed the idea of a Turkish and even pan-Turkish nation (Turkish: *millet*), and so the literature of this period came to be known as "National Literature" (Turkish: *millî edebiyyât*). It was during this period that the Persian- and Arabic-inflected Ottoman Turkish language was definitively turned away from as a vehicle for written literature, and that literature began to assert itself as being specifically Turkish, rather than Ottoman.

At first, this movement crystallized around the magazine

Genç Kalemler ("Young Pens"), which was begun in the city of Selânik in 1911 by the three writers who were most representative of the movement: Ziya Gökalp (1876–1924), a sociologist and thinker; Ömer Seyfettin (1884–1920), a short-story writer; and Ali Canip Yöntem (1887–1967), a poet. In *Genç Kalemler*'s first issue, an article entitled "New Language" (Turkish: "*Yeni Lisan*") pointed out that Turkish literature had previously looked for inspiration either to the East as in the Ottoman Divan tradition, or to the West as in the *Edebiyyât-ý Cedîde* and *Fecr-i Âtî* movements, without ever turning to Turkey itself. This latter was the National Literature movement's primary aim.

The intrinsically nationalistic character of *Genç Kalemler*, however, quickly took a decidedly chauvinistic turn, and other writers—many of whom, like Yakup Kadri Karao-smanoðlu, had been a part of the *Fecr-i Âtî* movement—began to emerge from within the matrix of the National Literature movement to counter this trend. Some of the more influential writers to come out of this less far-rightist branch of the National Literature movement were the poet Mehmet Emin Yurdakul (1869–1944), the early feminist novelist Halide Edip Adývar (1884–1964), and the short-story writer and novelist Reþat Nuri Güntekin (1889–1956).

Post-independence Literature

Following the Ottoman Empire's defeat in the First World War of 1914–1918, the victorious Entente Powers began the process of carving up the empire's lands and placing them under their own spheres of influence. In opposition to this process, the military leader Mustafa Kemal (1881–1938), in command of the growing Turkish national movement whose roots lay partly in the Young Turks, organized the 1919–1923 Turkish War of Independence. This war ended with the official ending of the Ottoman Empire, the expulsion of the Entente Powers, and the founding of the Republic of Turkey.

The literature of the new republic emerged largely from the pre-independence National Literature movement, with its roots simultaneously in the Turkish folk tradition and in the Western notion of progress. One important change to Turkish literature was enacted in 1928, when Mustafa Kemal initiated the creation and dissemination of a modified version of the Latin alphabet to replace the Arabic-based Ottoman script. Over time, this change—together with changes in Turkey's system of education—would lead to more widespread literacy in the country.

Stylistically, the prose of the early years of the Republic of Turkey was essentially a continuation of the National Literature movement, with Realism and Naturalism predominating. This trend culminated in the 1932 novel *Yaban* ("*The Wilds*"), by Yakup Kadri Karaosmanoðlu. This novel can be seen as the precursor to two trends that would soon develop: social realism and the "village novel" (*köy romaný*). The social realist movement is perhaps best represented by the short-story writer Sait Faik Abasýyanýk (1906–1954), whose work sensitively and realistically treats the lives of cosmopolitan Istanbul's lower classes and ethnic minorities, subjects which led to some criticism in the contemporary nationalistic atmosphere. The tradition of the "village novel", on the other hand, arose somewhat later.

As its name suggests, the "village novel" deals, in a generally realistic manner, with life in the villages and small towns of Turkey. The major writers in this tradition are Kemal Tahir (1910–1973), Orhan Kemal (1914–1970), and Yaºar Kemal (1923–). Yaºar Kemal, in particular, has earned fame outside of Turkey not only for his novels—many of which, such as 1955's *Ýnce Memed* ("*Memed, My Hawk*"), elevate local tales to the level of epic—but also for his firmly leftist political stance. In a very different tradition, but evincing a similar strong political viewpoint, was the satirical short-story writer Aziz Nesin (1915–1995) and Rýfat Ilgaz(1911-1993).

Another novelist contemporary to, but outside of the social realist and "village novel" traditions is Ahmet Hamdi Tanpýnar (1901–1962). In addition to being an important essayist and poet, Tanpýnar wrote a number of novels—such as *Huzur* (*"Tranquillity"*, 1949) and *Saatleri Ayarlamà Enstitüsü* (*"The Time Regulation Institute"*, 1961)—which dramatize the clash between East and West in modern Turkish culture and society. Similar problems are explored by the novelist and short-story writer Oðuz Atay (1934–1977). Unlike Tanpýnar, however, Atay—in such works as his long novel *Tutunamayanlar* (*"The Disconnected"*, 1971–1972) and his short story *"Beyaz Mantolu Adam"* ("Man in a White Coat", 1975)—wrote in a more modernist and existentialist vein. On the other hand, Onat Kutlar's *Ýshak* (*"Isaac"*, 1959), composed of nine short stories which are written mainly from a child's point of view and are often surrealistic and mystical, represent a very early example of magic realism.

The tradition of literary modernism also informs the work of novelist Adalet Aðaoðlu (1929–). Her trilogy of novels collectively entitled *Dar Zamanlar* (*"Tight Times"*, 1973–1987), for instance, examines the changes that occurred in Turkish society between the 1930s and the 1980s in a formally and technically innovative style. Orhan Pamuk (1952–), winner of the 2006 Nobel Prize in Literature, is another such innovative novelist, though his works—such as 1990's *Beyaz Kale* (*"The White Castle"*) and *Kara Kitap* (*"The Black Book"*) and 1998's *Benim Adým Kýrmýzý* (*"My Name is Red"*)—are influenced more by postmodernism than by modernism. This is true also of Latife Tekin (1957–), whose first novel *Sevgili Arsýz Ölüm* (*"Dear Shameless Death"*, 1983) shows the influence not only of postmodernism, but also of magic realism.

In the early years of the Republic of Turkey, there were a number of poetic trends. Authors such as Ahmed Hâþim and Yahyâ Kemâl Beyatlý (1884–1958) continued to write important formal verse whose language was, to a great extent, a continuation of the late Ottoman tradition. By far the majority of the poetry of the time, however, was in the tradition of the folk-inspired "syllabist" movement (*Beº Hececiler*), which had emerged from the National Literature movement and which tended to express patriotic themes couched in the syllabic meter associated with Turkish folk poetry.

The first radical step away from this trend was taken by Nâzým Hikmet Ran, who—during his time as a student in the Soviet Union from 1921 to 1924—was exposed to the modernist poetry of Vladimir Mayakovsky and others, which inspired him to start writing verse in a less formal style. At this time, he wrote the poem *"Açlarýn Gözbebekleri"* ("Pupils of the Hungry"), which introduced free verse into the Turkish language for, essentially, the first time. Much of Nâzým Hikmet's poetry subsequent to this breakthrough would continue to be written in free verse, though his work exerted little influence for some time due largely to censorship of his work owing to his Communist political stance, which also led to his spending several years in prison. Over time, in such books as *Simavne Kadýsý Oðlu Þeyh Bedreddin Destaný* (*"The Epic of Shaykh Bedreddin, Son of Judge Simavne"*, 1936) and *Memleketimden Ýnsan Manzaralarý* (*"Human Landscapes from My Country"*, 1939), he developed a voice simultaneously proclamatory and subtle.

Another revolution in Turkish poetry came about in 1941 with the publication of a small volume of verse preceded by an essay and entitled *Garip* (*"Strange"*). The authors were Orhan Veli Kanýk (1914–1950), Melih Cevdet Anday (1915–2002), and Oktay Rifat (1914–1988). Explicitly opposing themselves to everything that had gone in poetry before, they sought instead to create a popular art, "to explore the people's tastes, to determine them, and to make them reign supreme over art". To this end, and inspired in part by contemporary French poets like Jacques Prévert, they employed not only a variant of the free verse introduced by Nâzým Hikmet, but also highly colloquial language, and wrote primarily about mundane daily subjects and the ordinary man on the street. The reaction was immediate and polarized: most of the academic establishment and older poets vilified them, while much of the Turkish population embraced them wholeheartedly. Though the movement itself lasted only ten years—until Orhan Veli's death in 1950, after which Melih Cevdet Anday and Oktay Rifat moved on to other styles—its effect on Turkish poetry continues to be felt today.

Just as the Garip movement was a reaction against earlier poetry, so—in the 1950s and afterwards—was there a reaction against the Garip movement. The poets of this movement, soon known as *Ýkinci Yeni* ("Second New"), opposed themselves to the social aspects prevalent in the poetry of Nâzým Hikmet and the Garip poets, and instead—partly inspired by the disruption of language in such Western movements as Dada and Surrealism—sought to create a more abstract poetry through the use of jarring and unexpected language, complex images, and the association of ideas. To some extent, the movement can be seen as bearing some of the characteristics of postmodern literature. The most well-known poets writing in the "Second New" vein were Turgut Uyar (1927–1985), Edip Cansever (1928–1986), Cemal Süreya (1931–1990), Ece Ayhan (1931–2002), Sezai Karakoç (1933-) and Ýlhan Berk (1918–).

Outside of the Garip and "Second New" movements also, a number of significant poets have flourished, such as Fazýl Hüsnü Daðlarca (1914–), who wrote poems dealing with fundamental concepts like life, death, God, time, and the cosmos; Behçet Necatigil (1916–1979), whose somewhat allegorical poems explore the significance of middle-class daily life; Can Yücel (1926–1999), who—in addition to his own highly colloquial and varied poetry—was also a translator into Turkish of a variety of world literature; and Ýsmet Özel (1944–), whose early poetry was highly leftist but whose poetry since the 1970s has shown a strong mystical and even Islamist influence.

Book Trade

30 000 new titles are appearing yearly - in sometimes small numbers. Reading is not yet very popular; 70 000 of 71

Millionen inhabitants regularly read books. 9 versos 17 Euro (pro pocket book/hardcover) - at an averadge earning of less than 600 Euro monthly - are rather unattractive, where illegal copies at basars cost two thirds less. "Official Certificates" für legally published books do not definitely solve the problem (controlling stays difficult...). 5000 of 10 000 book shops are at Istanbul, with also the bookfair and growing licence trading. Turkey is guest of honour at the Frankfurt Bookfair in 2008.

Poetry Enjoys Pride Of Place among literary and artistic forms throughout the Islamic world. While this is no doubt due in part to its aesthetics, the mnemonic quality of poetry makes it easy to remember for people who cannot read and write—a significant proportion of the world's Muslim population today as in the past. It is simultaneously valued for the same characteristics by literate people, for, as something that you can carry in your memory, it is a cheap and portable form of art. One of the most satisfying marriages in world literature is the one between Islamic mystical (Sufi) experiences and teachings and poetry, which is capable of conveying these ideas in a manner that is as seductive as it is instructive.

The mystical poetry written in Persian by famous figures such as Rumi (d. 1273), Sa'di (d. 1292), and Hafiz (d. 1389) is very well known both in the Persian original and in its celebrated and widely circulated translations. But mystical poetry is composed and enjoyed to no less a degree in other languages spoken by Muslims all over the world. There is a rich tradition of Sufi literary composition in Arabic which is often used as a source of inspiration by the best known Persian poets. Similarly, Ottoman Turkish and Urdu poetry derive much of their literary style from Persian and much of their content from both Arabic and Persian alongside their native Turkish and Indian cultures. Persian Sufi poetry and its derivative genres in Urdu and Ottoman Turkish are representatives of a highly literate court culture, and have traditionally enjoyed a limited audience outside these circles.

Paralleling this "high culture" form of poetry there was a popular Sufi poetical literature in both Punjabi and other languages spoken by Indian Muslims (not to mention Arabic, vernacular Turkish, Kurdish, and many others}.

This form of poetry was often viewed as too rustic to enjoy court patronage, and received none of the encouragement or rewards enjoyed by "high culture" poetry. It is therefore a testament to the innate talents of these popular Sufi poets and to the magnetic attraction of their poetry that for every Ottoman court poet like Sheyh Galip there is a Yunus Emre, and for every Mughal court figure like Mirza Ghalib there is a Sultan Bahu. In fact, it is these popular poets, writing in the vernaculars of their own people, who are more renowned. The average citizen of a small town in Anatolia neither may nor even be familiar with Sheyh Galip's name, but more than likely would know some of Yunus Emre's poetry by heart. Similarly, an ordinary citizen of the Punjab is unlikely to be familiar with Mirza Ghalib's work, but could be moved to tears by listening to someone like Sultan Bahu.

Bahu's Religious Message

Sultan Bahu's mystical poetry is an expression of disillusionment with formal, legalistic and institutionalized forms of religion, and of optimistic faith in the possibility of a personal, individual spiritual relationship with God. Bahu is emphasizing a central tenet of Sufism: that an absolute love for and devotion to God can result in the experience of losing oneself within the divine. The major impediment to this union is human attachment to the physical world, an instinct ingrained in the human soul. Through systematic detachment from this world and the practice of asceticism under the guidance of a Sufi master—together with meditational exercises based on the repetition of God's name—the Sufi successfully tames the soul. The soul's passions, once harnessed, help transport the Sufi further along his or her journey The imagery used is often that of taming a horse, which then becomes the mount on which the mystic travels for the rest of the mystical path.

The ultimate goal of this journey is to lose one's identity within the greater identity of God, or to attain spiritual death before physical death. This quest for death before dying is based on a saying attributed to the Prophet: "Die before you die!" Sultan Bahu develops these central concepts in a manner which would be appealing and accessible to a wide audience unfamiliar with the more esoteric and philosophical dimensions of Sufism. He emphasizes the power of love and stresses that love is more important than learning. In order to show the danger of turning religious practice into a habit or a birthright, he juxtaposes the learned scholar, who is incapable of attaining God, against the illiterate person whose love-madness transports him or her to the divine.

The Lord was neither found on the exalted throne, nor is the Lord in the Ka'ba.

The Lord was not found in learning and books, nor is the Lord in the prayer niche.

He was never found swimming in the Ganges, nor met through countless pilgrimages.

In line with many other Sufi figures from the formative period of Sufism in the ninth century onward; Bahu uses an emphasis on the value of illiteracy not to undermine the importance of Islam as a religion but to underline it. According to Bahu, while religious scholars only observe the formal, outward aspects of Islamic ritual and doctrine, the illiterate lover understands their true meaning. In the heart of the lover, the Islamic creedal statement "There is no god hut Allah, and Muhammad is the messenger of Allah" takes on a magical significance. Bahu states that the only writing one needs to know is the letters mTtn and alif. The inim is the first letter of the name "Muhammad." The alif is the first letter of the Arabic alphabet and also the first letter of the name "Allah." It is written as a vertical line, bringing to mind a raised index finger and symbolizing the unity of God. Thus when Bahu speaks of knowing only the alif, he is positioning himself squarely in a Sufi tradition which uses this metaphor to emphasize the futility of becoming preoccupied with external forms while ignoring underlying meanings.

Those who find the Beloved in the letter alif need not open the Quran to read it.

Many of Sultan Bahu's metaphors are common to Sufi poetry in many languages. The divine beloved is haughty and distant, and the quest for this beloved is a source of great anguish to the Sufi lover. The lover is likened to a nightingale in love with the rose which sits unattainable in its bed of thorns, causing the nightingale to spend its life in lamentation and to risk capture in the rose garden of grief:

I pecked and ate many grains of wheat, now the string of eternity is around my neck.

I flutter, caught in the noose, like the nightingale in the garden.

Such metaphors and his references to famous Sufi figures of the past also place him squarely in a wider Sufi poetical tradition, as does his use of the term *faqir* (meaning beggar) to refer to a mystic, thus signifying the belief that material poverty is related to spiritual wealth. Sufi symbolism is apparent in Bahu's very name, which means "with Him" (i.e., God). Bahu used his given name to greater advantage than most other poets. Most of his poems end in the refrain "hu" ("He" or "Him"), a formula which simultaneously renders them instantly recognizable as Sultan Bahu's compositions and marks them as specifically Sufi poetry because "hu" is a common formula in the Sufi meditational exercise of zikr.

This refrain became so characteristic of his style that later generations added it to all his poems. Tn a similar fashion, his name "Bahu" appears in the final line of all his poems, even though in many instances it ruins the meter of the verse and was, undoubtedly, not included by the poet himself. On other occasions, not only is the name Bahu an integral part of the final verse, as is common in Islamic poetic traditions, but its meaning is also incorporated into the poem:

You will find the singular Beloved if you gamble your head.

Be drunk in the love of Allah, always saying "Hu! Hu!"

While contemplating the name of Allah, control your breath. When essence blends with Essence, only then will you be called "Bahu."

Many of the themes discussed by Bahu and the metaphors he uses are drawn from the literary bank of Sufi writing and are then adapted to the Punjabi environment. A striking example of this is his frequent reference to birds. In addition to the stock metaphor of the nightingale referred to above, Bahu made particular use of hawks and falcons. They are often used as symbols of the soul in its quest to return to God, just as a falcon desires to return to its master's hand:

How can the poor falcon fly, for its feet have been bound?

Whoever does not possess love, Bahu, loses both worlds.

In some of his poems Bahu refers to birds in a context which is comprehensible only if one is familiar with the Indian environment. This is true, for example, in his reference to the owl as symbolizing stupidity and in his images of birds singing as if to welcome the monsoon:

I wonder lamenting like the cuckoo, begging that my days don't go by in waste.

Speak, bird! The monsoon has come; perhaps God will she dsoem rain.

The cuckoo is traditionally believed to be singing a lament that means "Where is my beloved?" In the second line, I have substituted the generic "bird" for a species known as papeeha in Punjabi, the call of which is this same lament. Bahu's extreme reverence for his spiritual master is also a theme common in Sufism, particularly in the Indian context. Sufi writers traditionally emphasize the centraliry of a living spiritual guide, stating that it is almost impossible to attain advanced mystical states without the help of such a master.

The Sufi practitioner is supposed to surrender both his body and soul to this person, proverbially becoming like a corpse in the hands of a mortician.

This attitude toward Sufi masters has led to a very high degree of veneration, so much so that the tombs of dead Sufis function as the centers of saint and shrine cults which are visited by all sorts of devotees, most of whom have no formal Sufi affiliation. They also function as the centers for major religious celebrations, and many people come to these shrines to seek the intercession of Sufi saints—both living and dead—for critical events in their lives. Many legalistic scholars find this veneration suspect and speak out against the Sufi shrines. In pre-modern times such critics had limited success in curtailing the popular devotion to Sufi shrines, which occupy a more central position in the spiritual landscape of the Punjab and other parts of South Asia than do the mosques. Bahu echoes this sentiment in his many verses:

This body is a dwelling of the true Lord, and my heart like a garden to bow down in prayer.

Within it are fountains, within it are prayer grounds, within it places to bow down for prayer.

Within it is the Ka'ba, within it the qibla, within it cries of "Only Allah!"

I found the Perfect Guide, Bahu, He alone will take care of me.

One of the most intriguing features of Bahu's poetry, also characteristic of popular Sufi poetry in India, is his occasional use of the feminine gender when talking about himself. Sufi love poetry outside India (and even in the Indian high culture traditions of Persian and Urdu) represents the relationship between lover and beloved .is one in which an active human lover pursues a passive (or passive-aggressive) beloved. This dynamic traditionally genders the active partner as male. There is some ambiguity concerning the gender of the passive partner, in part because homoerotic love is widely accepted in Islamic literature and in part because of the lack of formal gender in both Persian and Ottoman. Most of Sultan Bahu's poems fit this pattern, but in a few of them the lover is explicitly female, something which is very clear since Punjabi does have gender:

I am ugly and my Beloved beautiful—how can I be agreeable Him?

He never enters my home though I use a hundred thousand ruses.

Neither am I beautiful nor have I wealth to display—how can I please my Friend?

This pain shall remain forever, Bahu, I will die crying.

There is little Islamic precedent for this form of eroticization of the relationship between the human being and God. On the other hand, it seems to share many elements with Hindu literature, in particular with the *virahini* tradition of northern India in which the poet addresses God in the voice of a girl or young woman. Similar to the devotional love poets of the *bhakti* tradition of *Krishnaite* Hinduism, the Sufi poet can be seen in the role of the herdswoman or Gopi who is in love with God. The death anniversary of an Indian Sufi saint is traditionally called an 'urs, an Arabic word for "wedding," and many of the rituals undertaken at such festivals clearly celebrate the saint's death as the occasion of his marriage to God. Such feminization of the Sufi is taken to an extreme in some popular Sufi groups where the men dress up in women's clothing.

Bahu evokes this image in one of his poems where he uses the term *sada suhagan* to indicate a level of blessed happiness; the term literally means a woman whose husband never dies and who therefore never becomes a widow. Some of the images evoked by Sultan Bahu are peculiar to his Indian environment. Islam and Hinduism were viewed by many legalistic religious scholars as mutually irreconcilable religious systems. This attitude sometimes combined with the administrative policies of Muslim rulers to create conditions of mutual hostility between Muslims and Hindus.

It was largely through the efforts of mystical figures such as Sultan Bahu that Islam gained popularity and converts in India. These mystical thinkers not only absorbed Indian ideas and values, they also consciously attempted to address an audience wider than the Turco-Persian settlers and the small number of Persianized Indian converts. Sultan Bahu's Punjabi poetry is clear evidence of this. The majority of his works are in Persian, but his fame derives from Punjabi verses that emphasize the sincerity of religious devotion irrespective of religious affiliation. It is no wonder that he is revered by Sikh and Hindu Punjabis as well as by Muslims.

The Translation

The Punjabi language has languished in comparison to the change in status of other northern Indian languages in the last two hundred years. Before the British colonization of India, its Muslim rulers had used Persian as their official language and ignored local vernaculars. Following the breakup of the Mughal Empire, the Sikh rulers of the Punjab continued to favor Persian as the language of state despite the fact that Punjabi is the Sikh scriptural language. By the time the British finally conquered the Punjab in 1839-41, the British administrative policy of using major ethnic languages to communicate with the colonized population was well in place, and the choice of Urdu (a language from north-central India) as the administrative language of Indian Muslims was an accomplished fact.

It is therefore no surprise that when British colonial rule was extended to the Punjab, Urdu was used as the medium of official commerce with the Punjabi Muslims (the use of Persian, the Islamic imperial language was simply never an option for the British). As a movement for Muslim self-determination took shape in northern India, the majority of Muslim activists, including those from the Punjab, willingly accepted Urdu as the language representing Muslim ethnicity.

This pattern, in which Punjabi was marginalized and trivialized to the benefit of Urdu continued after the establishment of Pakistan in 1947. The trivialization of Punjabi has meant that the government, which is the main sponsor of educational and cultural projects, has put virtually no effort into the standardization of Punjabi as a language or the preservation and dissemination of its literature. There is no standardized Punjabi grammar or script, and no good Punjabi dictionary. As a result systematic, critical studies of Punjabi literary works are all but impossible to do.

Greater Punjab is a vast geographical region, including the dusty flat lands surrounding Delhi, the rolling hills of Jammu and Himachal Pradesh, the narrow valleys of Hazara and Azad Kashmir, the salt hills and scrub of the Potohar plateau, and the rocky desert of the Deras in Baluchistan, Sindh, and Sarhad (the anachronistic North West Frontier Province of Pakistan). But the Punjabi heartland is the northwestern corner of the Indo-Gangetic plain, a flat region dominated by its rivers and from which the Punjab (Five Rivers) takes its name. Most of Islamic Punjabi literature comes from the center of this region, a place known as the Rechna Doab (Ravi and Chenab Twin River Region). The rivers dictate the rhythms of the romanticized Punjabi life. The major daily occupations of this life are farming and the care of cows and water buffaloes.

People live in villages surrounded by fields, rather than in homesteads located on private land. As a result, the daily march out to the fields or to pastures has become a motif in Punjabi literature. The rivers and the agriculture dependent upon them become the context in which the dramatic moments of Punjabi life are played out. Bathing, washing clothes and fetching water, grazing animals, fetching fodder, meeting mystics and mendicants, taking food to farmers and herdsmen—all become scenes of romance and intrigue. The Punjab is a place where poets can evoke images of birds pecking out the newly sprouted shoots of wheat, where buffaloes refuse to yield their milk until they hear the flute of their herdsman, and where (as mentioned earlier) a variety of lark is named after its plaintive cry, "Where is my beloved?"

This is a place where the rivers flood their banks with every monsoon, and where they mysteriously change course as they make their serpentine way from the Himalayas to the Arabian Sea. As the rivers make new channels, they create rich alluvial islands, called "*bela*." The bela is an important part of life as recorded in Punjabi literature. A good Ma is covered with grass, a bad bcla with marshes and quicksand; a good bela is a place to graze animals and meet lovers, a bad bela is where tigers hunt and where one dies of snakebite or drowning. It is on a bela that Hir meets her beloved Ranjha in thc famous Punjabi epic, and it is on the bela that she is betrayed. Thus when Sultan Bahu uses the imagery of the bela, he is not only evoking all that the bela represents in Punjabi rural life, he is also drawing on his audience's familiarity with the image of the bela in Punjabi literature, particularly in the epic of Hir.

It is in the wedding of Islamic mystical metaphors with the imagery of the Punjabi heartland that Sultan Bahu most distinguishes himself, and it is in this very aspect. Assuming that the majority of readers of this work will be unfamiliar not only with Punjabi but also with the Punjab, I have leaned toward more generic metaphors in my translation. Thus "bela" is translated as "marsh," "dune," and "river bank." One characteristic of the genre of Punjabi abyat is that the content of each line of a poem does not necessarily have anything to do with the next.

Furthermore, Bahu's Abyat are often in a very colloquial tone, and frequently reverse the normal Punjabi word order. These characteristics combine to give the translation an occasionally choppy and awkward tone. Keeping in mind the fact that these poems are normally sung, and are not expected to conform strictly to Indo-Persian metrics, I have rearranged the sentence structure only in a few extreme cases. The Punjabi

Abyat of Sultan Bahu are normally arranged in alphabetical order by the first letter of the Arabo-Persian alphabet. Since this arrangement is irrelevant in an English translation and has absolutely no relationship to the content, I have arranged the translations according to my own aesthetic sense.

Sultan Bahu's Life

Very little is known about Sultan Bahu's lite, and such information as exists is shaped by a three-hundred-year-long exercise in hagiography. He is mentioned in passing in biographical dictionaries of Indian Sufi figures, but these entries are extremely brief The only substantial account of his life is in the *Manaqib-i Snltani,* a work written six or seven generations after Sultan Bahu's death by one of his descendants by the name of Sultan Hamid. According to this text, which is extremely hagiographical in its tone? Sultan Bahu was born during the reign of the Mughal ruler Shah Jahan (r. 1628-58) in the town of Shorkot, located between Multan and Jhang in Pakistan. Shorkot had been given as a source of revenue to his father, Bayazid Muhammad, in recognition for military service to the Mughal government. His mother, Rasti, gave him the overtly mystical name of Bahu, meaning "With Him [God]." Bahu kept this as his pen name, to which his disciples added the honorific tide of "Sultan" which has been retained by both his spiritual and biological descendants. Prose works by Sultan Bahu suggest that he referred to himself as Bahu A'wan.

The A'wans are a tribe, based in the extreme western end of the Punjab, claiming descent from Ali (the cousin and son-in-law of the Prophet) through his son Muhammad ibn al-Hanafiyya. Ah is considered the fourth caliph by Sunni and the first imam by Shi'a Muslims. As a result, not only does the A'wans command high status in the Indian Muslim environment for being Arabs but they also claim descent from the household of the Prophet, albeit not through his daughter Fatima. Nothing is known of Sultan Bahu's early childhood or education.

It has traditionally been held that he received little or no formal schooling, and evidence in support of this view is drawn from some of his verses. Such verses are a formulaic part of the image of the love-infused Sufi; they deemphasize formal education in order to underline the transformative power of the love of God. Stories abound of early Sufis who could read nothing except the name of God but who worked miracles through it. Bahu's extensive writings would, in fact, suggest that he must have had at least some formal schooling. His lengthy and esoteric Persian writings show that he was familiar with the standardized Sufi teachings of the day. Furthermore, Bahu's prose works contain many traditions of the Prophet which are quoted in Arabic, a language and literature which could only be learned in the Punjab through formal education.

The *Manaqib-i Sultani* states that Sultan Bahu tried his hand at agriculture in his youth but gave it up and began to wander the forests and graveyards near Jhang. On one such occasion he encountered a Sufi on the banks of the Ravi. This man, named Habibullah Khan, became Bahu's first spiritual guide but quickly realized Bahu's unusual mystical potential and sent him to Delhi to study with his own master, Sayyid 'Abdur-Rahman of the Qadiri Sufi order. It is most likely that Bahu's formal knowledge of Sufism derives from the unspecified amount of time he spent in Delhi with this second Sufi master. During his time in Delhi, Bahu met the future Mughal ruler Aurangzeb at least once at the communal Friday prayer.

Some biographers have made much of his contact with Aurangzeb, the last of the truly powerful Mughals, but these contacts are no doubt exaggerated. Bahu does not appear to have wielded any influence over Aurangzeb's religion-, policies, nor did he benefit financially or politically from association with the future emperor. If anything, their relationship was most likely shaped by the fact that Bahu's Sufi master, Sayyid 'Abdur-Rahman, was related by marriage to Aurangzeb's estranged brother, Dara Shikuh. It is therefore unlikely that Sayyid 'Abdur-Rahman or any of his disciples would have had much to do with Aurangzeb.

Neither the date nor the reason for Bahu's return to Shorkor is known. The *Manaqib-i Sullani* states that he married four rimes, had eight sons (daughters are not mentioned), and never again left the section of the Punjab from which he came. He died in 1691 and was buried outside Shorkot at a place called Qilaqahrgan (or QilaqaV-gan). In 1775 the Chenab River changed course and threatened to wash away his grave, whereupon his coffin was dug up and moved to its present location where his shrine functions as a pilgrimage site for people from all over the Punjab.

Sultan Bahu's Written Works

Sultan Bahu's fame is almost entirely due to his Punjabi poetry, called the Abyat. This is despite the fact that he was a prolific writer of Persian prose and poetry-. The author of the *Manaqib-i Sultani* claims that Bahu wrote one hundred forty works, and twenty-six existing works are ascribed to him. Most of these have been published as nonscholarfy Urdu translations. Through a strange set of circumstances, the work of critical edition and study of the Persian texts is being thwarted by the heirs of one Malik Fazl Dm who, in the first quarter of this century, came to the realization that his vocation in life was to disseminate the teachings of Sultan Bahu.

Malik Fazl Din convinced the owners of what are believed to be the most accurate (and in some cases, the only known) manuscripts of Sultan Bahu's works to hand them over to him. He then commissioned a number of unskilled translators to render them into Urdu, which he published in a press he had opened in Lahore under the name *Allah wale ki qawmi dukkan* (The Godly One's Public Shop). The original manuscripts are in the hands of Malik Fazl Din's family which allows no one, not even the spiritual heirs of Sultan Bahu, to see them. This is very unfortunate, because the available translations suggest that Sultan Bahu's prose works are deserving of study. They are comprised of a number of book-length monographs and a majority of shorter treatises, containing general Sufi teachings, statements demonstrating the excellence of the Qadiri order, and didactic writings illustrating visions, stations, and states encountered along the Sufi path. A preliminary investigation suggests that the most important of these are *Mahik al-jaqr kalan* and *Nur al-huda-yi kalam.*

The Punjab1 Abyat

Bahu excelled as a mystical poet. There are frequent and extensive fragments of Persian poetry in his prose works, and he also has a Persian collection of poetry which has been published together with a versified Urdu translation. But his Persian verse has not gained popularity in any way comparable to his Punjabi poetry, which is regarded as one of the literary treasures of the language. At least fourteen editions of Bahu's Punjabi Abyat have been printed, in both the Perso-Arabic and the Gurmukhi scripts (the latter being the script used by Sikhs). It has also been translated into Urdu and English, although all the translations have serious shortcomings. Many problems of translation and redaction derive from the fact that there are no manuscripts of Bahu's Punjabi poetry known to predate this century. In fact, the oldest available collection of his Abyat is a lithograph edition printed in 1891 and containing 116 poems.

The most influential edition was published in 1915 by the aforementioned Malik Fazl Din and contains 183 poems. However, nothing is known concerning the written source of either of these versions. Malik Fazl Din's 1915 edition has become the basis for later editions and translations. Several attempts have been made to establish a reliable version of Bahu's Punjabi poetry, the most notable being by Sultan Altaf All (who has consulted the greatest number of sources) and Sayyid Nazir Ahmed (who has made a methodology). Although they are better than all other editions of Bahu's Abyat, both Sultan Altaf Ali's and Sayyid Nazir Ahmed's versions suffer from shortcomings, in large part due to difficulties endemic to the study of Muslim (as opposed to Sikh) Punjabi literature at this point in time.

Punjabi has traditionally been seen as an oral language and treated as unworthy ol being written down. As a result, the earliest known written examples of Bahu's Abyat date from two centuries after his death; there is, therefore, a certain futility to a text critical method of establishing an accurate version of his Punjabi poetry. It is conceivable that valuable manuscripts of the Abyat are waiting to be discovered in unattended private libraries, but the current written records of the Abyat have no textual connection with Sultan Bahu or his immediate disciples. Given the complete absence of a manuscript tradition, it would be methodologically more productive to take an oral, folkloric rather than a philological approach to studying not only the Abyat of Bahu but also the entire canon of premodem Punjabi poetry.

Bahu's poetry exists, is transmitted, and is appreciated almost entirely as an oral form accompanied by music. Anonymous poets have composed verses that have been attributed to Bahu, and his own verses have been modified in terms of vocabulary, meter, and style to suit the dialects and tastes of the audience. Attempts to recover Bahu's own poems require the establishment not only of a Punjabi grammar, but also a historical grammar of the Doabi Punjabi dialect of two centuries ago. Sayyid Nazir Ahmed's attempt at making the Abyat fit the standards of Urdu and Persian metrics is flawed in precisely this respect. In contrast, Sultan Altaf Ali's methodology of allowing the most popular versions to represent the text seems better, and I have followed him in this regard except when obvious Urdu words have crept into his edition. The literature is oral, and the most widely circulated variants should be considered the most representative.

There are two existing English translations of Sultan Bahu's Abyat. The first and better known one is by Maqbool Elahi. The second is a partial translation preceded by an uncritical study of Sultan Bahu's life and thought by L. R. Krishna and A. R. Luther. Both translations are somewhat date din their idiom and sacrifice accuracy of meaning in favor of rhyme and meter (this is explicitly stated as a goal by Maqbool Elahi). Furthermore, the number of verses in the poems in these translations does not correspond to those in the original Abyat, and the chosen rhyme has no similarity to that of Bahu's work. Both editions are out of print.

Poems of Uftade

Üftade is the name by which Mehmed is usually known. In fact, it designates a surname which was revealed during a vision, following an episode which was to mark the path of his future life. Üftade is a Persian word meaning "fallen", "perished", "and ruined". The story of the way in which he adopted the surname is celebrated. It is told by, amongst others, Ismail Hakki Bursevi, one of the most illustrious Celveti masters, in his work on the spiritual line of the Celvetiyye. In his youth, Mehmet had been chosen to perform the call to prayer in the Great Mosque of Bursa, the Ulucami, and in the mosque of Doganbey, whose name is not specified. His call to prayer was so beautiful that people gathered to hear it and some fell into ecstasy, as he himself records.

One day he was offered a sum of money to compensate him for his service. But the same night Mehmed had a vision during which it was said to him: "You have fallen (üftade) from your station"; following which he immediately returned the money which he had imprudently accepted. It is thus that after having used the name Muhyiddin, he abandoned it to use the name Üftade. This story was to have great importance in the care that he would take in future with money. In contrast to a large number of mystics living on gifts and other revenue taken from landed property granted by the State, as had become customary, Üftade would always refuse such a gift. One story at the end of his life well illustrates this position of principle.

The mother of Sultan Murad III, Nur Banu Sultan, had come to visit him and had brought a coffer full of money. Üftade, as ever, would not accept it, but try as he might to turn down the gift, at the lady's insistence; he ended up saying that she might leave the offering in a corner, where it remained untouched. One day, however, Üftade exclaimed to himself: "Since this money arrived in our house, the blessing has gone. May it (the coffer) disappear!" and the coffer vanished at once. Then soon after, Üftade said: "They have driven away our Presence! Let us set off at once on our travels, let us not stay another instant!" Üftade also gives advice to his disciples on the subject of money, when describing his attitude towards the salary he received as preacher in the Emir Sultan mosque. "I gave what I earned to the poor who searched for God, and I distributed to each poor person two dirhams, on condition that they would be content and would accept nothing from anyone else.

As for those amongst them who are not in need, let them eat only by taking from their own lawful estate once each day and night, and let them add nothing. Those that are in search of God should accept nothing from the exterior, for that gets in the way of handing oneself over in trust [to God]. As for the lovers of God, let them eat what is lawful but twice a day." He himself recounts also how, later on, he came to resign from his office of muezzin. "I became muezzin at a mosque, and for performing the call to prayer I earned three dirhams, with which I paid the rent on the house. One day I found myself flying close to the sky, and saw men such as I had never seen here in this lower world. Some said: 'look at him, how he flies!' Others said: 'If he didn't spend sacred money, he would cross the sky.'

After that I abandoned even the call to prayer." This story demonstrates the importance that Üftade gave to the relationship with money. Even lawful money could become a major obstacle in spiritual realisation. There was for him a fundamental incompatibility between religious duty, which can only be done for God alone, and payment, which one expects. Spiritual realisation enabled him to go beyond the apparent lawfulness of the act in order to enter truly into the ethical sphere of freely given service and handing oneself over in trust to God. The story of the coffer is emblematic, mirroring in a certain way Üftade's spiritual life.

It begins with losing a spiritual station which had been given to him by Divine Generosity, and then recovering it, as demonstrated by the recollection of the fall and the rule which it brought. Then it closes with accidentally breaching this rule, which was also to mark the end of Üftade's life and his return to the world of pure spirits. These two stories frame the whole of Üftade's spiritual life, and demonstrate the discipline which he put himself under. Üftade, then, was one of those masters whose rule meant that one should renounce the good things of this world, and we may recall here the rule of Najm al-din Kubra that one should renounce the two worlds to be counted amongst the men of God.

5

Sufism in Indo-Pakistan

Sufism and Mysticism

The mystic tradition of Sufism found home in Islam encompassing a diverse range of beliefs and practices dedicated to Allah and divine love to help a fellow man. Its not surprising, therefore, that Sufi orders associated with every branch of Islam exist. It is widely believed though that Sufi thought emerged from the Middle East in the eighth century, yet its adherents are now found every where in the world. Almost all traditional Sufi schools (orders) trace their "chains of transmission" back to the Prophet (PBUH) via his cousin and son-in-law Imam Ali ibn Abi Talib, except the Naqshbandi order which traces its origin to Caliph Abu Bakr. From their point of view, the esoteric teaching was given to those who had the capacity to contain the direct experiential gnosis of God, and then passed on from teacher to student through centuries.

Sufi is the Arabic word for "wool", in the sense of "cloak", referring to the simple cloaks the original Sufis wore, but the Sufis use the composing letters of the words to express hidden meanings, and so the word could also be understood as "enlightenment." Sufism became organised and adopted a form and institution in the 12th and 13th centuries A.D. The two great pioneers in this field were Sheikh Abdul Qadir Jilani and Hazrat Shahabuddin Suhrawardy. By introducing the system of *'silsila'* which was a sort of association / order, and *takia / khankha*, a lodge or hospice, they invested the movement with a sense of brotherhood and provided it with a meeting place. The *'silsila'* and the *takia / khankha* were the king-pins of the organization. With a stream of selfless workers available and with no dearth of devoted and assiduous leadership, the movement made swift progress and spread far and wide.

The character of Sufi movement was such that it did not require official patronage or military protection. It succeeded without both in a number of countries like Malaya, Indonesia, East and West Africa. The same is true of their work in Pakistan. In fact, power was a hindrance rather than a help to the progress of Sufi mission. Eminent Sheikh Nizamuddin refused to consider a proposal made by Mohammad Tughlaq to coordinate missionary activity with political expansion." (*Indian Muslim* by Prof. M. Mujeeb)

The Sufi Spirit

Sufism has universal appeal and its characteristics are universally acclaimed. Sufism on the whole is primarily concerned with direct personal experience, and as such may be compared to various forms of mysticism such as Zen Buddhism and Gnosticism. It negates rigidity and promotes free religious thought that emphasizes God's love and mercy that sustains the whole universe. Sufism stresses the essence of faith rather than mere observance of rituals. It shuns wealthy, monarchic and bureaucratic infestations of big cities and detests false values based on pelf and power and charters to restore morality in its proper place.

The Sufi Traditions in Pakistan

Pakistan and Sufism are inter-related, inter-woven and inseparable from each other. If Pakistan's beginning is traced back to the conquest of this sub-continent by Muslims armies, as is erroneously thought, then the whole sub-continent should have become Pakistan since Muslim arms were successful throughout the area. But Pakistan emerged only in those territories where Sufism met with success. Pakistan, therefore, can be described as the fruit of the Sufi movement.

Early in the 8th century A.D. when Mohammad Bin Qasim conquered Sind (which included most of Punjab), yet the general conversion to Islam in Pakistan, according to scholars, began on a sizeable scale two hundred years later from the 13th century. This period starts with the arrival of Hazrat Khwaja Moinuddin Chishti in the subcontinent followed by a large number of Chishti and Suhrawardy Sufis. The great pioneers of the 13th century Sufi movement in the areas of present-day Pakistan were the four friends known as 'Chahar Yar:' Hazrat Fariduddin Masud Ganj Shakar of Pak Pattan (1174-1266), Hazrat Syed Jalaluddin Bukhari of Uch-Bahawalpur (1196-1294), Hazrat Bahauddin Zakaria of Multan (1170-1267) and Hazrat Lal Shahbaz Qalandar of Sehwan (1177-1274). It is said that 17 leading tribes of the Punjab accepted Islam at the hands of Hazrat Fariduddin Masud Ganj Shakar.

But the Sufis did not do their work in a hurry. They first set an example of highest probity by their personal acts and propagated the message of Islam in a simple, yet forceful manner without exerting any political or economic pressure so that the work of conversion continued for centuries throughout the Delhi Sultanate, down to the days of the British Raj. Contrary to conventional Islam, music also played a significant role in spread of Islam through Sufi's creed. Classic music is the only art where a synthesis between Hindu and Muslim artistic traditions took place in the Indian subcontinent. Sufis with their spiritual preoccupations also remained in the forefront of this synthesis. Khawaja Moeenuddin Chishti, the founder of the Chishtyia order in the subcontinent and his successor Khwaja Bakhtiyar Kaki, both listened to music as a spiritual stimulant. In the assemblies of Nizamuddim Auliya, Amir Khusro's *ghazals* were sung along with the other pieces of music.

The Chishti tradition regarded music as an indispensable aid to ecstasy and a means to attain revelations through it. It relied on Persian verse as the content to musical composition but in some provinces it soon borrowed or adapted mixed Persian and Hindi wording. It is said that the Sufi practice of listening music first took place in the Indo-Pak subcontinent and then passed on to rest of the Muslim world. Our Sufi poets such as Baba Farid, Shah Husain, Sultan Bahu, Shah Latif Bhitai, Bulleh Shah, Sachal Sarmast, Khwaja Ghulam Farid, Mian Muhammad Bakhsh and Maulvi Ghulam Rasul continued the finest tradition of poetry and music. Still today, the shrines of these Sufi saints host classical music contests. Festivals and carnivals abound with *dhamal,* whirling in a ritual reverie. Men, and sometimes women, in bright traditional robes dance and shout around frantically following their own path to enlightenment. A traditional drum called *dhol* beats deafeningly and hypnotically, making everyone to dance to forget surrounding and tread in a voyage of ecstasy. Another popular genre of Sufi music is *qawwali,* the most important and widespread in the Khusrau tradition, which has remained alive for more than seven centuries.

Sufi Festivals and Tourism

The fairs at Sufi shrines or Sufi saints (popularly called the *Urs)* generally mark the death anniversary of a saint. At every Urs, devotees assemble in large numbers and pay homage to the memory of a saint. Soul inspiring music with *dhamaal* (when devotees dance in ecstasy on beat of a drum) on such occasions takes the colour of a folk festival and appeals to all and sundry. It forms a part of the folk music carrying mystic messages (verses) of the Sufi or saint which throbs the heart of every one and people from all walks of life throng the dargah or mausoleum. The countryside of Punjab but not excluding the urban centres or metropolises, abound with *Urses* like the ones of Data Ganj Bakhsh, Hazrat Mian Mir and Shah Hussain in Lahore, Urs of Baba Farid Ganj Shakar in Pakpattan, Urs of Hazrat Bahaudin Zakria in Multan, Urs of Sakhi Sarwar Sultan in Dera Ghazi Khan, Urs of Hazrat Bulleh Shah in Kasur and Urs of Hazrat Imam Barri Lateef in Islamabad. A big fair is organized at Jandiala Sher Khan in the Sheikhupura district on the Mausoleum of Syed Waris Shah.

A great festival of lights, called Mela Chiraghan, is held in the last week of March, outside the Shalimar Gardens, Lahore, in the memory of Sufi poet Madhu Lal Hussain. Every year, no less than 500,000 people come from across the country and from abroad to attend the festival. The touristic importance of these festivals is so strong that they need be incorporated in the overall tourism policy of the country. In the tourism year 2007 one of the slots was to organise Sufi Festivals in Multan and Sehwan. Such type of events directly relate to Islam's eternal message of peace, tolerance and international human brotherhood promoted through the works of our Sufi saints. These festivals could be held in the month of September, in synchronization with the Urs of our great Sufi Saint Lal Shahbaz Qalandar which is held every year from Sep. 3rd to Sep. 6th.

Multan is famous as the city of Peers and Shrines, and has some landmarks in this regard. Shams Tabriz's Shrine is a beautiful tourist attraction. The sky-blue engravings and glazed red bricks further add beauty to this monument. Shah Rukh-e-Alam Shrine is popular for its large domes. The shrine was built during the period of Tughlaq. The Sheikh Yusuf Gardez shrine is the other place worth visiting. Uch Sharif is another beautiful and the historical site. Located at the confluence of the two rivers Sutlej and Chenab, Uch Sharif is a wonderful tourist destination. Basically famous for its various beautiful shrines and tombs, the place offers another venue to host Sufi festival. Its beautiful shrines and tombs attract thousands of general tourists and people of Sufi following from almost every place in the world. Famous shrines in Uch Sharif include Hazrat Jalaluddin Surkh Bukhari, Makhdoom Jahanian Jahangasht, Hazrat Bahawal Haleem, Shaikh Saifuddin Ghazrooni and Bibi Jawandi.

Considerable ink has been used by modern writers on

the *"origins"* of Sufism in Islam, as to how it is *"genuinely"* Islamic and how a product, in the face of Islam, of outside influences. So far as the ideas of trust in and love of Allah are concerned, their rise to prominence is as a result of the developments within the intellectual and spiritual life of the community. Before the passing away of the Holy Prophet SAW; the community (Ummah) of the faithful, expressing the moral and spiritual quality of its faith, was firmly established, with the Shariah as the constitution. During the Ummayed Caliphs, many of whom behaved in strange contrast to the simple piety of the first four Caliphs, a full cleavage occurred between religion and state, facilitated by the shift of the capital of the Islamic empire from Medina to Damascus in 660 A.C.

Rise and Development

It was during the Abbasid Caliphate that this gulf was eased and the process of the intellectual awakening of Islam was hastened. It was during this period that Sufism emerged as an institution. For the first two centuries, Sufism remained spontaneous individual phenomena but, with the development of the formal disciplines of Islamic law and theology, and the gradual emergence, with them, of the class of Ulema, it rapidly developed into an institution with a tremendous mass appeal. Sufi teachings exemplify the life of the Holy Prophet SAW and the teachings of the Holy Quran in stressing the purity of the heart and inner life. The Sufi Saints always strove to uphold this excellence.

The earliest beginnings of Sufi organisation are indicated by informal and loose gatherings for religious discussions and spiritual exercises, called "circles" (halqa). The repeated recital of a religious formula, called zikr (remembrance of Allah) could take place anywhere, including mosques, which fact shows that Sufi practice was never at any stage regarded as rival growth challenging the formal disciplines of Islam.

Orthodox Sufism

During the 3rd A.H.\9th A.C. century, efforts began within the Sufis fold to bridge the gulf between orthodox Islam and Sufism with personalities such as Hazrath al Husayan al Mansur (al Hallaj) RA and Hazrath Maroof al-Kharki RA The reform movement aimed at integrating mystic consciousness with the Prophetic Shariah. The concept of *"subsistence"* or *"survival"* (baga) was introduced to amend and amplify Hazrath Bayazid Bustami's doctrine of *"annihilation"* (fana). Other major sets of category are *"intoxication"* and *"sobriety"*, and *"difference"*, *"absence"* and *"presence"*. This movement culminated in the monumental life-work of Imam al-Gazali RA who proved to be its genuine corner-stone.

This greatest figure in medieval Islam proved decisive for the future development of Islam, not so much through what he thought, as through what he taught on the basis of his personal experience. Endowed with a rare religious insight (developed through a series of spiritual crises and struggles that affected him even physically) and a keen perceptive mind, his mystic experiences enabled him to transform the formula of orthodox theology about the divine willpower and mercy into a living and moving personal reality that throbbed in his very veins. The influence of Imam al-Ghazali in Islam is incalculable. He not only reconstituted orthodox Islam, making Sufism an integral part of it, but he was also a great reformer of Sufism, purifying it of un-Islamic elements and putting it at the service of orthodox religion.

As such he represents a final stop in a long developing history. Sufism received, through his influence, the approval of Ijma or consensus of the community. Islam received a new vigour of life and a popular appeal which won large areas in Central Asia and Africa to the faith. One of the most remarkable lessons that he taught in the whole history of mysticism is that it is not a way of finding extra facts about Reality but is a meaningful way of looking at it, looking at it as a unity.

The Sufi Theosophy

Sufism exerted an irresistible pull on men's minds and during the 4th\10th and 5th\11th centuries won an increasing number of the ablest intelligentsia. The great systems of philosophical mysticism elaborated by the philosophers al- Farabi RA and Ibn Sina RA gave a fresh impetus to and were exploited by this theosophic Sufism. Other great philosophers that followed were Ibn al-Arabi RA (d. 638\1240), Moulana Jalal al-din Rumi RA (d 672\1273) and Moulana Nuraddin Abdul Rahman Jami RA (d. 898\1492). In the Persian Sufi poetry that blossomed so brilliantly, amorous images were employed in stark realism of spiritual love, which became the stock-in-trade of most of Persian, Turkish and Urdu poetry.

Sufism and Popular Religion

Just as the doctrine and practice of Sufism arose out of early pietism and the activity of the preachers so the movement of popular religion which, from the 5th\11th century onward developed with an astonishing rapidity into Sufi orders throughout the length and breadth of the Muslim world, is directly associated with the doctrines of the Sufi schools. The early development and formulation of the Sufi ideal and its broader techniques had taken place at the hands of the individual Sufis who were centres of limited and close circles of disciples. These circles with their differing doctrines may justifiably be called Sufi schools of which the chief mystic doctrines have been recorded by the 5th\11th century Sufi al- Hujwiri RA (more popularly known as Hazrath Data Ganj Baksh, whose tomb in Lahore is an object of public veneration) in his work *"Kashf al-Mahjub"*.

In the middle of the 3rd\9th century Sufism began to be publicly taught in Baghdad and elsewhere. The overwhelming attraction that it came to exert over the masses has to be explained by several factors-religious, social and political. First, Sufism claimed to lead it and adapts to a direct communion with Allah, a thesis which the orthodox Ulama rejected. The religious fascination was so powerful that Sufism, in course of time, became a religion within a religion with its own exclusive structure of ideas, practices and organisations. But the directly religious motivation was not the only factor in the spread of the Sufi movement. Its socio political function, and at times more specifically its protest function, were even more powerful than the religious one. Sufism offered a pattern of social life which satisfied the social needs of especially the uneducated classes. It was through socio- religious cults that Sufism came to be connected with organised professional groups.

This was pre-eminently the case with medieval Turkey where the Sufi movement was associated intimately with the professional guilds and military organisation of the "Janisarries" (yenicheri). All organised professions of craftsmen and artisans were connected with some saint or the other, thus deriving their spiritual patronage. At the same time, the Sufi organisations were a kind of bulwark against the state authority especially since the 5th\11th century when the political unity of the Islamic world began to crumble; giving place to the ever insecure masses against autocratic and ever despotic sultans whose authority was also accepted by the Ulama. Sufism in its organised form therefore functioned also as a protest against tyranny. This has been pre-eminently the case both in medieval Turkey and in modern times in North and West Africa and the Eastern Sudan.

In Turkey the Sufi movement has been associated with the numerous rebellions against the state from the 7th\13th century (when a certain Shaykh Baba Ilyas rose in rebellion against the last Seljug Sultan) to the 11th\17th century. In Africa the Sufi orders of various kinds have constantly put up a fierce military resistance against the penetration of the European colonial powers. And it is the same with the Malaysian Archipelago. From its informal and loose beginnings in the 2nd\3rd century, when they gathered privately to recite the Quran aloud, this zikr (remembrance of Allah - certain passages of the Quran are appealed to in this connection) developed into an elaborate congregational ritual during the following centuries. In the Sufi orders of Africa especially, the term wird has normally replaced zikr, both of which came to mean not the recitation of the Holy Book but of short religious formulas, usually containing the ninety-nine *"beautiful names"* of Allah, and repeated on a chain of beads.

The absolute authority, both in matters spiritual and material, of the Sufi leader, called Shaykh (pir or murshid in Persia and India, muqaddam in Negro Africa) over his disciples called faqir (poor) darwish, murid (disciple) or ikhwan and khwan (brothers) or ashab (companions), is a cardinal constitutional principle of organised Sufism. The history of Sufism is rich with personalities of outstanding integrity and genuine moral greatness. However the doctrine of complete surrender to a fellow human being could not be reconciled with Islamic orthodoxy which rejected even when orthodox Ulama cautiously joined the movement and participated in some of its moderate forms. Besides Sufism's "appeal to the heart" at the higher spiritual level, it unfolded a tendency of compromise with the popular beliefs and practices of the half converted and even nominally converted masses. It allowed motley of religious attitudes inherited by the new converts from their previous backgrounds, from animism in Africa to pantheism in India.

Although this strong tendency to compromise with local ideas and customs of the converts has assisted tremendously in the spread of Islam by Sufism, it has also divided Islam into a variety of religious and social cultures, and militated against the forces of uniformity represented by the orthodox Ulama. Thus Sufism proved the greatest channel for the spread of Islam precisely by the virtue of the same compromise. In India, Central Asia, Turkey and Africa, it brought millions within the fold of Islam with astonishing rapidity and still a proselytizing force in Africa. Further, the fact that Sufism came to be linked with Sunni Islam caused a severe diminution in the ranks of the Shia.

The Sufi Orders

Although the Sufi orders, as we know them, date from the 6th\12th and 7th\13th centuries, one important feature of this movement goes back much earlier. This feature is the genealogy of spiritual authority commonly called Silsila. In the 4th\10th century, Sufi al-Khuldi RA (d. 348\959) traced the genealogy of the mystic teaching to Hasan al-Basri RA (d. 110\728) and thence to the companion Anas ibn Malik RA, to the Holy Prophet SAW himself. Later chains started going to Hazrath Ali RA, in most cases through Hasan al Basri RA, The Naqshabandi order traced its genealogy to the first Caliph, Hazrath Abu Bakr RA, and the Suhrawardis traced their source of authority to the second Caliph, Hazrath Umar ibn al Khattab RA. Before the advent of organised Sufism, there existed tariqas which were merely schools of Sufi doctrine. The Sufi orders, in their rise, are connected with this early phase of schools of mysticism; and the term *"tariqa"* has therefore retained this original concept being ideally a method or way with doctrinal overtones through rites and external practices.

The pivot of a Sufi fraternity is obviously the Shaykh whose residence or place of teaching called zawiya (or ribat) in Arabic, khanqah in India and Persia and tekke in Turkey, serves as the centre of the spiritual activities of his congregation. The membership is normally of two kinds; besides the proper initiates or the immediate circle, there are usually a large number of associates or lay members who pay visits from time to time in order to get fresh instructions but are otherwise allowed to carry on their normal way of life. To teach and treat people, according to their capacity and individual needs is a cardinal principle with Sufi Shaykhs, who often show a remarkable insight into practical psychology. While an able disciple may succeed in obtaining *"the robe"* (khirqa, the insignia of graduation) and the privilege to teach the master's methods as his khalifa (successor or deputy), other initiates, during the first stages of their apprenticeship, may be required to render prolonged services at the khanqah, such as gathering food or collecting food-grains or cooking for the congregation, etc.

The number of the individual orders throughout the Muslim world is so large that only a few will be mentioned. Among the non Africa orders, a broad line of division may be drawn between urban orders, with an educated and cultured following and the "rustic" orders of the countryside. In North West and Negro Africa especially, there are variations with regard to political attitude and whether a particular order is militant or peace-loving. The orders also interact with one another and especially in the later centuries it has not been possible to keep a rigid line of division. Among the very few exceptions which have been able to keep exclusive membership, if not an exclusive character, are the Tjanya in Africa and Mawlawiya in Turkey (suppressed since 1925). The most widespread and probably the oldest existing Sufi order is the Qadiriya. It overarches most of the other orders which have been related to in terms of influence at one stage or another if they have not directly descended from it. Indeed, with regard to most of the other orders it has acted as a kind of lever, because of its looseness and adaptability and its own congregations have spread from one end of the world to the other.

The order is named after Hazrath Abd al Qadir Gilani RA (b. 470\1077) of Baghdad, whose famous work, entitled sufficiency for the seekers of Truth, contains his sermons as well as an account of Muslim sects. He possessed striking piety and philanthropy and manifested a powerful sincerity in his sermons. His writings are orthodox in character with some mystical interpretations of the Quranic passages. The chief underlying traits of his teaching are dissuasion from being immersed in worldliness and an emphasis on charity and humanitarianism. All kinds of miracles are attributed to him. The central nucleus at Baghdad, which is still managed by a descendant of Hazrath Abd al-Qadir al-Gilani RA, spread to North Africa and then into Negro Africa, eastwards as far as Indo-China and northwards into Turkey. The Qadiriya order is among the most peaceful of the Sufi orders and is distinguished by piety and humanitarianism, the ethos inculcated by the Shaykh with whom it is associated. It is on the whole orthodox avoiding the excesses of more extreme popular orders.

A still more refined but far less widespread order, the Suhrawardiya, grew from the mystic doctrine of Hazrath Umar al-Suhrawardi (d. 632\1236) of Persia. This order is to be found only in Afghanistan and the Indo-Pakistan continent. The order did not spread very far, probably because of its rigorous spiritual discipline. But towards the end of the 8th\14th century it inspired an important orthodox order, the Khalwatiya, founded in Persia by Hazrath Umar al-Khalwati RA (d. 800\1398). This order, noted for its strict discipline (Khalwati-seclusionist), spread into Turkey and during the 12th\18th century was introduced into Egypt and the Middle East. Towards the end of the same century, a disciple of the same order founded in North-West Africa the new Tijani order. The Khalwati order also gave rise to several branches within itself and it especially attracted the adherence of the orthodox Ulama.

A younger contemporary of Hazrath Abd al-Qadir al-Gilani RA, Hazrath al-Rifai (d. 578\1182) founded another important order in the district of Basra in Iraq, called after him Rifaiya. It spread into Egypt, Turkey and some parts of South-East Asia. Hazrath Ahmad al-Badawi RA (d. 675\1276), the founder of the Badawiya or Ahmadiya order, has been venerated as the greatest saint in Egypt for centuries. The other two popular orders in Lower Egypt, the Dusuqiya and the Buyyamiya, are offshoots of this order. Hazrath Sa'ad al-Din RA (d. 700\1300) is the founder of the Sadiya (or Jibawiya) fraternity in Damascus, whose origins are shrouded in mystery. But the order is said to have spread to Egypt and

Turkey, during the founder's life time. In North-West Africa, the diffusion of Islam with political overtones among the Berbers and in Negro Africa took place in close association with Sufism. The most important point of radiation for Sufism in North Africa was Abu Madyan of Tlemeen (6th\12th century).

The order of Shadhiliya is associated with the name of another disciple of Abu Madyan, Hazrath Abul Hasan al-Shadhiliya RA (d. 656\1258). Although he did not leave any written work, his disciple, the Alexandrian Ibn Ata Allah RA (d. 709\1309), compiled a collection of his *"wise sayings"*. These sayings, which have been commented upon by Shaykh al Rundi RA (d. 796\1394), constitute the main mystic text book of this order which has been propagated also in South-East Asia. In the 9th\15th century a reformed Shahdili order called al-Jazuliya came into existence in Morocco. One of the branches of the latter is the Isawiya; another is the orthodox Daqawiya of Morocco. The Shahdiliya, although it penetrated into Eastern Sudan, has had no impact on West African territories.

A much more recent order is that of the Tijaniya, founded about 1195\1781, by an ex-Khalwati disciple Ahmad al-Tijani RA at Fez. This order considerably simplified the ritual and laid greater stress directly on good intention and deeds, a fact which has contributed to its rapid success at proselytization and has also given it, at times, a more militant outlook. It makes no separation between the spiritual and the temporal. Whereas in Algeria it has been on good terms with the French colonial administration, it has resisted actively the foreign domination in Morocco. From Morocco it spread into French West Africa and into French Guinea during the 13th\19th century. The history of the origins of the early Sufi fraternities in central Asia, that eventually spread to Turkey on the one hand and to the East, South and South-East Asia, on the other, remains obscure. Ahmad Yasawi (d. 562\1167), a disciple of Yusuf al- Hamadhani (d. 534\1140), who belonged to the Persio-Central Asian Sufi circle called the *"Khawjagan"* (the masters), laid the foundations of the oldest Turkish order called the Yasawiya.

The Bektashi order founded by Baba Bektashi RA during the 6th\12th century was the most important popular *"rustic"* order in Turkey, spread into Anatolia and was fully organised and established towards the end of the 9th\15th century. Among the established orders, the Bektashiya are the furthest removed from orthodoxy, caring little for the obligatory laws of Islam. Through their associations with the military Janissaries they required political power in the Ottoman Empire and from time to time rose in revolt against the secular authority. Crushed in 1242\1826 by the government, they revived towards the end of the century but were disbanded finally in 1343\1925 by the modern Turkish state along with other orders, and now survive in Albania. Another order which spread from Central Asia into Turkey and Eastern Muslim lands but also has a spiritual connection with the Khawjagan is the Naqshabandiya founded in the 8th\14th century in Bukhara by Hazrath Baha al-Din Naqsha-band RA (d. 791\1389). Although he was an immediate disciple of the Sufi al-Sammasi and of the latter's disciple, Amir Khulal, he adopted the method of zikr of an earlier Sufi, Khaliq al-Ghujdawani RA (d. 575\1179), who was the disciple of the same Yusuf al-Hamadhani who guided Ahmad Yasawi.

The Naqshabandiya, which spread in India, China and the Malayan Archipelago, is an orthodox order and, in general, appeals to the elite. It was introduced into India by Hazrath Baqi Billah RA in the 10th\16th century and was started afresh and reinvigorated by his important and influential pupil Hazrath Ahmad Sirhinidi RA. The main sophisticated or *"urban"* order among the Turks, however, has been that of the Mevleviye (Mawlawiya), instituted by the famous mystic poet Hazrath Jalal al-Din Rumi RA (d. 672\1273). The Mathnawi, his great poetic work of surpassing beauty and profound thought has achieved immense popularity and has, indeed, been hailed as the *"Quran of the Sufis"*. Since their suppression by the Kemalist revolutionary regime, the Mevleviye are confined to the Middle East, chiefly Aleppo. In the Indo-Pakistan subcontinent, besides the universal orders of the Qadiriya and the Naqshabandiya, the chief Sufi brotherhood is that of the Chistiya, founded by Hazrath Mu'in al Din Chisti RA (d. 633\1236) of Ajmer whose tomb (Dargah) is famous for popular pilgrimage (Urs).

After a long line of famous representatives, the order suffered a period of eclipse, but was revived about a century ago. Besides these orders, the Indian subcontinent teems with a host of other orders which are but very loosely organised. These range from lesser off-shoots of regular orders, through more or less organised *"irregular"* orders (the chief of which are the Qalandars) to individual mendicants, called faqirs or malangs. In Indonesia, Islam reached relatively late and had little time to consolidate its impact before Western colonialism made its appearance. The heyday of the Sufi movement in Western Asia lasted from the 10th\16th century to the 12th\18th century, which was roughly also the period covered by the Ottoman Empire from its establishment to its zenith.

During the 13th and 14th A.H. (19th and 20th A.C.) centuries, forces were set in motion to take control or weaken the Sufi movement which is the cornerstone of Sunnism and the Ahle Sunnat Wal Jam'at. These forces took a double form. Firstly, there are those who have genuinely attempted to reform Sufism from within by excluding those indigenous beliefs and practices that do not confirm to Islamic doctrines. Secondly, there are those, especially non-Muslims who have been using unsuspecting Muslims, under the guise of reform, to bring about an onslaught on the different Muslim countries and communities where Sufism is closely associated with popular religion.

Glimpses of Sufism

Sufism is an Islamic institution which derives its sources and validity from al-kitab wa al Sunna (i.e. the Quran and the

Hadith) and the Sufi doctrines in no way conflict with the orthodox Muslim theology or Sharia.

Hadith-e-Ihsan and Sufism

In the wider sense Sufism means the perfection of Imaan (faith) and Islam (submission), which can be attained by Ihsan (literally goodness, but implies sincerity in one's conviction and practice). The Holy Prophet SAW said "Imaan is that you believe in Allah, His angels, His books, His messengers, in a life after death and in Qadr, in the good of it and the evil of it. Islam is that you bear witness that there is no Allah but Allah and that Muhammad SAW is the Messenger of Allah, keeping up prayer, fasting in the month of Ramadhan, paying zakat (poor tax) and the pilgrimage to Makkah. Ihsan is that you worship Allah as if you see Him; and if you see Him not Surely He sees you"

This hadith is well-known by the following names or captions:

Hadith-e-Gabriel, because it was Gabriel who had come to teach peoples their religion;

Hadith-e-Ihsan, because it is a prominent hadith;

Umm-ul-ahadith, because it is the root and mother of all ahadith:

Ummul-ul-Jawmi, because it is a complete and comprehensive hadith, dealing with the articles of Imaan, pillars of Islam and the importance of Ihsan in Imaan and Islam.

Thus Imaan relates to matters of faith or conviction - the theoretical side - and Ihsan to the state of sincerity in one's conviction and practice - to feel oneself in the Divine presence. According to the Prophet SAW there are two requisites of Ihsan, which, the Sufis call Mushahida (vision of Allah) and Muraqaba (meditation). The former implies that one should worship Allah as if one sees Him; while the latter signifies that if one cannot see Him, one should meditate that *"surely He sees you"*. This is in a sense the epitome of Sufi practice, which can be achieved by zikr (remembrance), fhikr (meditation) and suhbat (companionship of the righteous persons). It was because of this realization, that the Sufis described ihsan as Umm-ul- Tasawwuf (the mother of Sufism) and therefore the basis of Sufism.

Quran, Hadith and Sufism:

Tadhkiya Zahir refers to purification of external self such as Taharat, Wudu, Ghusl, Salaat, Saum, Zakat, Haj, Lawful Earning, Nikah, Rights of Man and the like. Tadhkia Batin signifies that one should purify ones inward-self such as Taqwa, Trust in Allah, Sabr, Fortitude, Gratitude, Sincerity, Modesty, Contentment, Humility, Decent Manners, and the like. It also implies that one should purify the inward-self by abandonment of vices such as Falsehood, Backbitting, Envy, Pride, Anger, Malice, Carnal Passions, and the like.

Sufis lay great emphasis on Tadhkiya Batin, which they refer to as Tadhkiya Nafs (purity of self), Tadhkiya Qalb (purity of heart) and Tathir-e-Akhlaaq (purity of character), to which the Quran refers in these words:

"He loves those who purify themselves". (2:222)

"He indeed is successful who purifies himself" (87:14)

The traditions of the Prophet SAW are on the same lines.

"The most excellent Jihad (holy war) is that of the conquest of self".

Thus tasawwuf is founded upon the Quran and Hadith and that is not an undesirable innovation (bidat) in Islam. Although the use of the word *"tasawwuf"* was not in vogue at the time of the Prophet SAW or his Companions, it is unwise to question the general wisdom of an institution which is undoubtedly based on the foundations of and in tune with the true spirit of Islam. According to Ibn Khaldun, the companions and the successors followed this path of tasawwuf of unfailing perseverance in worship, utter devotion to Allah, turning away from the adornments of this world, renunciation of what most men seek in the way of pleasure and dignity, and isolating oneself from all mankind in spiritual retreat. Later, when worldliness spread and men tended to become more and more bound up with the ties of this life, those who dedicated themselves to the worship of Allah were distinguished from the rest by the title As-Sufiyya (Sufis) and Al-Mutasawwifa (those who aspire to be Sufis).

Sufism may be defined as Taaluq-be-Allah (connection with Allah), Ikhlaas-e-Amal (sincerity in deeds), Tabkhia Nafs (purity of self) Tasfia Qalb (purity of heart), Tartair-e-Akhlaq (purity of character) and Rida-e-Ilahi (satisfaction) in order that Qurb-e-Ilahi (nearness to Allah) may be attained. All the prominent Sufis are agreed that Sufism is the purification of the heart from associating with created beings, separation from natural characteristic, suppression of human qualities, avoiding the temptations of the carnal soul, taking up the qualities of the spirit, attachment to the sciences of reality, using what is more proper to the eternal, counselling all the community, being truly faithful to Allah, and following the Holy Prophet SAW according to the Law. It teaches us how to purify soul, heart and character, and how to adorn our exterior and interior life in order that perfect happiness maybe attained. There is, according to Khaja Nasiruddin RA, an eminent Indian Sufi, three essentials of Sufism, namely: Tadkhia Nafs (purity of self), Tasfia Qalb (purity of heart) and Tajalia Ruh (purity of soul).

Sufism, according to Shaik Abdul Qadir al-Jilani RA is based on the following characteristics:

The generosity (sakhawat) of the Prophet Ibraheem;

The satisfaction (rida) of the Prophet Ishak;

The patience (sabr) of the Prophet Ayub;

The suppliant (munajat) of the Prophet Zakariya;

The expatriation (ghurbat) of the Prophet Yahya;

The wearing of robe (khirkha) of the Prophet Moosa;

The travel (safr) of the Prophet Isa;
The poverty (faqr) of the Prophet Muhammad
May the peace and blessings of Allah be upon them?

Derivation of the Term "Sufi"

The most probable derivations of the term "Sufi", according to which the Sufi received their names, may be described as under:

Because of the purity (safa) of their hearts (qalb) and the cleanliness of their acts (athar).

Because they were in the first rank (saffa) of the congregational prayer.

Because their qualities resembled those of the people of the Bench (Ashab Suffah), who lived during the time of the Holy Prophet SAW.

Because of their habit of wearing wool (suf).

The word "Sufi", according to Allama Lutfi, resembles the Greek word "Theosophia" meaning hikmat-e-ilahi (the wisdom of Allah). Wherever Tadhkiya and Hikmat are spoken of in the Quran, the Sufis ascribe them to Tasawwuf.

Various meanings have been assigned to the word "Sufi" such as a Sufi is he whose conduct towards Allah is sincere, and towards whom Allah's blessings descends, who neither possesses nor is possessed and if he possesses anything spends it. A Sufi is one who is clean of impurity, and full of meditation, which is cut off from humanity for Allah's sake, and in whose eyes gold and mud are equal.

Abu al-Mawahib al-Shadhili mentions the following characteristics of Sufis:

"The saint is a servant, worshipping and fulfilling the duties of servantship; he is truthful, faithful and righteous. The poor man he prefers to the rich, the small quantity to the large, and the low to the high; he is of genuine feeling in the opinion of men. The saint is one who smiles if saluted; in conversation he is pleasant; when asked he shall give; when others divulge secrets, he conceals; of princes he knows he is not proud, and the poor he does not disdain; the next world he does not sell for the present. Through Allah he is rich; before Him he is humble; from Him he takes; to Him he gives; on Him depends; he fears none other than Allah; his trust is only in Allah".

The ultimate aim and object of Sufism is rida-e-Ilahi (satisfaction or pleasure of Allah) and qurb-e-Ilahi (nearness to Allah). All his actions as a Sufi must lead to the attainment of ride- e-Ilahi and the Quran says:

"Say, 'Verily, my prayer and my sacrifice, my life and my death are all for Allah, Lord of the Worlds'." (6:163)

"This is a day when their truth will profit the truthful ones. For them are Gardens wherein flow rivers abiding therein forever. Allah is well-pleased with them and they are well- pleased with Allah. That is the mighty achievement". (5:119)

The Prophet's traditions, too, bear testimony to this, as for instance: "Whoever is pleased with Allah, Allah is pleased with them."

The mystical verses in the Sufi life also make interesting and instructive reading. The following verses, attributed to Dhu 'l-Nun RA (d, 859), the great Egyptian Sufi, come very close to expounding the doctrine of rida:

"To Thee alone my spirit cries;
In Thee my whole ambition lies;
And still Thy Wealth is far above
The poverty of my small love"

Rida, according to Ali Hujwiri RA renowned Indian Sufi, also known as Data Ganj Baksh is to two kinds:

Allah is pleased with His servant, and in token of His pleasure, He bestows upon him His blessings;

The servant of Allah is pleased with Allah, and this manifests in his obedience to all the Commands of Allah.

The attainment of qurb-e-Ilahi (nearness or proximity to Allah), is in a sense the epitome of Sufi practice. A Sufi believes that Allah is nearer to him than anything else - and that Allah is always with him. This is in accordance with the Quran:

"Allah is in the East and the West, so wheresoever you turn, there is the face of Allah." (2:115)

"We are nearer to him than his jugular vein." (50:16)

"And He is with you wherever you are." (57:4)

The Prophet SAW has said that whosoever remembers Allah, Allah will remember him and whosoever walks towards Allah, Allah will walk towards him. The Sufis and the mystical poets are all unanimous on the basis of the doctrine of Qurb. The following lines (rubai) composed by the illustrious poet Umar Khayyam sums it all:

"My body's life and strength proceed from Thee!
My soul within and spirit are of Thee!
My being is of Thee, and Thou art mine,
And I am Thine, since I lost in Thee!"

Sufism and Sufi Orders in Islam

Sufism is known as the Way of the Heart, the Way of the Pure, the Mystical Path of Islam. By whatever name it is called, it is the path which takes the seeker to the Divine Presence. In essence Sufism is a means and a way by which the seeker will move from the gravity of his or her lower self, to ascend, with the assistance of a mystical guide, and through the methods and practices defined by the Way he or she has chosen, to the state wherein the Vision of God is presented to her or him. The ways to God are as numerous as the breaths of mankind. Each individual person has his or her own, personal and private way to the Divine Presence.

Mystical Path to the Divine Presence

Among human beings, there must always exist those, whom through Divine Grace have received their Trusts from God in this worldly life. They move about in the world as if they were part of it, yet inside, their hearts and souls are in the Divine Presence. If they ask of God, their request is accepted, and if they look at mankind, it is always with the eye of mercy to those less fortunate than themselves. They are known as the Friends of God, called *Awliya* in Sufism. It is Sufism which is related to them and they are product of Sufism.

"There is no doubt that Sufism [=Tasawwuf] is an important branch of Islam. The word itself may be derived form the Arabic word "Sool" (Wool) or form "Sata" (cleanliness). But its foundation lies in one's personal sincerity in seeking to be close to Allah and to live a life pleasing to Him. Study of the Quran, the Hadith, and the practical life of the Holy Prophet and his faithful Companions provides unmistakable support to this reality" (An Objective Appraisal of the Sublime Sufi Path) by Shaikh Allah Yar Khan.) "Kashf (visions) and Karamah are not essential to Tasawwuf (Sufism) though charlatans claim such gifts as Sufis in order to gain advantage in commerce, or win cases in the courts of law. Nor is Sufism in any way involved in hocus pocus and talisman trading.

Sufism has also nothing to do with prostration on tombs or the lighting of lamps on them. To predict the future is not Tasawwuf either, nor is calling the aulia in absentia (with the belief that they hear such a call), nor belief that they have the power to deliver mankind from its sufferings. No Tawajjuh of a mentor can edify and enlighten a disciple and direct him toward the Straight Path without his own efforts and his own adherence to the Prophet's Sunnah. Claims for the veracity of kashf and ilham are not Sufism, nor are taken to be essentials of Sufism, whereas in fact they are its opposite.

The spirit or Ruh of every person originates what is

known as Alam at Amar or Realm of Command and is a created reflection of the Divine Attributes, Its food is the Light of Allah or the Divine Refulgence which it acquires form the Realm of Command through the Holy Prophet Muhammad (SAW), whose position in the spiritual world is like the sun in the solar system. The Quran refers to him as a bright lamp. Indeed, he is a divinely selected channel of all blessings or Baraka, and all Exalted Messengers themselves receive this Baraka form him.

Naqshbandiyya Order

Like the vital organs of the physical body, the human spirit also possesses the equivalent of vital organs, called lataaif (sing: lattefa, or subtlety). The research scholars of various Sufi orders have associated them with specific areas of the human body. The Naqshbandiah Owaisiah Order identifies this la-teaif in ascending order of power, as follows:

First – Qalb: This spiritual faculty is associated with the physical heart. To strengthen it is to increase ones general or basic capability for contemplation or zikr.

Second – Ruh: The site of the Ruh, which is a distinct facility of the human Ruh or spirit, is on the right hand side of the chest at the level of the heart. Its primary function is total concentration on Allah.

Third – Sirri: This is above the Qalb and functions to make possible kashf or physical visions associated with spiritual insights.

Forth – Khafi: This located above the Ruh, and functions to perceive the presence of Allah wherever one is.

Fifth – Akhfa: This is located at the centre of the first four lataaif and makes it possible for the human spirit to perceive the closeness of Allah's presence, which the Quran informs us is closer than faculties of both body and sprit.

Sixth – Nafs al Natiqa: This is located at the forehead

and functions to influence the human soul, towards higher states leading to perfection.

Seventh – Sultan-al-Azkar: This serves to absorb the Baraka of Allah into the entire body to that one's zikr of Allah will emanate from every cell in a single and continual act of worship.

There are five Exalted Messengers among the many known and unknown Messengers of Allah. These are Hadhart Muhammad, Hadhrat Ibrahim, Hadhrat Musa (Moses), Hadhrat Nuh (Noah), and Hadhrat Esa (Jesus), peace be upon them all, A sixth, Hadhrat Adam, is the first Prophet of ALLAH and the father of mankind. Each is associated with a particular lateefa. Thus the Baraka and lights from Hadhrat Adam, peace be upon him, descend on lateefa known as Qalb. Observed through kashf, its lights are yellowish, reflected from the first heaven. Those with kashf observe Prophet Adam, peace be upon him, during the decent of this Baraka from Allah.

The second lateefa is connected with Hadhrat Nuh and Hadhrat Ibrahim, peace be upon them. Its lights descend from the second heaven and appear to be golden red. The lights descending upon the third lateefa are from Hadhrat Musa, peace be upon him, and are white. One the fourth lateefa the lights of Hadhrat Esa, peace be upon him, descend from the fourth heaven and are deep blue, the fifth lateefa receives its baraka directly from the Holy Prophet Muhammad (SAW). The lights associated with this special Baraka are green, descend from the fifth heaven, and overwhelm the entire first whose color and states cannot be determined. It is like a flash of light that defies comprehension. If ALLAH blesses one with intrinsic vision or observation, (kashf) all of this can be seen. In the beginning it is slightly diffused, but as the vision develops its clarity increases.

Or method is called Pas-an-Fas, which in Persian means guarding every breath. This zikr is performed with the heart through breathing. If not carried out attentively and vigorously, the normal achievement of one day might take many years. The method is very simple. Sit down facing the Qiblah, fully attentive toward ALLAH and close your eyes. Start the zikr after reciting the Taawuz (a'uuzu bi Allahi min al shaitan al rajim) and Tasmiah (bism Allah al Rahman al Rahim). When you breathe in, concentrate on letting the word ALLAH penetrate the depths of your heart so that it calls out "ALLAH" when you breathe out, the pronoun for Allah, namely "Hu," again uttered by the Qalb, is carried by the breath to strike the lateefa for which the zikr is being performed. Zikr of suitable duration should be made for each lateefa. When all seven lataaif have been covered, return to the Qalb.

After a few more breaths, start the meditation. The body should now be relaxed and the mind set at ease, while breathing outwards (Exhaling) "Hu" strikes His Sublime Throne. This illuminates the path for the Ruh facilitating its flight toward ALLAH in subsequent meditation. Remember that progress will not be made without the attention of the Shaikh because the Baraka leading one along the Sufi path is transmitted only through him. The Companions attained this from the Holy Prophet, peace be upon him and transmitted it to the Tab'ain, who in turn passed it on to the Tb Tab'ain. The Aulia (sing. Wail or friend of Allah or saint) acquired this wealth of Baraka from them and it has been transferred through the generations from one person to another.

ALLAH willing, this process will continue forever, and every believer, whether male or female, scholar or uneducated, rich or poor can acquire this Baraka. The only prerequisites are sound beliefs and sincerity to the efforts is in religious propagation though literature or by word of mouth, no positive change in life can be realized without Baraka. Zikr, invokes Baraka, and this in turn transforms the heart and init-iates the journey from vice to virtue toward perfect goodness.

The *Daily Awrad* (Spiritual Practices) of the Initiate in

Naqshbandiyya -as an example:

Shahada three times [*ash-hadu an La ilaha illAllah wa ashhadu anna Muhammadan* c*abduhu wa rasuluh*];

"*Astaghfirullah*" 25 times;

Fatiha one time with the intention of participating in the blessings sent down with it when it was revealed in Makkah.

Ikhlas (Surat 112) 11 times;

Falaq (Surat 113) 1 time;

Nas (Surat 114) 1 time;

La ilaha illAllah 10 times, the last time completing it with *Muammadun Rasulullah.*

Salawat ash-sharifa 10 times [*Allahumma Salli* c*ala Muhammadin wa* c*ala ali Muhammadin wa Sallim*];

"ihda'," that is, presenting the reward of the above recitation to the Prophet (s) and to the Shaykhs of the Naqshbandi Tariqat;

Wrapping it up with Fatiha, with the intention of sharing in the Divine Graces and *tajalli* which were sent down when it was revealed in Madinah the second time.

Dhikr of the Glorious Name *'Allah'* 1500 times;

Salawat [same as (h)] 100 times; 300 times on Mondays, Thursdays and Fridays.

One-thirtieth *(juz')* of the Quran, or instead Ikhlas 100 times;

One chapter of *Dala'il al-Khairat* or instead Salawat 100 times.

The Sufi Orders

Islam, as a complete code of life or din, was perfected during the life of the Holy Prophet Muhammad (salla'Allahu alaihi wa sallam). He was the sole teacher and his mosque was the core institution of the community. Although Islam in its entirety was practiced during that blessed era, the classification and compilation of its teaching into distinct branches of knowledge, like 'Tafsir' (interpretation or exegesis of the Quran), Hadith (traditions or sayings of the Holy Prophet, SAW), Fiqh (Islamic law), and Tasawwuf (the inward aspect), were undertaken later. This din of Allah passed from the Holy Prophet (SAW) to his Companions in two ways the outward and the inward. The former comprised the teachings of Islam enunciated by speech and conduct, i.e., the Quran and Sunnah. The latter comprised the invisible blessings or the Prophetic lights transmitting so purified their hearts as to instill in them a great love of his teachings and an ardent desire to follow them with utmost sincerity and devotion. Tasawwuf is the effort to acquire this Baraka.

The Companions handed down his teachings and blessings to the Tab'ain. Their strong hearts were capable of infusing these blessings into the hearts of their followers. Both these aspects of Islam were similarly passed on by the Tab'ain to the Tab'a Tab'ain, the former in writing and the latter from heart to heart. The compilation of the teachings (the outward aspect) and their interpretation led to the creation of many schools of religious thought of which four have survived, namely, the Hanafi, the Hanbali, the Maliki, and the Shaf'i, named after their founders. Similarly, in order to acquire, preserve and distribute his Baraka (the inward aspect), an organized effort was initiated by four schools of Tasawwuf: The Naqshbandiah, the Qadriah, the Chishtiah, and Suharwardiah. These schools were also named after their organizers and came to be known as Sufi Orders.

All these orders aimed at purifying the hearts of sincere Muslims with Prophetic lights, hut they adopted somewhat different means to accomplish this goal. Khawaja Naqshband (d-1389 A.C) organized the Naqshbandiah Order of Bukhara [now in Central Asia (Turkestan), Republic of Uzbekistan]. This Order has two main branches – the Mujaddidiah and the Owaisiah. The former is identified with Shaikh Ahmed Sirhindi, Mujaddad Alif Sani (literally reviver of the first Muslim millenium), who was successor of Khawaja Baqi Bilah, who introduced the Order to the Indo-Pakistan sub-continent. The method of zikr employed by the Naqshbandiah is "Zikr-al-Khafi-Qalbi" (contemplation of Allah's name within the heart) and is termed "Pas an Fas", which in Persian means guarding every breath. The Owaisiah Order employs a similar method of zikr but acquires the Prophetic blessings in the manner of Khawaja Owais Qarni, who received this beneficence from the Holy Prophet (SAW) without a formal physical meeting.

In the Subcontinent, the Sufis made untiring, selfless and incessant struggle for the spread of Islam. They devoted their lives and gave up their homes to champion the cause of Islam in a miraculous way. Neither did they resort to arms nor to swords for this. It was their affection, sympathy, fraternity and unlimited philanthropist actions that won the hearts of people. The spread of Islam stems from the invasion of Muhammad Bin Qasim in the Subcontinent, but roots of Sufism can be traced to the time when the first Sufi, Muhammad Alfi, came to the Subcontinent. However, with the passage of time, many Sufis made their way here following the invasions of Muslim conquerors. They came from Central Asia and the Arabian Peninsula in order to establish an Islamic society. Sufism took shape and became an institution in the 12th and 13th century. The two great pioneers in this filed were Shaikh Abdul Qadir Jilani and Hazrat Shahabuddin Suharawardy.

Four branches of Sufism, namely Qadriya, Chishtiya, Suharawardya and Naqshahbandya were introduced in the Subcontinent by Syed Bandqi Mohammad Ghosh, Khwaja Moinuddin Chishti, Shaikh Bahawaldin Lakariya and Khwaja Mohammad Baqi Billah respectively. There is an established myth that the Sufis followed the Muslim warriors. But now it is clear that Shah Abdul Rehman had settled in Ajmer before Khwaja Moinuddin. Shaikh Ismail Bukhari came to the Subcontinent before Mahmud Ghaznavi. The Ismail missionary Adbullah landed near Cambay in AD1067 and worked in Gujarat when the country was governed by

Sindhraj Jai Singh. He and his Jain teacher, Huma Charya, are said to have converted to Islam when there was no Muslim invasion recorded at the time.

During Ghazanavid rule, there was massive influx of important spiritual leaders like Hazrat Shaikh Ismail and Hazrat Ali Bin Osman Hujweri, popularly known as Data Ganj Bux. The latter was among the leading Sufi philosophers of the day. He did immense missionary work in his individual capacity and set an outstanding example for future generations. Many scholars are of the view that the general conversion to Islam in the Subcontinent started on a sizable scale from the 13th century, after the Ghurid rule. This period coincides with the arrival of Hazrat Khwaja Moinuddin Chishti and the Suharawardy Sufis. This period also witnessed the expansion of Muslim power across the Sutlaj into northern India. In addition to Punjab, Sindh also claims the distinction of being the centre of Indian Sufism. According to Hassan Nizami, Suharawardy Sufis were the first to arrive in India and made their headquarters in Sindh. This order achieved much success under the leadership of Hazrat Bahwaldin Zakriya in Multan.

The famous Qadriya order entered India through Sindh in AD1482. Syed Bandagi Mohammad Ghouse, one of the descendants of the founder (Shaikh Abdul Qadir Jilani, 1078-1116) took up residence in Sindh at Uch (now in Bahawalpur) and died in AD1517. Sakhi Sultan (Mangopir), Hazart Abdullah Shah of Karachi, Hazrat Shah Inayat of Jhok Sharif, Hazrat Shah Abdul Latif Bhittai, Sachal Sarmast and Qalandar Lal Shahbaz were saints of high stature in Sindh who converted many Hindus. In Bengal, saints and servants accompanied the administrators and warriors, and established their own darghas and khanqahs. Shah Jalal of Sylhet, Makhdumul-mulk Sharfuddin and Shaikh Nur Qutb may be particularly mentioned. Shah Jalal did much for the spread of Islam in Bengal, while Shaikh Akhi Sirajuddin propagated Islam in Gaur and Pandua.

Other notable figures of the 13th century Sufi movement in Indo-Pak were the four friends known as 'Chaharyar' — Hazrat Fariduddin Masud Ganj Shakar of Pakpattan (1174-1266); Hazrat Syed Jalaluddin Bukhari, ulma of Uch Bahawalpur (1196- 1296); Hazrat Bahawaldin Zakariya of Multan (1170-1267); and Hazrat Lal Shahbaz Qalendar of Sehwan (1177-1274). It is said that 17 leading tribes of the Punjab accepted Islam at the hands of the Sufis. Fortunately, the list of Sufis does not end here. Their exact number is beyond the capacity of this chapter, so only a few noteworthy Sufis can be mentioned. Mohammad Ghose, Hazrat Mian Mir of Lahore, Hazrat Syed Yakub Zanjani of Lahore, Ruknuddin Rukne Alam of Multan, who was grandson of Hazarat Bahauddin Lakariya whose family migrated from Sindh. Syed Ahmed Saqi Sarwar of D.G. Khan, Pir Jalaluddin Qutb-al-Aqtab, who died at Uch in AD1923 converted Mazaris and several other Baloch tribes to Islam, Hazarat Khardari Baba Mulla Taher of Ziarat (the visit to his tomb led to the place becoming known as Ziarat) Pir Hinqlaj of coastal Makran, Pir Baba of Swat, and Kake Sahib of Nowshero played important roles in the spread of Islam.

The Sufis were well-read, widely travelled and spiritual leaders of the masses. They succeeded in their mission because they had both the strength of character and the courage of conviction, and were selfless and devoted to their cause. Their movement made inroads in the Subcontinent and it grew powerful and successful for a number of reasons. Firstly, before they started preaching, they set noble and brilliant example through their behaviour and conduct. Secondly, Islam was preached by them in a simple, pragmatic and flexible way, contrary to the ulemas who laid much emphasis on the rigidity of rules. Thirdly, they highlighted Allah's positive and merciful attributes to ignite a love of God in people's hearts. The Sufis disliked formalities and ceremonial acts, preferring to lead simple lives, and their lofty and admirable principles became guidelines for the people. They were against suppressions and social evils, condemning the use of force to gain power. Then their khanqahs were always open for everyone, and those with money had to donate generously to the needy. People flocked from time to time to the Sufis for solace and comfort.

The Sufis were triumphant because of their noble deeds and the marvellous examples they set. They never imposed their beliefs on non-Muslims. The khanqas provided protection to wanderers, institutions for those who wanted to quench their thirst for knowledge, food to the needy and love to all. People rallied round the ideology of Sufism which was simple to digest, practicable to exercise. The Sufis converted a civilisation into a better one, which is beyond the imagination of ordinary people. The small pockets of Muslim society in towns and villages after the invasion of Muhammad Bin Qasim changed into large cities and provinces. Above all, it was the sheer straggle of the Sufis which paved the way for the future Islamic state in the Subcontinent. Had the Sufis shunned their practice of Islamic teachings in the 13th and 14th century, it would have been difficult to implant a Muslim civilisation in the country where a well-organized Hindu community had lived for centuries.

Early Sufis in the Chishti Order

Many people think that Khwaja Mo'inuddin Chishti is the founder of the Chishti order. This is not correct, so in the following chapter I intend to tell something about his spiritual ancestors and briefly something about their teachings. The Chishti order of the Sufis derives its name from Chisht (pronounce: Chesht, hence Cheshti). Chisht is a small town near Herat in Afghanistan. When travelling and arriving in Herat I intended also to visit Chisht, but it was said that the road was not safe, because of dacoits, so I abandoned the idea.

The first one to call him Chishti was Abu Ishaq Shami. As the name Shami implies he came from Syria or even from Damascus (ash-Sham). He met a Sufi who directed him to settle in Chisht and from that day on he is known as Abu

Ishaq Shami Chishti. He died in 940 C.E. in Damascus and lies buried on mount Qasiyun, where later on also Ibn al-'Arabi was buried. Looking at the date of his death we can say that the Chishtiyya order is one of the oldest, if not the oldest now still existing Sufi order.

Some of his sayings are:

1. Starvation excels all in bliss (this shows the ascetic character of classical Sufism).
2. The worldly people are impure while the dervishes are pure in their souls. These two different natures cannot therefore mingle.

The spiritual successor of the founder of the Chishtiyya order, Khwaja Abu Ishaq Shami Chishti, is called shaykh Abu Ahmad Abdal Chishti. The father of the shaykh for some time tried to keep him back from the Sufi path. He of course did not succeed as his son became an eminent Sufi. It is related about the shaykh that he did not sleep for thirty years. He was absorbed in meditation. He breathed his last on the 3rd of Jamada II at the age of ninety-five in 356 A.H. (corresponding to the 16th of May 967 C.E.). He was buried at Chisht in Afghanistan.

One of his sayings is:

'Fire does not affect the true believer in God'.

Shaykh Abu Muhammad Chishti was invested as the head of the Chishtiyya order by his father Abu Ahmad Chishti about whom we have already reported. The appointment of a son as a successor is an exception with the Chishtis, but in case of genuine spiritual capacities there is nothing against the appointment of one's son. When succession from father to son becomes an automatic procedure, then of course Sufism degenerates. The shaykh passed away from this world on the 4th of Rabi II at the age of seventy (lunar years) in 409 A.H. (which corresponds to the 18th of August 1018 C.E.).

His sayings:

1. Cherish music to enlighten your heart.

2. Indulgence in sama' (audition of Sufi music) for a moment is as prolific as the penitence for hundreds of years, but the worldly people do not realise it.

Khwaja Abu Muhammad Chishti was the maternal uncle of Khwaja Abu Yusuf Chishti who became his successor. He was a descendent of the prophet Muhammad (Allah's blessings and peace be upon him). He breathed his last on the 3rd of Rajab at the age of 84 in 459 A.H. (20th of May 1067 C.E.). He was buried in Chisht, the cradle and the grave of the early Chishtiyya.

Saying:

Indulgence in sama' (audition of Sufi music) achieves more than long enduring penitence. The next in the silsila of the Chishtiyya is Khwaja Mawdud Chishti. He had learnt the Quran by heart and could recite it very melodiously at the age of seven. Afterwards he learned the other things. When he was only 26 years old his father's life came to an end. According to the will of his father he became his successor. He was the first to salute others and used to stand out of respect to others. He was famous for his hospitality. He was kind to his servants. He bade farewell to this world in the month of Rajab at the age of 97 in 533 A.H. (March 1139 C.E.). He was buried at Chisht like many of the early Chishtiyya.

Sayings:

1. The lover of sama' (Sufi music) is a stranger to the outside world, but is a friend to God.
2. The mysteries of sama' are inexplicable. If you reveal them you are liable to punishment.

Khwaja Mawdud Chishti visited Balkh (the place of birth of Jalaluddin Rumi) and Bukhara, a place mentioned in the famous line of Hafez:

If that Turk of Shiraz would take my heart in his hand,

I would give for his Hindu mole both Bokhara and Samarqand.

Khwaja Hajji Sharif Zindani, his successor, renounced all and everything. He led a life of strict seclusion for forty years and hated society. He used to live on the leaves of trees. Although several of the Chishtiyya stressed the value of asceticism, in general they say that seclusion and ascetic practices is for short periods of time only. You should live in the midst of society and then keep up your spiritual ideals. Khwaja Hajji Sharif Zindani passed away from this world on the 10th of Rajab at the age of 120 in 612 A.H. (4th of November 1215 C.E.). Zindani means from Zindana. He was also buried in Zindana. I do not know where this place is situated. How about you?

The following saying is very characteristic of him:

Riches are the enemy of a dervish; they should be shunned.

The successor of Khwaja Hajji Sharif Zindani has been Khwaja Uthman Haruni. Here is a poem translated from the Persian:

I do not know why at last to have a longing look, I dance!

But I feel proud of the fondness that before the Friend, I dance!

You strike the musical instrument and see, everytime I dance!

In whatever way you cause me to dance, o Friend, I dance!

Come o Beloved! See the spectacle that in the crowd

of the intrepid and daring,

With a hundred ignominies in the heart of the market, I dance!

Blessed is recklessness that I trample underfoot

the very many acts of virtue.

Hail to piety, that with the robe and the turban I dance.

I am Uthman-e-Haruni and a friend of shaykh Mansur,

They revile and rebuke and on the gallows I dance.

Khwaja Uthman Haruni came from Harun in Iran. According to some people he was born on 526 A.H./1131-2 C.E.). There are others however who hold that he was born in 510 A.H./1116 A.D. He received the name Uthman at birth, but his nickname is Abu Nur. He was also called Abu'l Mansur. As is the custom among the Muslims when he attained the age of four years, four months and four days his 'Bismillah' was performed. At this function the child recites some portion of the Quran and is sent to school. He became a hafiz, one who has committed the Quran to memory. He met an absorbed person, a majdhub, called Chirk. This meeting proved to be the turning point in his life. He went in search of spirituality and asked Khwaja Hajji Sharif Zindani to be enrolled as his mureed.

The shaykh accepted his request and with his own hand placed a four-edged cap on his head. He gave this explanation of this four-edged cap:

First is the renunciation of the world

Second is the renunciation of the world hereafter

Third is the renunciation of the desires of the self

Fourth is the renunciation of everything other than God.

Khwaja Uthman Haruni lived in the company of his shaykh for over thirty years. Thereafter he undertook long tours and travels and also performed the hajj. His close disciple Khwaja Mo'inuddin Hasan Chishti was with him for more than twenty-two years. In order to help his mureeds Khwaja Uthman Haruni gave discourses in order to guide them. He died on the 5th of Shawwal in the year 617 A.H. (3rd of December 1220 C.E.). His tomb in Mecca nowadays no longer exists. Khadim Hasan visited it in the beginning of this century, but it is said to be destroyed thereafter. I do not know if this had to do with the anti-Sufi attitude of the Wahabi movement or if there were other reasons. Khwaja Uthman Haruni made a prophecy about his own grave stating that it would not remain in tact, but the grave of Mo'inuddin would remain until the Day of Judgment.

Once he disclosed the secret that when the Friend becomes your friend then the whole universe in fact becomes yours. But it is necessary then that you should be unmindful of everything else and be ever with the Friend and follow Him faithfully and assiduously. At another time he showed contempt for those mendicants who ate to their hearts content and took themselves to be mendicant and wore the khirqa – the robe of the dervishes. If you feed the hungry, God will fulfil your thousand wants and will free you from hell fire. For you a house is built in heaven. The lover of God should be charitable like the river, generous like the sun and hospitable like the earth.

He indeed is close to God, who is ever steeped in His submission,

Who interprets every event as coming from God?

And who is content with it and who takes it as a blessing.

This is the main object of all prayers and worship.

The history of the Chishtiyya Sufi order continues with the successor of Khwaja Uthman Haruni: Khwaja Mo'inuddin Hasan Chishti. It is therefore clear that Mo'inuddin Chishti is not the founder of the Chishtiyya. He is the one who brought the order to India and there is no doubt that he is the most outstanding wali of the sub-continent of Indo-Pakistan and Bangla Desh. He belonged to the house of the prophet Muhammad (s.a.) both from the paternal side (He is Husaini) and the maternal side (He is Hasani). He is closely related to shaykh Abdul Qadir Jilani. His great grand-father, Khwaja Ahmad Husain, migrated from Usqar (Iraq) to Sanjar. His father Khwaja Ghiyasuddin Hasan was well-educated and trained. He was an accomplished man and a great Sufi of his time. His mother, Bibi Mah Nur, alias Ummul Warah, was the daughter of Dawud ibn Abdullah al-Hambali. Khwaja Mo'inuddin Chishti was born in Isfahan in the year 530 A.H.

Khwaja Gharib Nawaz (= Helper of the poor) as Mo'inuddin Chishti was known received his early education at home. When he was 9 years old he committed the Quran to memory. Subsequently he was admitted in a maktab (school) in Sanjar. He concentrated mostly on hadith and fiqh. His father passed away in 1150 C.E. Gharib Nawaz was hardly fifteen years old then. One day in the same year when he was watering his garden a mystic named Ibrahim Qanduzi all of a sudden entered the garden. Mo'inuddin Chishti was very courteous towards him and offered him a bunch of grapes. Ibrahim Qanduzi was very pleased with his behaviour and wanted to repay him. He took out a piece of oil-cake and chewing it, gave it to the young man. As soon as he ate it, he underwent a strange transformation. He felt disgusted with mundane affairs and was enamoured of a higher life. He had inherited from his father a grinding-stone and a garden, which constituted his source of income. He sold them and distributed the proceeds thereof among the poor.

In pursuit of knowledge he visited Khorasan first. Then he proceeded to other centres of Islamic learning like Samarqand and Bokhara. You may be reminded of the famous line of Hafez:

If that Turk of Shiraz would take my heart in his hand,

I would give for his Hindu mole both Bokhara and Samarqand

He stayed there for about five years, i.e. from 1150 up to 1155 C.E. He continued receiving his education up to the age of twenty years. He counted as his teachers two outstanding scholars of his time, namely Maulana Hissamuddin of Bokhara and Maulana Sharafuddin. What happened afterwards to him? What happened to the Chishti Sufis who succeeded him?

Sufi Saints in India

India is the land of spiritualism. Some of the major religions of the world have been started over here. Sufism has also been present in India since a long time and even today we find a number of Sufi followers here. Some of the popular Sufi saints of India have been discussed below.

Khwaja Moinuddin Chishti

Khwaja Moinuddin Chisti was one of the most famous Sufi saints in India. He is the founder of the Chishtiya order in India. He was born in Persia and is said to be a direct descendent of Prophet Muhammad. He settled in Ajmer in India from where he preached the principles of Sufism to all. He had a massive following and even today, people irrespective of their religions are adopting his principles of Sufism. Every year, his death anniversary is celebrated in Ajmer at his tomb when thousands of believers gather to pay respect to this great Sufi saint.

Hazrat Nizam-Ud-Din

Another famous Sufi saint of the Chisti order in India was Hazrat Khwaja Nizam-ud-din Auliya, who was popularly known as Hazrat Nizam-ud-Din. His real name was Mohammad and at the age of 20, he became the student of Fariduddin Ganj-i-Shakkar. He was revered saint who is supposed to have been the master of Amir Khusro. His shrine located in Delhi is a popular attraction for Sufi followers.

Bulleh Shah

Baba Bulleh Shah was a revered Sufi saint of India whose real name was Abdullah Shah. He preached his teachings and principles in Punjab. During the time he was at his peak, there was much unrest between Muslims and Sikhs. He preached nothing but the truth and his words of wisdom pacified those affected by the constant tiffs between Muslims and Sikhs. Through his poems, he criticized the orthodox religious systems that were prevalent during his time. His poems were written in Punjabi and Sindhi as these were languages that common people could read and understand.

Sufi Practices

Given below is information about the various practices in Sufism that form a part of this religion.

Dhikr:

Dhikr is basically about remembering God for all Sufis. According to Islam, one who engages in Dhikr has awareness of God. It basically includes chanting of God's name and reciting sections of the Quran. It has similarities with the Jewish Merkavah practice of meditation used to attain a higher level of consciousness. This can be done through singing, dance, meditative music, swirling, etc. that finally leads to a trance.

Hadhra:

The Hadhra basically consists of various forms of Dhikr, songs and dances that are used to appeal God and Angels. The word Hadhra is Arabic and it means "Presence".

Qawwali:

In Sufism, Qawwali is the devotional form of music, which is common in Pakistan, India, Afghanistan, Turkey, Iran, etc. The Qawwali is known for its worldly appeal and transcends all bounds and limitations of countries and different regions. Some of the modern day masters of Qawwali are Nusrat Fateh Ali Khan and Sabri Brothers.

Sama:

Sama is Arabic word which means listening. In Sufis, the holy ritual of whirling dance is known as Sama. It is basically an act of devotion that takes a person to a higher level of consciousness. The right kind of music invokes the right kind of emotion which is elated when one does the whirl dance. This helps in the process of contemplating the divine force.

Khalwa

Khalwa basically refers to a kind of retreat that a person can experience under the guidance of a Sufi teacher. There is a belief in Sufism that all prophets must have retreated into seclusion at some point of time in order to derive inspiration and divine power. Thus, the Sufis practice retreat in order to concentrate on the divinity of the Almighty. Many books have been written on 'Sufism in India' and depending on how original their sources are and the intention of the writer/ translator, some books must be read with caution. The difficulty of obtaining original sources is one of the factors contributing to the perpetuation of myths and practices about certain Sufis and other aspects of Islam in India.

Very few books mention and write about the great Reviver of the 14th Century, Imam Ahmed Raza Khan al-Qadiri (may Allah be pleased with him). His Eminence stresses that without this great Sufi and Reviver; there would be no real 'Sunnism' today. Under his pen, the language of love between Almighty Allah, the beloved Prophet Muhammad (Allah bless him and give him peace), and the poet (himself) became a tool which to condemn those 'others' with whose views he disagreed. Under his leadership from the 1880s until his demise in 1921, the debates in which the Ahle Sunnat Wal Jamaat engaged do not deal specifically with politics. They deal instead with issue such as the noble qualities of the beloved Prophet Muhammad (Peace and blessing be Upon Him), the permissibility or otherwise of the intercession of deceased 'Saints' (Pirs), or the correct manner of calling believers to the Mosque for the Friday congregational prayers.

Many writers use the term 'Barelwis' to describe Imam Ahmed Raza Khan al-Qadiri (may Allah be pleased with him) followers; our members and seekers for Truth are brethren who follow the Qadiri Tariqat, reject the name and it was not a term they used for self-identification. Studies show that the Ahle Sunnat Wal Jamaat under this great spiritual leader and scientist had a strong Sufi dimension, in affiliation particularly with the Qadiriyya Tariqat, and many of the leading lights of the Ahle Sunnat Wal Jamaat leadership in the late 19th and early 20th century were caretakers of Sufi Shrines, and belonged to a world where intercessionary power of Saints and family ancestors (baraka) were taken for granted. Imam Raza's (may Allah be pleased with him) conceptions about the beloved Prophet Muhammad's (Allah bless him and give him peace) role as mediator with Almighty Allah and his miraculous achievements were in line with Sufi concepts of spiritual authority and power.

The Influence of Sufism

Dedicating their whole being to the Absolute, the Sufis in the Indian subcontinent achieved their spiritual goal through intuition, esoteric knowledge, and experience of the mystical world. Theirs was naturally the antithesis of the solely intellectual experience fostered by some of the philosophers. Some Suhrawardî leaders and other dervishes played an important role in the power struggle of the ruling classes and aristocracy and pressured the government into taking a very narrow view of Islam. However, the large number of eminent Sufis whose vision of Islamic spiritual life was broadly based gave moral courage to the people by awakening in them spiritual values and reliance on God during calamities such as drought, floods, and panic due to protracted wars and foreign invasions.

The early Chishtiyyah believed that contact with the saintly was the only means by which people would renounce evil or convert to Islam. The social and economic position of the masses of Muslim converts who accepted Islam under a variety of pressures was in fact no better than that of the Hindu masses, because of the dominance of the discriminating ruling classes. Nevertheless, the khanqahs did offer peace and comfort to the thousands of Muslims who crowded the towns. The lack of literary evidence is the most formidable obstacle to the presentation of any pictures of village khanqahs, where the tombs of local Pirs and the graves of local martyrs both real and fake offered the sole spiritual comfort to the inhabitants in their sufferings and anguish. The ʻurs (death anniversaries) and other ceremonies celebrated in khanqahs developed into significant cultural institutions and were eagerly awaited by both poor and rich alike.

Not only was Sufi poetry an expression of the mystic

love of thirsty soul seeking an intuitive understanding of God, but it was also avenue for the outlet of emotions and spiritual feelings which would otherwise never have been expressed because of the fury of the orthodox, social, inhibitions, and political repressions. Sufi poetry in Hindi and regional languages opened a fresh avenue for a new spiritual, serene, and colorful way of life. The Natha Panthî and Vaishnavite symbols did not necessarily make them syncretic, for a number of Sufis who used such symbols enjoyed a reputation for excessively deep devotion to Islam. They were designed to be shared with the experiences of their countrymen whose spirits passionately loved to attain the higher reaches of Reality. Both the Sufi poets of the regional languages and the pioneers of Hindu bhaktî (devotional) movements rebelled against all forms of religious formalism, falsehood, hypocrisy, and stupidity and tried to create a world in which spiritual bliss was the all-consuming goal.

The devotion of some of the rulers and members of the governing classes to the Sufis went a long way toward making possible the erection of such masterpieces of architecture as the tomb of the Suhrawardî Shaykh Rukn al-Dîn in Multan, the khanqah of Mir Sayyid 'Alî Hamadânî in Srinagar (Kashmir), and the tombs of Shaykh Muhòammad Ghawth in Gwalior and Shaykh Salîm Chishtî at Fatehpur Sikri. Eve the Mughal miniatures did not neglect the Sufi landscape; some of them integrate Sufi themes with the bhaktas (Hindu devotees). The most serious threat to the survival of Sufism was the presumptuous claims of Sufi charlatans and impostors. The latter exploited Sufi influence to their advantage. Their poetry and music promoted immoral practices, the use of drugs, and thaumaturgy and was a great threat to a spiritual world view of the genuine Sufis. But genuine Sufism survived this and other threats and has managed to keep alive to this day.

The *dargah* (shrine) of Khwaja Moinuddin Chisti, more popularly known as *Garib Nawaz* or the comfort of the poor, is considered, after Mecca and Medina, to be the most sacred shrine of Muslims from the Indian subcontinent. The hospice of the great saint and founder of the *Chistiya silsilah* (Chisti strain or tradition) of Sufism in India goes back several hundred years, almost to the earliest period of the Muslim conquest of India. What is more, it serves as an interesting parallel, if not contrasts, to the "official" Islam that clerics and kings in Delhi usually espoused. This *dargah,* representing years of Sufi traditions, which is open to everyone regardless of caste, creed, faith, age, or gender, twenty-four hours a day, not only posed a powerful challenge to the Hindu orthodoxy of the time, but also to the Muslim orthodoxy represented by the *ulema* (orthodox Islamic clerics).

While the dominant Hindu practices emphasized caste hierarchies and exclusion, the *dargah* of the saint was the refuge of the lowliest, humble, and oppressed people of the land. While the Muslim priestocracy preached the supremacy of Islam, the religion of the conquerors, the Chistis demonstrated their love and acceptance of people of all faiths. The Chistis, unlike many other Sufi traditions or orders, always kept a healthy distance from the power politics of the court. They practiced extreme poverty and simplicity. Their fondness for music soon endeared them to the masses. Like the shrine of any Hindu saint, the *dargah* of the Sufis became a center not only of the worship of the pir or guru, but also a place of healing, refuge, and wish fulfillment. No wonder, people of all faiths, Hindus and Muslims alike, flock to these shrines even today.

My recent visit to the great *dargah* at Ajmer Sharif, India was memorable. It was a Thursday and the whole sanctuary was clogged with devotees. As we approached, we were confronted and solicited by the inevitable money-mongering middlemen who flock such places. But we managed to escape their clutches. Once inside, we seemed to have entered a medieval world. Men, women, and children in all kinds of attire hurried about here and there. There was a long line of people trying to get inside the shrine to pay their respects at the saint's tomb. We too were ushered into the rather full, even sticky chamber. So many people jostled to kiss the cold marble or the silver railing. At the head of the grave were two *khadims* or servants of the shrine. They were collecting heaps of notes for a brief genuflection.

A peace descended into my being. I remembered the other saints of the lineage, not only Khwaja Kutbutddin Bakhtiyar Kaki of Mehrauli, but also Baba Farid Ganjeshakkar, Hazrat Nizamuddin Aulia, Khwaja Nasiruddin Chirag-e-Dilli, Khwaja Bande Nawaz of Gulbarga, and the other great masters of the *Chistiya silsilah* at Khuldabad, Hyderabad, Aurangabad and elsewhere in the subcontinent. Coming to this root shrine was like bowing to them all. Just then one of the attendants beckoned to me. Placing my head under the green *chadar* or sheet, he invoked, in the most moving and sincere manner, the blessings of the saint on me. I felt loved and protected; my heart welled up with gratitude and compassion. I knew that my visit had been successful.

Outside, the *qawalis* (Islamic devotional music) were going on. Seated in front of the shrine, the present *gaddi nashin*, heir to the lineage, Syed Umuruddin Baba, son of Syed Kutbuddin Sakhi, sat solemnly. He was the present *Khalifa* (representative of Prophet Muhammad or Allah on earth), and therefore the object of devotion of all those who sat in the courtyard. While all of us looked at him, he looked only at the shrine or the sky. The most interesting thing was that he was dressed in saffron and looked just like a Hindu sage or holy man. Even the *chaubdars* or attendants wore saffron turbans! Sufi traditions of peace and coexistence are indeed very powerful as an expression of people's Islam in our subcontinent, but unfortunately the ruling clergy has never given them either recognition or validity. It was interesting that Pakistani president Pervez Musharraf and his Begum were unable to visit this *dargah* of *Garib Nawaz* during their visit to India last year. "How could they," someone said, "The Khwaja did not call him because he did not come with peace in his heart."

Sufism is akin to mysticism. Much before the advent of Islamic culture (and Sufism) in India, mysticism existed in Buddhist philosophy, *Hatha Yogic* System, Vedantic thought, Vaishnava tradition and at a much later stage in Bhakti movement, a very strong wave had emerged in the form of Sikh spiritualism in Punjab. IGNCA hosted a three-day seminar on "The Sufi Tradition" from January 2-4. The objective of the seminar was to discuss the all-round impact of Sufism-not merely on the religious aspect but also on the life and culture in India. The seminar was inaugurated by Prof. Siraj Hussain, Vice-Chancellor, Jamia Hamdard, New Delhi. Nearly 25 scholars participated in the discussions. Dr. L.M. Singhvi, President IGNCA Trust, was among those who shared their views in the seminar. Sufi literally means 'one who is pure.' In Greek, Sufi is an enlightened person. Sufism was born in Arabia, very early in Islamic history. The Sufis came to India following the Muslim conquerors. India, with her multi-racial, multi-religious and multi-lingual society has always welcomed men imbued with high moral and spiritual ideas who could, in the words of Tagore, "set at naught all differences of men, by the overflow of their consciousness of God".

The Sufi saints of India belong to this category of "Good-conscious men" who stood above all narrow and parochial divisions of society and strove to find a unity for the heterogeneous elements that make up its totality. The Arabs laid stress on asceticism and disciplining of the body, while the later Sufis in Iran and India, under the influence of Greek philosophy, Platonic ideology, Christian faith, Vedantist thinking, Buddhist lore, etc. believed in leading an emotionally rich life. They wrote poetry, read it aloud in the *Dayars* (Circles), sang and danced. They had faith in God; they loved the Prophet but they maintained that the *Murshid* or *Guru* could also lead to realization of the Divine Reality. The Indian Sufis laid stress on repeating the holy name (*Jaap*), concentration (*Dhyan*) and mediation *(Habs-i-dam)*. Sufi maintained that the soul has been separated from the Divine Reality and supreme mission of human life is to achieve reunion with God. They believed that there are four stages in one's journey to realization: (a) leading a disciplined life as prescribed in Islam *(Shariat)*; (b) following the path delineated by the *Murshid* or *Guru (Tariqat)*; (c) attaining enlightenment *(Haqiqat)*; (d) on realization of truth, getting merged into Divine Reality *(Mariat)*.

The Sufis believe that God exists in all and all exist in God. Religion is only a way of life; it does not necessarily lead to liberation. It is *Murshid (Guru)* whose grace shows the way and leads to union with God. All happenings take place only as per the Will of God. It is the faith of the Sufis that the soul is distinct from the physical body and will merge into Divine Reality according to a person's deeds. Sufism in India was not confined to influencing a specific place or a shrine or a mosque and its units. Its impact was felt on the culture of the people, on the entire interlocking aspects such as environmental, geographical, social, economic, artistic and devotional. The seminar provided a forum for a creative and critical dialogue on the Indian Sufi tradition in general and art and culture in particular. At the conclusion of the seminar the participants agreed that there was an immediate need for the holistic studies of different Sufi centres having secular and value based traditions. They also mooted the idea of an international seminar of scholars, social activists and practicing Sufis. It many greatly contribute to social harmony and peaceful co-existence, and also help in identifying Sufism as a discipline. Believing in mysticism and teachings of tolerance the Sufis may help in bringing peace and security at National and International level. The concluding remarks at the seminar were given by Khwaza Hasan Sani Nizami of Dargah Sahib, Nizamuddin.

6

Sufi Orders and Fraternities

Sufi order (fraternity - *tarika*) established in Asia Minor at the end of 13 or at the beginning of 14 centuries C.E. primary among the native Turkish nomadic and non-nomadic population. The name of the order has been connected with Hadji Bektash Rumi. In the secret literature of Bekta-shiya, i.e. *wilayat-name* (existed since 20s of 15 century), *silsila-name* and *arkan-name* (since 16 century and later) this person was regarded as patron, saint and symbol of Bekatashiya order. According to the scholarly opinion the real founder of the order was itinerant preacher (baba) and kalandar Hadji Bektash Wali Nishapuri Horasani (1208-1270), who proclamed his spiritual silsila (lineage) to be originated from Turkestan shaikh Ahmad Yasawi (d. 1166), and through that person - to Shiyitic Imam Musa al-Kazim. Hadji Bektash soon obtains wide popularity in Asia Minor.

In 1240 he took active part in the uprising of "Turkish Free-men" led by dervish-kalandar Baba-Iskhak (against Konya sultan Giyas ad-din Kai-Husrau). There are no authentic sources or writings of Hadji Bektash and we can not have judgements about his teaching (the Bektashiya tradition believes that he was an author of Arabian treatise "Maqalat", but we have no its original text; there exist only two its Turkish poetical translations of 14 and16 ceturies). But according to the later prayer books, rite manuals and rules it can be supposed that Hadji Bektash (as many other Turkish itinerant preachers) preached the ideas of the kalandariya and (possible) notions of the radical Shiyits (gulat). Bektashiya became widespread among the rural population. Gradually, the Bektashiya became an established unit with developed net of "monasteries" and communities with strict hierarchy, uninfected ritual system and the rites of initiations as well as with definite symbols and special garments.

This transformation of the order into established organization was connected with the activities of "Grand Master" Balim-Sultan (d. 1516) whose religious title among the believers was "The Second Elder" (*Pir-i sani*). Balim-Sultan proclaimed him to be the descendant of Hadji Bektash Rumi and reformed structure of the communities and "monasteruies", subsequence of the rites of initiation and (probably) established the practice of celibacy. But some members of the Order rejected the reforms of Balim-Sultan. There appeared two fighting groups of the followers. The first one consisted of Chelebis, i.e. the descendants of Hadji Bektash Rumi and the followers of the reforms of Balim-Sultan. The second one consisted of babas, who were sure that just they themselves were true followers of the teaching of the Founder of Bektashiya; they struggled against the reforms.

This schism led the Order to serious conflicts and struggling. In result, Chelebis preserved in their hands the place of the head of the maternal tekke ("monastery") Pirevi as well as the leading role in the Order including the rank of the head of the Order (until the second half of 17 century there existed elections of the head of the Order; after this date this place became hereditary). At the second part of 16 century the head of Bektashiya Order Sersam-'Ali-baba (d. 1589) established the highest apostolic position of the Order-Dede-baba. Though, the Chelebis preserved their real power within the Order (control over wakfs, distribution of the profits, nomination of the heads of the local tekke, etc.), only Dede-baba could give somebody permission to be appointed to the position of the head of Bektashiya. This position was elective, and eight babas of the central "monastery" participated in the elections of Dede-baba. The members of Bektashiya participated in a number of uprisings against the Ottoman regime (e.g., in the movement of Kalendar-oglu in 1526 which was supported by 30 000 members of Bektashiya).

After the Ottoman conquests Bektashiya spread in Syria, Palestine, Egypt where its "monasteries" and communities had been established. During the leadership of of Balim-Sultan the Bectashiya propaganda enjoyed the greatest success among the members of the Janissary corps. Bektashiya was exceptionally influential among the Janissary soldiers. This circumstance determined the growth of the political importance of the Bektashiya Order in the Ottoman Turkey. In its turn, the connection between elite Janissary corps and highly organized fraternity of Bektashiya transformed the Janissary corps into closed separate institution. In 1826 sultan Mahmud II deleted the Yanissary troops and began to perscute Bektashiya Order: its activities were forbidden, three leading heads of the order (Dede-baba, Chelebi and Dede, who was the leader of the celibate dervishes) were executed, new "monasteries" were destroyed (in the capital the old "monasteries" were also destroyed), the real estate (wakfs, land, buildings, etc.) of the Order was confiscated, many shaikhs and simple members of the Order were exiled, and the local "monasteries" were given to the Sufi Nakshbandiya Order.

These persecutions stimulated the emigration of the Bektashiya memebers to the Balkans, especially, to Albania where new important tekkes has been established in Tirana and Akche Hisara; the whole communities of the native people became there the members of the Orders, protesting against the Sunnite Islam of the Turkish conquerors. But during the reign of sultan Abdul-Medjid (1839-1861) the Order revived and returned back its lost centers. During the leadership of Ahmad Jalal ad-din Chelebi there took place the final conflict between Chelebis and Babas. The fraternity became (unofficially) divided into three branches: the proper Bektashi, Dedes (their enemies called them "kajars", i.e. "bandits", "gangsters") and Chelebis (who were called by the first group as "murtadds" - "apostates", "schismatics"). In 1925 the Republican government of Turkey abolished all the Sufi orders, including Bektashiya. There is information that in Albania the Bektashiya was active even in 1967. It is active in Yugoslavia. Until 1965 there existed the Albanian tekke in Cairo. In Turkey (1952) there existed about 30 000 members of Bektashiya. In 1953-1954 they initiated strong political activities in Istambul which caused the governmental repressions.

In its formatting period Bektashiya was closely connected with the movement of gazi which did much for the victory of the Ottomans. This circumstance gave to the Order a reputation of a Sunnite fraternity the silsila (lineage) of which goes to the righteous caliph Abu Bakr (7 century). But in the course of time the doctrine of the Order became an object of powerful influences of ascetico-mystico-esoteric trends (such as Kalandariya and Malamatiya), Shamanistic beliefs of the Turkmen (kyzylbashian) rural and nomadic groups, entering the fraternity as well as the ideas of Anatolian Christian sectarians and Shiyitic doctrines (from moderate to extreme) and the teaching of Khurifits. Therefore it is difficult to speak about the unitary system of the Bektashiya's doctrines. Religious eclecticism/syncretism is a very important feature of its doctrine. Besides this, very complex and controversial relations between different Bektashiya groups must also be noted. These groups entered the Order as its units to obtain its protection from the persecutions but even in the Bektashiya's clothes their members continued to preach their own ideas. Here lay origins of Bektashiya's religious tolerance.

The essentials of the syncretic doctrine of Bektashiya and related practices are: only uninitiated into the secrets of the mystical way must hold the norms of Shariat (the Moslem Law); the hidden meaning of the Quran is attainable only for the initiates; negation of the Namaz - fivefold prayer; ritual bathing is necessary only during the rite of initiation; it is necessary to fast only first ten days of the month of Mukharram (in this period the members of the fraternity do not drink water but eat fruits, vegetables and other simple vegetarian food; in this time in the nights they also celebrate the memories (matem gedjeleri) of the Shiyite martyrs); the cult of the Alidic infants-martyrs (ma'sum-i pak); especial cult of Jafar as-Sadik; thesis that " Ali (the last righteous caliphimam and Prophet's relative - 7 century) is the incarnation of God, and miraj, the ascension of Muhammad, is a sign of exalted place of the Prophet near to Ali; Christian New Year is Ali's birthday, it must be celebrated for three days: they have sacred gatherings where the members of the Order drink milk and listen to the music; initiation (ayinjam', ainjem) is the glorification of the Prophet's family (ahl-i bait), the believers must pray for this family in mornings and evenings as well as for Ali himself; after the month of Muharram (when there is no repentance) a believer must one time in a year confess to the head (baba) of the "monastery" his sins to get absolution from him.

The women in Bektashiya also could participate in their services. Some Bektashiya members take the Trinity of Ali, Muhammad and Allah to be the symbol of their fraternity. The other take as such symbol the Trinity of Ali, Hadji Bektash and FazlAllah Astarabadi (he was a founder of hurufism, which was a mystical Gnostic Shiyitic Sufi teaching; FazlAllah Astarabadi was executed in 1394 or 1401; his followers believed that he was an incarnation of God). The Bektashiya also deified FazAllah and took his book Javidan-name (Turkish - Ashik-name) as the sacred writing. The Bektashiya believe in the magic power of the numbers, especially such numbers as "4" ["four gates", or stages of the mystical way - Shari'a (Law), Tarika (Way of practice), Ma'rifa (Gnosis), Hakika (Truth) as well as four kinds of people coming through these gates, i.e., 'abid, zahid, 'arif and muhibb], 12 (a number of Imams, or Apostles), 32 (a number of letters of Persian alphabet, as well as of lines of the human face which determine fate and destiny of a person).

The Order consisted of rural communities and communities of the initiated ones. Adults from the rural communities passed through the initiation rite (ikrar ayini, ayindjem) which was performed by a hereditary leader of the local community. Thus they became the members of Bektashiya order. The completely Initiated members lived in the convents located in the rural districts but not far from the towns. If they would like to obtain right to wear special ritual hat (taj), hirka (Sufi cloak) and other sacred accessories, they had to pass through the ceremony of the sacred vow (tauba, wakfi wudjut). The complex system of communities and convents was governed by Chelebi whose residence was located in the maternal tekke (Pir-evi) in the place of Hadji Bektash Koyo (founded in 16 century); it was called by Bektashi as Hazrat (His Holiness). Primary the maternal tekke consisted of 12 departments (maidan, hana) which were later limited to the number of eight. These places were: a hall for collective Dhikr and mystical sessions, different places of the house holding (such as kitchen, etc.), garden and Baba-dede's apartments. These departments were headed by special Babas appointed by Baba-dede; they worked only under Baba-dede's strong control.

At the head of the local chapters and convents (in Cairo, Kerbel, Rumeliya and Tirana) stood the so called caliphas. Such convents consisted of four departments. The local tekke were under the supervision of Babas (hereditary, as a rule).

The members of the Order were divised into six principal categories:

Ashik - associated member without initiation;

Mukhip (muhibb) - ashik, passed through the ceremony of initiation and received right to participate in some ritual meetings of Bektashiya;

Dervsh - mukhip, completed the stage of service to the initiational elders, obtained some skill in the practice of the

Way, given the vow and received the permission to wear hirka, taj and other symbolic accesoirs of Bektashiya;

Baba- was appointed to their position by Dede-baba or Calipha of the local tekke (convent; the Calipha appointed babas only for local convents) from the number of Dervishes by special credentials (idjazet-nama) as a head of the local community or of the chapter of the central (regional) tekke. Babas wore taj with white cloth around the top of this hat, he had right to control the common members of the fraternity (such as muhip and dervish);

Dervish-i mudjarrad - dervishes taken the vow of celibacy. They participated in a special closed, or esoteric rite of initiation (mudjerred ayini) taken place in the maternal tekke as well as in the Bektashiya tekke in Kerbela or in the tekke of Balim-Sultan in Anatholia. They lived only in convents, shave mustache, beard and head and wore silver or copper ring in the right ear as a special sign;

Calipha - vice-Chelebi as a head of a regional tekke (abbot). He may be appointed to his position from babas only by a special decree (idjazet-nama) signed by Dede-baba.To this document had to be attached symbols of authority: lamp, large flag, small flag and table cloth. Calipha wore taj with black cloth around the top of this hat and had rights to control common fraternity members as well as to appoint the babas of the local tekkes.

The solemn rite of initiation and taking the vow was followed by a ritual banquet with eating of sherbet and cheese; after it general dinner took place including wine drinking and listening to the music. Bektashiya practiced loud Dhikr but in general ecstatic services (sama, hadra) only initiated members took part. Members of the Order wore taj (conical hat) of white colour, as a rule. Since 18 century there used two types of hats: made from four cloths and made of 12 cloths in the upper part and of 4 cloths in the lower one.

On the neck they wore tigband - thick thread woven in the wool of a sheep, killed in the day of possessor's initiation;

on the chest the Bektashiya members wore a specially prepared stone (taslim-tashi; seng-i taslim) which symbolized the absolute submission of the adept on the chosen path; in the center of a broad embroidered belt there was a kambariya (drop-like agate) and in the side of the belt - jilband, or a having a number of divisions skin bag, two sided axe-teber and a knife; across the shoulder they wore a vessel for charity (kashkul) and a horn. All these accessories were called "wasla". Syncretic by its roots teaching of Bektashiya exerted powerful influence not only on the formation of the religious world-view of the Turkish people but also influenced the development of the Turkish culture, music and, especially, literature.

Formative Years

The formative years of Sufism were between 620 -1100 AD. It was during this time the Sufi masters, known in Arabic as "*Shaikhs,*" started to form the first Sufi fraternities. These early fraternities, and indeed some individual Sufis, met with great hostility and resistance from certain sections of the Muslim community; on points of interpretation of Islamic Theology and Law. Some early Sufis were even persecuted on account of their mystical utterances and beliefs. The most famous Sufi-martyr was Al Hallaj of Basra in Iraq. Nevertheless, individual Sufis achieved great eminence because of their piety and practices. The well-known among them are Rabia Basri (a [female] Sufi Teacher), Junad, Ibrahim, Adheim and Hasan Basri.

Perhaps the most notable one was the great theologian and philosopher Al Gazalli who lived in Syria around 1100 AD. His famous treatises, called the "Reconstruction of Religious Sciences," the "Alchemy of Happiness," and other works; set off to convince the Islamic world that Sufism and its teachings originated from the Quran and were compatible with mainstream Islamic thought and theology. It was Al Gazalli who bridged the gap between traditional and mystical Islam. It was around 1000 AD that the early Sufi literature, in the form of manuals, treatises, discourses, and poetry, became the source of Sufi thinking and meditations.

Orders and Lodges

Around 1200 AD Sufism was institutionalized into Sufi orders. Generally, the political atmosphere from North Africa to India was "ripe" for the formation of Sufi orders. Under the patronage of kings and sultans, prominent Sufi masters received financial grants to build lodges and hospices to house the master; his disciples, students, novices and even travellers. The lodges soon became schools of Sufi learning and scholarship. Attached to the lodges were other places of learning, such as colleges and universities; where students could learn Islamic law and theology, philosophy, and natural sciences. The most prominent Sufi master of the day became the "founder" of a particular Sufi order. One of the well-known orders is the "Qadiryya" founded by the great Sufi-master Abdul Qadir Gilani in Iraq. Others were founded in different parts of the Islamic world by Sufi-masters such as Jalaluddin Rumi in Turkey, Suharwardy in Asia Minor, and Muinuddin Chishti in India. Although each order had a regional flavour, their basic teachings and practices remained fundamentally the same. Because of this, a mutual respect and admiration exists between various orders. Hence, a Sufi may belong to more than one order.

It was between 1200 - 1500 AD that Sufis and Sufism enjoyed a period of intense Sufi activity in various part of the Islamic world. Hence this period is considered as the "Classical Period" or the "Golden Age" of Sufism. Lodges and hospices soon became not only places to house Sufi students and novices but also places for "spiritual retreat" for practicing Sufis and other mystics. Some of the original orders, which I mentioned before, along with new ones are to be found in the Middle and Far East, India, Africa and various parts of Europe and North America. It is estimated, that presently, there are some 40 Sufi Orders in the world.

Rituals and Practices

Now, I should like to talk about the Sufi rituals and practices. It is rather difficult to summarize all the practices and rituals associated with the various orders. However, there are certain practices common to all the orders. They are:

1 Ritual prayer and fasting according to Islamic injunctions.
2. Remembrance of the "spiritual lineage" of each order.
3. The practice of "*dhikr*," an Arabic word for remembrance of God, by invocation.
4. Meditative and contemplative practices, including intensive spiritual training, in "spiritual retreats" from time to time.
5. Listening to musical concerts, to enhance mystical awareness.

The ritual of "initiation" into the order is ordained by the Sufi master of that particular order. Aspiring novices had to undergo a period of intense training in self-discipline, learning to control one's instincts and desires, guided by the Sufi-master. It was the master who would eventually decide if the novice was ready to be initiated into the order. The "initiation" was and still is a "solemn pledge" by the novice to obey the master implicitly in all matters, spiritual and moral. The master in turn pledges to instruct, teach and guide the "new initiate" along the Sufi path. The initiation really symbolizes that the initiate or disciple is now ready to understand the "inner truth" of spiritual realities. Realities which can only be experienced and understood by "intuitive knowledge," Knowledge which stems from the "heart," rather that the "mind." The practice of "*dhikr*" is the central feature in all Sufi orders. "*Dhikr*" is the Arabic word for the devotional practice of the "remembrance of God," It is performed by the repeated invocation of the Names and Attributes of God. It is based on the Quranic verse in which God says "*Remember Me and I will remember you,*" The practice of "*dhikr*" may vary in different orders; but its ultimate object is to create spiritual awareness and love for God. It can be practiced individually, or collectively. Some orders perform it silently and some loudly; all under the direction of the Sufi master.

It should be noted that *"dhikr"* is not exclusive to the Sufis [for] it is practiced by all Muslims as part of Islamic prayer and devotion. Another important practice in Sufism is what is called *"Sema,"* or *"Sama' "* which literally means "listening," These auditions may be a recitation from the Holy Quran, or devotional poetry. Throughout the centuries, Sufi poets have written mystical poetry for devotional purposes and some have even been set to music. Listening to musical concerts, as part of Sufi devotion, is permitted and practiced by certain Sufi orders. A Sufi Order known as the 'Mevlevi Order" founded by the Sufi master Jalaluddin Rumi, who lived in Turkey around 1200 AD, permits a "mystical dance" known in the west as the dance of the Whirling Dervishes. To appreciate the significance of this dance,it is necessary to be aware of its symbolic interpretation and meaning. Veneration of Sufi Saints is a common practice amongst Sufis. Devout Sufi masters who led highly devotional and spiritual lives were elevated to sainthood.

The Sufis believe that a Sufi saint (although dead for hundreds of years) can still make his "spiritual presence" felt to his disciples Hence, it is common practice among Sufis to visit [the] tombs of Sufi saints to pay homage, recite Sura Fateha and/or other Quranic passages, pray to God for *isa-e-thawab* (i.e. praying to God that the rewards of such recitations be bestowed on the dead), and ask for the deceased saint's blessings. There is no formal procedure, or official appointment, or proclamation, similar to the practices of other religions used for the canonisation of saints. Other practices include ritual prayer, fasting, and meditation, as directed by the master. Finally a Sufi may, under the strict guidance of his master, enter into a "spiritual retreat," for a fixed period (usually between 3 to 40 days, or for 24 hours) for intensive prayer and meditation, and daytime fasting. It is best to remember here that all these practice are to prepare the Sufi for the "spiritual journey" along the Sufi path; a path which leads towards God through love and devotion.

The Path - Its Teachings and Tenets

The Sufi firmly believes that each individual spirit desires union with the Universal Spirit, namely God, after death. Furthermore, he believes that it is possible to "experience" God in this life! This kind of experience is described by Sufis as supra-sensory, ultra-mystical, and even "visionary," It must be emphasized here that this kind of "experience" has been achieved by only the elite! Nevertheless, this is the goal of every Sufi. Sufism teaches that the Sufi who seeks God, must advance by slow "stages" along the Path. The "stages" relate to repentance, followed by abstinence, renunciation, 'poverty', patience and trust in God. These stages constitute the ethical and ascetic disciplines of Sufism. Total commitment at each stage is vital towards the spiritual progress of the Sufi. The individual soul is called "*nafs*" in Arabic. Sufism teaches that the soul initially is a "demanding soul," which can be and should be disciplined into a "contented soul," and subsequently into a "soul at peace." These characteristics of the soul are described at length in the Quran and commented upon by Sufi teachers and scholars.

Sufism's primary teaching is based on the Unity of God called "*tawheed*" in Arabic. Its emphasis is on the "Oneness" and "Uniqueness" of God. This concept of Unity leads to the realization of Unity which embraces multiplicity in the Universe. This may sound paradoxical, but Sufi writers and theologians (both classical and modern) have written volumes on this subject, with particular emphasis on explaining various aspects, or grades of manifestation, in terms of immanence and transcendence. Sufis believe that God's earliest creation was the human "intellect." Giving humans the knowledge to discern and to choose between right and wrong, good and evil. This knowledge in Sufism is raised to a higher level, which arises from the "heart" rather than the "mind." It is this intuitive knowledge that distinguishes a mystic from a philosopher. It is through the practice of intuitive knowledge that a Sufi experiences mystical phenomena and visions.

The central doctrine of Sufism however is love, divine love. The Quran teaches that *"God's mercy is greater than His wrath"* and that *"God's love is His supreme attribute."* The Sufi does NOT reject, but instead believes in the doctrine and the concepts of the 'Fear of God' and 'God's wrath of the Day of Judgement." The Sufi maintains that obedience to God's commands should ensue NOT out of the fear of punishment of Hellfire or for the desire of the pleasures and bounties of Paradise as a reward, but rather with the sincere motive and intention of attaining proximity to God - purely for the sake of, and solely for the pleasure of God.

To the Sufi, Paradise (as a reward) and Hell (as a punishment) are but graphic terms to make us understand a state of things which is beyond all our notions of life in this world. The Sufi longs for what is beyond Paradise, the vision of God Himself - the ultimate reward after entering Paradise. And nothing would be lovelier than gazing upon the Lord when He removes his 'veil' (His 'garb of grandeur'). The Sufi attests that God has created man with a mind, free-will, and love. Therefore the mainspring of Sufism is love. Based on this, the Sufi path becomes a 'Path of Love,' where the Sufi becomes the 'lover' and God the 'beloved.' This love affair ends only with the ultimate union with the Beloved. This love relationship is depicted in most volumes of Sufi literature and poetry.

Sufi Literature and Poetry

As has been previously mentioned, earlier Sufism was based on an oral tradition, but around 1000 AD, its teachings and doctrines were put into writing. For the next four centuries, Sufi literature flourished in the form of manuals, mystical tales and anecdotes, treatises on Islamic theology, philosophy, metaphysics and mystical poetry. Sufi manuals were for the instruction and practice of new "initiates," in various orders.

They took a form of "master-disciple" instruction on correct behaviour and conduct within the order. They also dealt with strict "obedience" to the master, methods of "*dhikr*" and meditation, and also with piety and devotion to God. A famous classical manual is by Ibn Arabi called, "*Journey to the Lord of Power,*" which is a handbook on spiritual retreat. Tales and anecdotes in the form of literature are really meant as "teaching tales," with the purpose of driving home a moral or mystical point. Some of the tales are elaborate and allegorical in their content. A classical example is Attar's "*Conference of the Birds,*" and SA'DI's "*The Rose Garden,*" and many others by Arabic and Persian authors and poets.

Classical Sufi treatises on the nature and essence of Sufism and Islamic theology were written by the famous Sufi philosopher Al Gazalli, who lived in Damascus, Syria around 1100 AD. His famous work called "*Reconstruction of Religious Sciences,*" and "*Alchemy of Happiness*"' is classic examples. Another Sufi master Ibn Arabi, born in Spain around 1160 AD, is perhaps the most profound Sufi author of his time. Two of his famous works are called "*Bezels of Wisdom,*" and"*Meccan Revelations.*" They deal with theories on pantheism and monotheism, such as the theory that asserts that "God is Nature, and Nature God." The other theory differentiates God from Nature, by asserting that "God is above Nature, which He created." Yet other theories deal with the "Unity of Being," and the "wisdom of prophecy," and so on. Studies based on such works are still subjects for Sufi contemplation and meditation.

Sufi poetry is recited by Sufis to enhance mystical awareness. Such poetry written in the "classical era" was by Arabic poet Ibn-Al-Farid, and Persian poets such as Hafiz, Sa'di, Jami and Rumi. Rumi perhaps is the best known in the West for his monumental poetic works called the "*Masnavi*" and "*Divan-i-shams.*" Poetic imagery both symbolic and mystical, depicts the central themes with which all Sufis are familiar with, are the "pangs of separation of the lover from the beloved," the "individual soul's" desire for mystical union with the "Universal soul," These are some of the important themes. Classical and modern Sufi poetry can be found from North Africa and Middle East, to India and Indonesia.

Sufi Music and Dance

The practice of music and dance in Sufism is rather contentious. It is by no means universally accepted by all Sufis as some Sufi orders frown upon it. Others [may] rejoice in the recitation of mystical poetry, accompanied by musical instruments and performed as part of their prayers and devotions. Some Sufis consider such music conducive to "mystical ecstasy." These Sufis maintain that music can arouse passion - either sensual or spiritual. It is spiritual passion (longing for God) which is the Sufi's goal. Hence musical concerts are a regular feature of some Sufi orders. The Sufi dance that is much talked about in the West, belongs to one Sufi order, founded by a Sufi master Jalaluddin Rumi who lived around 1100 AD. This dance is known in the West as the dance of the "whirling dervishes." Actually, the dance is performed by the Sufis from that order under strict and controlled conditions, led by a Sufi master. The "steps" and "motions" symbolically depict the "cosmos in motion."

Contemporary Sufism

There are two aspects of Sufism, one is called "practical Sufism" and the other [is] "philosophical Sufism." One deals with the actual practice, while the other deals with the 'way' and how it is practiced. By way of analogy, it has been said that the "philosopher" looks at "water," and describes its properties, whereas the "Sufi," on the other hand, drinks it to quench his thirst. Sufism was brought to the West within the last two hundred years by several western scholars, who were generally Christian missionaries. This gave a rather biased view of Sufism, which is now being corrected. Contemporary western scholars now study Sufism within the framework of Islamic theology and tradition and are therefore able to present it as "the mystical dimension of Islam." Some of the contemporary authors and scholars are Frithjof Schuon, Titus Burckhardt, Martin Lings, S.H. Nasr, and Annemarie Schimmel.

As previously mentioned, a "schism" exists today within the Islamic world. A certain section of Muslims believe that Sufi practices are too radical,[and are] a departure from the fundamental teachings and practices of Islam. This is debatable and I do not propose to go into it here. There are also two schools of thought within the Sufi community. One believes that Sufism is firmly entrenched in Islamic thought and tradition, and cannot be uprooted from Islam. The other school believes that the Sufi message is a "universal message," and therefore transcends any one religion. However, an overwhelming majority of practising Sufis belong to the first group. They maintain that the so-called "Sufism" of the second group is a mere misnomer and that it should really be designated as "mysticism" mainly because the word 'Sufi' has an essential Islamic connotation.

It is obviously for this reason that genuine Sufism is correctly referred to as *Islamic mysticism*. In other words, one must distinguish between genuine-Sufis and pseudo-Sufis who appear to have mushroomed in the very fertile land of California and other places such as Europe and even Asia. I should like to conclude by summarising a Sufi as one who is a mystic, empowered by the Quran and the Prophet, guided by the Sufi master and Saints and belongs to one of the many Sufi orders. In addition to ritual prayer and fasting, he practices various techniques of meditation. He recites poetry and delights in music all towards one goal, namely union with God, the Divine Beloved. Finally it is said that Sufism in the olden days was a "reality without a name," today it is a "name without reality."

Sunni Mystics

Sufis have a firm in the Quran and the *hadith* (traditions of interpretation), but are a fervent people, and in contrast to traditional Sunni believe belief strongly in a personal relationship to God (Allah). They are "mystics. There are within the movement many different schools of method and discipline, providing techniques or principles for meditation and worship, devotion and union with Allah, and having different theological systems, or sometimes specific "non-systems." The Sufis emphasize the Spirit and the relaof the Muslim (devotee, believer) to Allah, the goal of oneness with Allah, the depth and completeness of personal relationwith Allah.

Yet the movement has progreat social activists, like Abd al-Qadir al-Jilani of the 12th century, founder of the Qadiriya fraternity of dervishes. His collected sermons show a man of "noble, religious and philanthropic spirit.... He was a powerful preacher who was said to have converted many criminals in Baghdad and organized relief for the poor and needy." The theologian Abu Hamid al-Ghazali, of the 11th century, recognized universally as a great Islamic systematic theologian, was converted to Sufism in 1095, yet continued in his theological reflection and writing. Ibnul 'Arabi was a Spanish Sufi who elucidated the doctrine of Reality (wahdatu 'l-wujud the unity of existence) in the eleventh century, using a concept of *logos* (the "word").

Spiritual Union

The movement has often emphasized asceticism in various forms and degrees, and the concept of discipline in devotion is prominent. The familiar term "dervish" (*darwish*) refers to one caught up with God in personal devotion, approaching spiritual union with the Divine, caught up out of the world, leaving evil and pain behind. The various schools have their particular techniques for inducing or enhancing the mystical trance, one of which is popularly referred to in the phrase "whirling dervish," depictthe whirling dancing orders, or fraternities, of mystical devotion. These dervish orders spread all over the Muslim world from the twelfth century. These were mostly semi-monastic fraternities, with many brothers returning to their normal occupations after meetings of "litani" or "ecstacy" (*dhikr*).

The Sufis get their name from the asceticism of the early mystics. The name comes from the Arabic word *suf* (wool), used to refer to the garments made of the fiber. The countrymen of the early Persian mystics called them by this nickname because they wore a garment of undyed wool like the Chrismystics. Sufism as an ascetic discipline reflected the strong asceticism of "the more serious of the early Muslims, who were disgusted at the wide-spread luxury and loose living which marked the Caliphates of Damascus and Baghdad. They enjoined austerity and prayer and gave themselves up to a life of contemplation and religious exercise." The Sufis have existed from the earliest days of Islam. They spread to all areas of Islam. In reference to East Africa, most Somalis in Somalia and Kenya are attached to various Sufi groups.

Personal Relationship

Performance of ritual observances is important, but held to be meaningless witha personal relationship with God. The Sufis often spoke of a need for personal conversion, followed by development of true Islam (submission to Allah, and in Sufi terms oneness of spirit with Allah). The sense of mystical relationship to Allah went far beyond the trance of transcendent union, however, and formed a basis of continuing relationship and life commitment to Allah — very similar to the evangelical Christian concept of the new birth, a personal inner communion with the Creator. Thus the Sufis had conflicts with the orthodox Sunnis who did not think of God in terms of redemption and personal relationship. For Allah was above all creatures and man was so unlike Allah, that it was inconceivable that the created might be unified with the Creator.

Yet it was this sense of personal devotion and spiritual communion (relationship) with Allah that led so many mystics to apply themselves to serious theological reflection as a part of their testimony and service. This devotion was the basis of their prophetic role in calling the Muslim community to return to true active religion. As al-Ghazali proposed, love of God leads the believer to make all actions an expression of love. The motive for all actions is to increase one's knowledge of God, which in turn leads to a greater love of God. "When the Sufis accepted the scholastic theology and law as defining the rational and moral imperatives of Islam in external terms and set themselves to seek out and to practice their inner content, they raised the whole level of religious thought and action in Islam to a higher plane of consciousness and purpose."

Role of Jesus

Because of this emphasis on love, Jesus figured prominently in Sufi thought, philoso and devotion. This book will examine briefly the place of Jesus in Sufism. Because the Quran is basic to such a study in Islam, we will begin our investigations there, and after basic insights, we will progress to the thought of al-Hallaj, who, more than any other mystic took Jesus as a model. Sufism belongs in spirit to the modern age. It has an affinity with it; it is in tune with secularism, with the modern thirst for objective knowledge. Yet the Sufi tradition is immensely old. In some quarters a belief still persists that it is a mystical offshoot of Islam, but most reliable sources claim it is far older than the Muslim religion. Evidence is emerging that suggests that the tentacles of the brotherhood reach out to many religions and cultures and extend thousands of years into the past, and that its members were once better known as the Friends of Truth, the Builders, the Masters, the People of the Way and numerous other appellations that had been circulating for far longer than the lifetime of Islam.

The Friends, it is said, were already present in Medina during Muhammad's lifetime and adopted the name Sufi after taking an oath of fidelity to the Muslim cause. A number of derivations of the word Sufi have been put forward, including Ain Soph, the Qabalistic term for the unknowable, and Sophos, meaning Wisdom. This is in line with the view held by many students of Sufism, who claim that it corresponds with the hidden esoteric wisdom-dimension that underlies all religions. Thus the British Sufi fellow-traveller and author Ernest Scott believes the Sufi tradition has impregnated Western culture to a degree we rarely realize, leading him indeed to call it the Invisible Tradition. Its covert influence, he says, has been strong in Manichaeism and the Cathar faith, in the Troubadour and Jester traditions of medieval Europe, in the evolution of Jewish Qabalah, in alchemy and in Christianity itself. Scott quotes the Afghan Sufi teacher Idris Shah as saying that "there is evidence that at the deepest levels of Sufi secrecy, there is a mutual communication with the mystics of the Christian West."

Scott further quotes Hakim Jami, a twelth-century Sufi master, as implicitly denying Sufism's Islamic origin by declaring that Plato, Hippocrates, Pythagoras and Hermes lay on an unbroken line of Sufi transmission, thus making a causal connection between Sufism and the Greek Mystery schools of antiquity. The British esotericist J.G. Bennett goes further, claiming that the Sufis are the descendants and spiritual heirs of the old master magicians of Altai, and that Central Asia has been their heartland for forty thousand years or more. He says that it was from the Altaic shamans that the Sufis inherited the religious tolerance, supremely practical expertise and democratic ideals that are their hallmark today. And it was from the Siberian schools of wisdom that they learned their unique way of surrender, the way of total obedience to a higher principle than man which has earned them the soubriquet "the slaves of God."

Bennett gained much of this knowledge of Sufism's hidden history from his mentor George Ivanovitch Gurdjieff (1877 – 1949), the Armenian-Greek mystic and spiritual teacher who travelled extensively in the Caucasus and Central Asia and who received Sufi training in the dervish schools he encountered there. In *The Masters of Wisdom,* Bennett recounts:

Gurdjieff told me that he had learned about these ancient schools of wisdom from researches he himself had made in caves in the Caucasian mountains and in the great limestone caverns of the Syr Darya in Turkestan. I have since learned that there is a Sufi tradition in Central Asia that claims to go back forty thousand years.

Gurdjieff also told Bennett that the paintings in the Lascaux caves in the Dordogne, France, which the great authority on parietal art, the Abbé Breuil, has dated to about thirty thousand years BCE, were the work of later Sufi descendants of the shamans. Gurdjieff took the story of Atlantis literally. He associated it with pre-sand Egypt and believed the Lascaux artists were members of a brotherhood that survived after Atlantis sank seven or eight thousand years ago. They were highly evolved Masters of Wisdom, "'psychoteleios' who had learned the secret of immortality," and whose centres of initiation on the now submerged Atlantic continental shelf have left us, in their paintings of deer, bison and auroch, a magical message of prehistoric spirituality that lay undeciphered for many thousands of years. In that palaeolithic age art and religion were still one; secular and religious consciousness had not yet separated out, and spirit and matter were not yet in opposition; nor was evil an absolute force seeking the overthrow of good.

All things and all attitudes to things were filled with the magnetic, synthesizing radiance of hypercosmic energy, which Gurdjieff called *conscious energy*. In such a unified world the great Initiates developed the unique type of spirituality that still distinguishes Sufism today, wherein the polarizing activity of mind is submissive to the over-riding Spirit that ever seeks a return to the One. Only in the later more alienated religious systems, Gurdjieff believed, do we find the divisive seeds of philosophical dualism. At the apogee of the Sumerian civilization, Bennett continues, the Sufis are believed to have founded a brotherhood called the Sarman or Sarmoun Society, which, according to Gurdjieff, met in Babylon as far back as

c. 2500 BCE and was responsible for preserving the inner teachings and initiations of the Aryan tradition in a period of religious decline.

Sarmoun is a word meaning bee in Old Persian, and refers symbolically to the practice of the brotherhood of storing the "honey" of both the traditional wisdom and the supernatural energy or *baraka* enabling it to be understood, and sending this double "nectar" out into the world in times of great need. The word Sarmoun can also mean "those who are enlightened." The Sarmouni are believed to have secret training centres hidden to this day in the most remote regions of Central Asia. In *Gurdjieff: Making a New World,* Bennett conjectures that around 500 BCE the Sarmoun Society migrated from ancient Chaldaea to Mosul in Mesopotamia, moving north into the upper valley of the Tigris, into the mountains of Kurdistan and the Caucasus. There it became active in the rise of Zoroastrianism under the Persian monarch Cambyses I.

According to Gurdjieff, the Society later moved eastward to Central Asia, twenty days' journey from Kabul and twelve days' journey from Bokhara. "He [Gurdjieff] refers," says Bennett, "to the valleys of the Pyandje and the Syr Darya, which suggest an area in the mountains south-east of Tashkent." Although Gurdjieff was never explicit about his relationship to the Sarmouni or the precise locality of the monasteries in which he trained towards the end of his travels, he provides many hints in such autobiographical writings as *Meetings With Remarkable Men* that this Sarmoun brotherhood, whose monasteries were situated on the northern slopes of the Himalayas, was the custodian of the most ancient wisdom known and the primary source of his extraordinary esoteric knowledge and powers.

Gurdjieff came to the West as a man with a mission. He had journeyed extensively in the Caucasus, where it is thought he first entered the *tekkes* of the Yesevi dervishes of Sheikh Adi in the Kurdish foothills and later those of the Sarmouni in Afghanistan, receiving a number of initiations by the remarkable age of twenty two. Those closest to him maintain that he remained in touch with hidden Sufi sources throughout his life and received help and support from them. He clearly believed that he acted on their authority in setting up schools in the West that transmitted the cosmological and psychological teachings he himself had learned during his travels. Yet while freely recounting his many Central Asian adventures in his search for wisdom, Gurdjieff managed to draw a permanent veil of secrecy and ambiguity over all details of these intimate encounters with the dervish tradition. This of course is in line with the extreme reticence of the Sufi orders themselves.

A charismatic hypnotist, carpet trader, Russian spy and mystic *extraordinaire,* George Gurdjieff was the son of a Greek-Armenian bard and was deeply impressed by his father's songs concerning the great spiritual luminaries of a vanished past. The boy apparently began his search for the lost wisdom of the ancients at the early age of fifteen, and maintained it at huge cost to his health and material resources until he emerged, nearly thirty years later, a magus of mysterious yet undeniably charismatic authority. Possessed of enormous personal courage, during World War I Gurdjieff led a large posse of Russian followers across Eastern Europe to safety, through the raging battle lines of Bolsheviks and Cossacks in turn, eventually establishing a school in Fontainbleu, outside Paris, for the study and practice of methods of spiritual self-transformation. These methods, revolutionary in their day, are believed to have included the sacred dance and music exercises of the shamanistic Yesevi dervishes of Kurdistan, a community in which Gurdjieff seems to have received his initial training in Sufi techniques of "soul-making."

The Yezidis, a secretive Kurdish religious sect from which the Sufi Bektashi order has sprung, live to this day in the foothills north of Mosul in Iraqui Kurdistan pursuing a cult of angels. According to the British baroness E.S. Drower, who in 1940 published a detailed paper on the sect, the chief Yezidi angel is Malek Taus, the Peacock Angel who has some likeness to Lucifer, the fallen angel of Christian fame. A black serpent is also held in special reverence in the Yezidi religion as a symbol of magical potency – no doubt ultimately a symbol of kundalini and the spinal system of energies elaborated in spiritual physiology. While paying lip service to the Muslim faith, the Yezidi have own unique cosmogony, mythology and ritual practices, which have more commonality with the Magian or Gnostic belief-systems than with either Islam or Christianity.

Ceaselessly persecuted and destroyed by Kurdish Muslims and Ottoman Turks as well as Islamic armies of both Iraq and Iran, the once powerful Yezidi tribes have been almost wiped out as heretics of the first order. Only isolated groups are now left. These include small pockets in Central Kurdistan, the Russian Caucasus and in satellite communities in Syria, Lebanon, Anatolia and Iran. Sheikh Adi, a noted mystic of the thirteenth or fourteenth century, was a Median Magi, and although he is regarded as the founder of the Yezidi faith and an incarnation of the Peacock Angel, both the religion and the tribe are ascribed a far earlier date of origin. They are believed to be heirs to an ancient ancestral tradition going back to Noah. Adrian G. Gilbert comments:

> It is my belief that they [the Yezidis] are descended from the ancient Chaldaeans. Their own tradition is that they migrated from the South, and they may well be the lost remnants of the Babylonian Magi who disappeared after the time of Alexander of Macedon.

This is certainly in line with Gurdjieff's belief that the roots of Sufism lie in a spiritual tradition of extreme antiquity such as is found in the Yezidi faith, and that it was probably centred in the Caucasus and Central Asia. Nevertheless, there are many evidences that Sufism has continually developed beyond its initial form and has amplified its teachings over the ages. The late Hugh Schonfield, a noted Jewish scholar and author, says that by the third century CE Sufi schools were well established in the Middle East, particularly in Mosul, the heart of the old Assyrian kingdom, under the auspices of the Zoroastrian Magi. There the Sufis were joined by many Jewish refugees from Egypt fleeing Roman persecution.

Among these were the Therapeutae, members of an Essene Order of contemplatives strongly imbued with a revolutionary New Covenant with God. The covenant involved a Judaic reformation that forbad militarism and animal sacrifice and embraced the principles of gender equality and an equitable distribution of wealth. The Therapeutae brought to the Sufi tradition not only these enlightened social ideals which were actually already enshrined in its own constitution, but much of the new Hermetic and Kabbalistic mysticism fermenting in Alexandria. Thus, says Schonfield, throughout Egypt and the Middle East there were religious fusions and amalgamations, and the emergence of spiritual hybrids... Zoroastrianism and Mithraism lent their characteristics to Jewish Essene teaching, and found a Greek expression in the Hermetic and Christian Gnostic. The coverage of the Roman Empire right round the Mediterranean carried the cults with it, and opened the way to new blendings.

In this way Sufism was continually invigorated by new trends and in turn invigorated others. Then, when in the seventh century CE civilization was in danger of total collapse through the ravages of global pestilence, war, earthquakes and the suppression of all Greek learning by Byzantine Christianity, the Sufi masters transferred their allegiance from Zoroastrianism to Islam, the latter offering the greater hope of rehabilitation for humanity. Thus the wisdom and science of Persia, with its great heritage of Greek learning, passed into the Muslim culture and was carried by Muslim sages into every quarter of the globe. The Dark Ages were halted and Islam, supported by the Sufis, brought about a brilliant revival of the Graeco-Roman arts and sciences. The conquest of Spain by the Muslim Moors meant Jews, Muslims and Christians were able to live there harmoniously until the fifteenth century, creating a culture of superb beauty and intelligence which lasted until the Jews and Muslims were banished to Byzantium, and which gave Sufism entrance into the rest of backward Europe. During the same centuries Crusaders such as the Templars encountered the rich Saracen culture in the Holy Land and secretly brought back the cream of Sufi thought to Europe to enrich Christian theological scholarship, art and sciences.

With the Mongol invasions, however, came difficult days for European civilization as many sources of Sufi wisdom withdrew. The Sufi Masters of Wisdom known in Central Asia as the Khwajagan lineage withdrew at this time to the Trans-Himalayas, where their schools still persist. The Khwajagan were neither savants nor mystical ecstatics. They were practical men who assiduously practiced the breathing and mantric exercise of the *zikr,* fought their own weaknesses by means of trials based on humiliation and abasement, and during the Mongol depredations of the conquered western cities built new schools, hospitals and mosques. Some say these Masters, who may be synonymous with the Sarmouni, have continued to this day to head the Sufi hierarchy – which Bennett has called the Hidden Directorate - from its hidden Trans-Himalayan headquarters. Meanwhile, the Sufi orders left behind continued to strengthen their ties with other esoteric systems, such as the Magian secret societies in Persia and the Copts in Egypt, and to extend their formidable influence across the world into South-East Asia.

In the Sunda Islands they amalgamated successfully with the indigenous shamans, Hindu-Buddhists and Taoists and were instrumental in establishing in Java one of the most influential schools of Tibetan Kalachakra Tantra in the world. The result was a chain of hybrid secret societies around the globe whose roots were buried deep in a freedom-loving soil compounded of Sufism, Magian wisdom and the Solomonic and Hermetic wisdom of the Egyptian Essenes. It was these pan-religious amalgamations that produced over the centuries initiatic schools like the Templars, the Chartres masters, the Rosicrucians, the Illuminati, the Freemasons and the Theosophists, all dedicated to working for the religious and scientific dawning of a new age free from religious intolerance. Throughout the long Sufi saga, the West had been unaware of intervention in its affairs, or indeed of the very existence of a powerful organization in its midst that was monitoring the course of history and at the same time maintaining its own hierarchy, objectives and worldview independently of the visible political and religious structures of society. But the Sufi masters knew that this unconscious condition, mainly imposed on the people by repressive forces outside their control, must end, and that the time of awakening was drawing near.

The two Rosicrucian manifestos pseudonymously published in Germany in the early years of the seventeenth century marked the first Sufi venture into the public domain and caused a sensation. The manifestos purported to advertise a mysterious order called the Fraternity of the Rosey Cross which had been founded, it was claimed, by one Christian Rosencreutz; and a third publication called *The Alchemical Wedding of Christian Rosencreutz,* written in high Dutch, came out soon after. The manifestos declared that Fr. Rosencreutz had obtained the inspiration for his brotherhood from Arabia, Fez (the home of Sufic alchemy since the eighth century) and Egypt, all centres of Sufi activity. And Rosicrucian tradition has it that Fr. Rosencreutz was initiated in Palestine by an Arabic sect. Observes Ernest Scott:

> When it is realized that the Sufi teacher Suhrawardi of Aleppo had a teaching method called the Path of the Rose and that the Sufic word for a dervish exercise has the same consonantal root as the word for a rose, the Sufic origin of the Rosicrucians may be inferred with some confidence.

As we now know, the series of Rosicrucian publications

with their visionary and reforming talk of an invisible college, a "winged academy" dedicated to a commonwealth of man, created a furore in Europe. Some saw the publications as a hoax, others as a God-given sign of the millennium. As ever, the Sufis were not directly mentioned: but, sweeping like a rejuvenating wind through Protestant and Catholic lands alike, the movement stirred up by the mysterious manifestos became a potent though short-lived catalyst for change. It instigated a religious and intellectual uprising that sought reform in education, religion and science, promising a coming utopia in which the dignity and worth of every man and woman would be recognized.

Frances A. Yates, a foremost Renaissance scholar, believes this period in the seventeenth century can rightly be called the Rosicrucian Enlightenment and that out of its "great reservoir of spiritual and intellectual power, of moral and reforming vision" came the Royal Society and the age of scientific revolution. Full of Christian mysticism yet also permeated with Hermetic-Kabbalistic angelology and alchemical religious philosophy, the Rosicrucian teachings proclaimed that this age of enlightenment, in which religion and science would no longer be antithetical, was at hand; great advances were to be made and a reformation of the whole wide world would presage "a great influx of truth and light" into fallen society such as shone on Adam in paradise. For a time large factions of the Church espoused these ideas, and the Jesuits, themselves of occult and hermetic origin, took over much of the Rosicrucian symbolism and emblematics.

Yet, in the event the whole programme was aborted by the fiercely reactionary response of the Spanish Inquisition and its political ally, the Hapsburg dynasty, which instigated the Thirty Years' War, forcing thousands of religious dissidents to flee with the seeds of the new vision to the New World. The Sufi programme had to incubate in secret for several more centuries. Not until the twentieth century, in a more tolerant and receptive age, were the Sufis finally able to reveal themselves openly. In 1921 Gurdjieff, the emigré and entrepreneur from Armenia, was the first to make this possible. He came with a crucial message for the twentieth century and, as we shall see, for our own era in the third millennium. Of great personal magnetism, drive and unusual psychic powers, Gurdjieff burst upon the western scene with his programme for spiritual development, bringing to the European cognoscenti for the first time an awareness of the sacred ritual dances and dervish exercises of the East. These, he said, had strong links with Altaic shamanism and Tibetan and Chinese Tantra.

But Sufis have never regarded spiritual exercises alone as adequate. Generally speaking, little is said in Sufi literature about *Baraka,* the effective grace that makes spiritual development on this path possible, yet its importance is primary. Baraka, as transmitted from teacher to pupil, is said to be a high emotional energy associated with the heart centre, and according to Bennett, enables the pupil to do what would be quite beyond his unaided strength. It is this inner infusion of conscious energy - energy of a high spiritual nature - that enables the *zikhr*, the Sufi invocatory exercise, to be fruitful. Discipline, austerity and voluntary suffering, which Gurdjieff translated as conscious labour and intentional suffering, were also needed. By intentional suffering he meant exposing oneself to painful situations in order to help others. While the southern Sufi orders embraced the mystical doctrine of love and union with God, these northern Sufis were strongly influenced by Buddhism and, like the Khwajagan, were concerned with a total liberation from self and the world of appearances.

They were regarded by the more conservative southern Sufis as unorthodox, even being accused of magical practices learned from the Siberian shamans to the north. Nevertheless, Gurdjieff saw great benefit for the West in the dervish practices, disapproved though they were by the more purist brotherhoods such as the Nach'shbandi and the Qadiri, and made his unique programme available to all those wishing to develop their human potential. At his Institute for the Harmonious Development of Man in Fontainbleu, Gurdjieff trained his students in group dance movements set to dervish rhythms that demanded of them intense physical effort and coordination and which raised the body to a "high state of consciousness" conducive to a transformation of energies. He also encouraged his pupils to observe intensively their own psychic centres of thinking, feeling and instinct as a means of achieving a degree of self-government that man at present entirely lacks – but without which, Gurdjieff insisted, it is impossible for him to govern and maintain the planet. Public performances of Gurdjieff's dervish dances were put on at various theatres, even in the prestigious Carnegie Hall in New York, and Europe and America marvelled: nothing like it had ever been known. Sacred dances, Gurdjieff said, have always been one of the vital subjects taught in esoteric schools of the East... Such gymnastics have a double aim: they contain and express a certain form of knowledge and at the same time serves as a means to acquire a harmonious state of being.

At one time it was his intention to use the movements in the traditional way for which they were principally intended in the ancient temples of initiation – that is, as a means of transmitting knowledge directly to the higher centres without passing through the mind, which is the way of Tantra. But a car accident in which Gurdjieff's physical health was severely damaged put an end to his wider plans for the movements and turned his attention to writing and training selected people to carry on his work at a more intellectual level. Sufi prescience, Sufi aptitude for the right teaching in the right time and place, is well attested. In many respects, Gurdjieff's writings contributed enormously to the familiarization of the West to the radical idea of the psyche or soul – the dynamic centre that mediates between the spiritual and the sensory functions – which at that time Sigmund Freud was also bringing to Western notice.

Recognition of this unifying centre of relativity, which modifies the traditional absolutes of philosophy and religion on one hand and the physical sciences on the other, was just then opening up, and Gurdjieff's psychological brand of theosophy, which became the vogue at the same time as Freudian and socialist theory, made a very great impact. The Gurdjieff schools of self-development spread to numerous countries and his ideas became common coinage in the new enlightenment of the sixties. Through the interest aroused in his methods and teachings, in which the centrality of individuation was paramount, Gurdjieff was able to give out for the first time a certain amount of information about the Sufi *tarekats* hidden in Eurasia. And in his train came a school of eminent Sufi writers like Guénon, Bennett, Ouspensky, Schuon, Hazrat Inayat Khan and Idris Shah, all of whom further opened up the world of Sufism to a vast reading public.

One of the central strands in Gurdjieff's belief-system was the principle of world-creation and world-maintenance, which he said was derived from "an old Sumerian manuscript" discovered by a great Kurdish philosopher. The doctrine can be summed up very simply: "Everything that exists maintains and is maintained by other existences." Peculiar to Sufism and appearing in no other religion, it states that the whole of the universe is a web of mutually supporting systems, "apparatuses for transforming energy", each one of which produces the means of sustenance for others. This law of reciprocal maintenance governs all of life and applies to man as well as in his relation to Mother Nature. The world is not made for man, as we have been taught; both are made for each other. Man's destiny and the destiny of the earth are interdependent. The evolution of the one depends on the evolution of the other, the survival of one on the survival of the other. Man is not separate from the cosmic process; he is himself part of the ecosystem he observes out there, and he must serve the evolution of the world as well as his own. That is the law of the cosmos, even as the palaeolithic shaman defined it many millennia ago.

From the Sarmounis, Gurdjieff learned that man is at present an automaton, a mere mechanism driven by the blind forces of action and reaction, his sense of identity fragmented his will almost non-existent. Yet even work on himself will not redeem him without an acceptance that he is here to serve the world. Through Gurdjieff, therefore, the Sufis gave out to the twentieth century a new teaching, a new outlook on life that was revolutionary seventy years ago: man cannot advance spiritually unless he fulfils his obligation to planet earth, and through planet earth to the solar system. He must "pay the debt of his existence" by nurturing that which nurtured him. For men cross is a two-fold spiritual destiny; to evolve as an individual, but also to serve the evolution of kingdoms other than his own, lives other than his own. Out of the friction these opposed drives generate, said Gurdjieff, there comes a transcendental third, the birth of conscience.

This suffering of the tension between the opposites is the law of true religion and is alleviated only by the awakening of the mediating force inherent in the soul; that is, conscience or love. The Sufi theory of world-creation and world-maintenance – "a new master idea for the coming age", as Bennett called it – has become increasingly relevant as the planet's ecological crisis has worsened over the decades; and now, looking back from our vantage point in the new millennium, we can see how it has indeed become the hallmark of our time, perhaps the key to its essential meaning. Wherever the next civilization is centred it must be where the third and reconciling power can operate; where conscience can find a home. That is the prime Sufi message for our generation, as it was Gurdjieff's.

Suhrawardi's was the only other silsila (principle) which had a considerable following in medieval India. This Islamic order is considered one of the four prominent orders in Sufism. Shihab-ud-din Suhrawardi, a teacher in Baghdad, was the founder of this silsila which was introduced in India by his disciple Jalal-ud-din Tabrizi and Oaha-ud-din Zakariya (1183-

1262). The former took his abode in Bengal where he converted a large number of Hindus and established a Khanqah. However, Zakariya was mainly responsible for organising the Suhrawardi silsila in India. His Khanqah at Multan became one of the important centres of religious learning in India. After Sheikh Ziaudin Jahib Suhrawardi founded the Suhrawardi Order, his nephew Abu Hafs Umar al-Suhrawardi (1145 - 1234) took the responsibility to spread the Suhrawardi Order in various parts of the world. He was sent as emissary to the court of Ayyubid Sultan Malik al-Adil I of Egypt, to Khwarezm-Shah Muhammad of Bukhara and to Kaiqubad I, the Seljuk ruler of Konya by the Khalifa of Baghdad, Caliph an-Nasir.

He had done a great job, as numerous Sufis from all over the Islamic world joined the order under his guidance. After his death, Hazrat Jalaluddin Surkh-Posh Bukhari and Hazrat Baha-ud-din Zakariya worked hard to spread the Suhrawardi Order into India. Though the Suhrawardi Order originated in Iraq, it succeeded only in India for taking the shape of a fraternity, along with its infrastructure, internal hierarchy of members and cloisters and a single centre in Multan and Uchch. The Sufis of the Suhrawardi Order have played the principal role in the formation of a conservative 'new piety' and in the initiation of urban commercial and vocational groups into mysticism. The Suhrawardiyya is a strictly Sunni order and it is mainly guided by Shafi'i madhab. Apart from Abu Hafs Umar al-Suhrawardi, another famous Sufi saint of the Suhrawardi Order, Fakharuddin Iraqi also played a pivotal role in the spreading of the Order. He received formal initiation into the Sufi way under Shaykh Baha'uddin, the head of the Suhrawardiyya Sufi Order. Iraqi was deeply devoted to Qunawi and to the teachings of Ibn El-Arabi and he also got inspirations from a series of speeches, delivered by Qunawi on the esoteric meaning of Ibn El-Arabi's great works. Inspired by the speeches, Iraqi composed one of his own masterpiece works of commentary and poetry, named the Lama'at or Divine Flashes.

Yet another disciple, Jalal-ud-din Surkh Bukhari (died 1291), settled in Ucheh and set up a Khanqah there. His grandson and successor Sayyid Jalal-ud-din organised and strengthened this centre. He converted a large number of tribes. He played an important part in the political and religious life of Sind. Shaikh Rukn-ud-din Abul Fateh, grandson of Shaikh Bahaud-din Zakariya, was the most important Khalifah of this order. He occupies the same high position in the Suhrawardi silsila as Shaikh Nizam-ud-din does in the Chishti order. The whole population of Sind held him in high esteem. Shaikh Ruknuddin also contributed considerably in popularizing the Suhrawardi Order. In fact the Sultans of Delhi, such as, Alauddin Khilji and Muhammad Tughlaq highly respected him. However, though the Suhrawardi Order declined in Multan after his death, it became remained well accepted in the provinces of Uchch, Gujarat, Punjab, Kashmir and even Delhi. The Suhrawardi Order also became popular in Bengal, at a later period. Apart from the above mentioned great Sufi saints of Suhrawardi Order, some of the other saints and philosophers like Shaikh Sharfuddin Yahya Manairi and Shihabuddin Yahya as-Suhrawardi also made their own contributions to the development of the Suhrawardi Order.

As far as the practices of Suhrawardi Order are concerned these vary from the production of mystical ecstasy to the completely quiescent exercise for 'perception of Reality'. The legends or works of fiction have laid the foundation of the instructional materials of the Suhrawardi Order. However, they contain some materials to the devotees and the materials are essential for preparing the ground for the experiences which the disciple must eventually undergo. It is believed that without those materials, there is a possibility that the disciple may simply develop altered states of mind that make him unfit for ordinary life. Moreover unlike the Chishtis, the saints of this order led a comfortable life. They made ample provisions for their families and even employed teachers on handsome salaries for the education of their sons. Suhrawardis believed that there was no harm in owning property and dispensing of wealth if the heart was detached.

Suhrawardis actively associated themselves with the government and accepted the posts of Shaikh-ul-Islam and Sadr-i-Wilayat. They exhorted their followers to be nearer to the kings who are the chosen of God, the Almighty. Under no conditions, showing disrespect to them or disobeying their orders is permitted or proper in Shariat. One of the Suhrawardi saints Shaikh Rukn-ud-din Multani was of the view that it was essential for a shaikh to have money, learning or scholarship besides spiritual attainments to satisfy the variety of people who visited him.

7

Theosophical Sufism

Mysticism in Islam has two distinct origins. The first is the Quran itself, which postulates an intensely personal and direct relationship between the individual and God. This fervent devotion was expressed in the early practice of Hasan al-Basri (d. 728) and the poetry of Rabi'a al-Adawiyya (d. 801) and gave rise to spiritual Sufism. Practiced by preachers who embraced a simple - almost ascetic - life, it also included celibacy and extensive religious worship and contemplation carried out individually or, more often, in a *halaqa,* or circle of devotees. The second source is the mystical doctrines of other religious traditions, including Gnosticism, Christianity, Zoroastrianism, and Hinduism, which converts to Islam brought into their new faith, giving rise to theosophical Sufism. These traditions had elaborate theosophical doctrines, at the heart of which lay the concept of the unity with the divine, the ultimate goal of the mystic. However, the principle of *tawhid* (divine unity), the cornerstone of orthodox Islamic belief, establishes God's absolute unity and absolute transcendence, thereby precluding any possibility of the creature joining with the Creator.

Theosophical Sufism eventually resolved this contradiction through the elaboration of a number of paradoxical concepts that maintain at once unity and difference, annihilation of self into the divine *(fana)* and self-persistence *(baqa),* presence and absence, intoxication and sobriety. The analogy of seeing God in a mirror image of oneself is often used to explain this unity with the divine. The reinterpretation of *tawhid* as unity of being, according to which the mystic could claim unity with divine existence or attributes while preserving the transcendence of divine essence, allowed Sufism to claim adherence to fundamental orthodox Islamic dogma and gave Islamic mysticism its distinctive flavor. On the basis of this new interpretation, divine truth *(haqiqa)* became the ultimate object of the Sufi gnosis, which was called *marifa* (intuitive knowledge) to set it apart from the rational and exoteric discourse of the law; the law itself became secondary - either a mere step to reach unity with the divine or a hindrance that could be dismissed after a certain level of illumination.

Knowledge of the divine nature was called *kashf* and was considered to be infallible, a characteristic that in orthodox Islam is attributed only to Prophetic revelation. The concept of the unity of being was tied to the Hellenistic understanding of God as a First Intellect from whose self-contemplation the world emanates, and that was reinforced by the Greek-inspired Muslim philosophers, who adopted that understanding against the dogma of the Muslim theological schools. The articulation of theosophical Sufism and its harmonization with the *shari'a* (Islamic law) was carried out by Muhyi al-Din ibn al-Arabi (d. 1240), who systematized a sainthood hierarchy that culminated in a "seal of sainthood" parallel to the Quranic "seal of prophecy" that he attributed to himself.

Although at first fought by the orthodox, this process of presenting the theosophical concepts in Islamic terms and justifying them through the esoteric interpretation of the Quran eventually made Sufism legitimate. The process was furthered by the elaboration of a body of Sufi prophetic sayings *(hadith)* that justified Sufi practice (although that led to the elaboration of anti-Sufi *hadith.*) The full adherence by theosophical Sufism to the *shari'a* and the nominal adherence to the concept of *tawhid* met the main legal requirement of the faith. In addition, the materialism that accompanied the economic, technological, and cultural expansion of the Islamic empire in Umawi and Abbassid times, as well as the tendency among literalist jurists and theologians to reduce the law and the faith to a numbing amalgam of rules and rituals, helped the spread of Sufism by causing a popular reaction against these trends.

In the eleventh century, Abu Hamid al-Ghazzali (d. 1111), who dominated the orthodox movement with his powerful intellect, strongly defended the spiritual dimension in Sufism against the impoverished literalist views of its most vocal opponents and integrated it into the theological expression of the faith; and although he opposed the unity of being and the asceticism and withdrawal preached by some Sufis, the stature of al-Ghazzali helped validate Sufism. Sufism could now spread unimpeded in all its various expression, although any unambiguous claim of having achieved unity with the divine met with retribution or persecution from the orthodox theologians (as happened to Husayn bin Mansur alHallaj, executed for heresy in 922.)

Partly because orthodox resistance precluded its integration in the theological disciplines and partly because of its very nature, Sufism did not become an organized discipline and came to refer to anything from intense piety to specific devotional steps to mystical philosophy. Most often, however, a Sufi cell (called *tariqa* or *zawiya* or *ribat*) was formed around a teacher, and spiritual doctrine and practice could vary widely from one cell to another. Generally, the Sufi experience centers on a number of practices (including *dhikr* or recitation of the Quran, contemplation, prayer, singing, dancing, and fasting) prescribed by the Sufi shaykh, who determines the progress of the disciple through the *maqamat* (stages of spiritual development, codified by Dhu Nun, d. 859.) Sufism contributed greatly to Islamic art in poetry (that of Jalal al-Din al-Rumi, d. 1273, is the best known in the Muslim world as well as in the West) and in literature and music.

By the middle of the ninth century, Sufi orders had established schools throughout the Muslim world. Since any teacher could establish a cell, these were innumerable. However, the main Sufi schools established a *silsila* (chain) through which the master's teachings were transmitted from teacher to disciple, and a loose lineage was traced back either to Abu al-Qasim al-Junayd (d. 910) in the Arab world or to Abu Yazid al-Bistami (d. 874) in Central Asia and Iran. Within the Arab tradition, the Rifa'iyya, became know for some wild practices and spread widely until overtaken in the fifteenth century by the Qadiriyya (Abd alQadir al-Jilani, d. 1166), whose orthodox bent and more flexible teachings became popular. Less famous because of its emphasis on strict mystical discipline was the Suhrawardiyya (al-Suhrawardi, d. 1168), which gained favor with the upper classes.

Within Central Asia and Anatolia, were the Mawlawiyya, an introspective order known for its use of chanting and its dancing dervishes, the nomadic Yasawiyya, and the powerful and orthodox Naqshbandiyya, which was popular with the elite in India and Central Asia. Also popular in the Indian subcontinent was the Chishtiyya (Mu'in al-Din Chishti, d. 1236). In Africa, the Badawiyya in Egypt (Ahmad al-Badawi, d. 1276) and the Shadhiliyya had emerged from the Rifa'iyya, though the latter was more insistent on following the Sunna (tradition of the Prophet) and discoura-ged asceticism. The Tijaniyya (Ahmad al-Tijani, d. 1815) became very active in fighting European colonization in Northern Africa in the nineteenth century. Amongst the Shi'a, the most popular orders were the Safawiyya (Safiy al-Din, d. 1334), which originally had been a Sunni movement, and the Ni'matullah. The orders shared the same general structure, an initiation ceremony during which the disciple (or the affiliate) was inducted in a similar path, marked with individual and collective rituals that focused on total obedience to the Sufi master.

These orders contributed greatly to the spread of Islam and often served as social protest movements, through their association with craft and commercial guilds, against state authority and abuses of power. But the veneration of the saints and the belief in their power to perform miracles (a claim that was eventually sanctioned by orthodoxy) slowly degenerated in popular practice into a muddle of saint worship, fatalism, superstition, and magic and cultic practices. This was accentuated by the excesses of the more extreme Sufi organizations, which demanded profession of faith in the saints as part of the *shahada* (Muslim creed); other organizations allowed followers to use illicit substances and disregard the law in the pursuit of the loftier goal of achieving knowledge of the divine; still others preached extreme asceticism and withdrawal from the world.

Such excesses had always met with strong disapproval from orthodox jurists, although all of the jurists accepted the spiritual dimension of Sufism, but it was not until the reform movements of the eighteenth century that a reaction against these excesses took place. Building on the criticism of theosophical Sufism by Taqiyy al-Din ibn Taymiyya, Muhammad ibn Abd al-Wahhab (d. 1792) introduced a strict return to the pristine sources of Islam, namely the Quran and the *Sunna* (the Prophet's tradition), and condemned the morally lax practices and quasi-worship of the saints and the Prophet that were practiced by Sufis. In India and North Africa, reform was also under way, although for different reasons. The Sufi movements, whose active preaching had brought massive conversions to Islam in those areas, had adopted beliefs and practices from their converts that were at times clearly in opposition to Islamic belief and to the *shari'a.*

Alarmed by this syncretism, Sufi masters including Muhammad al-Baqi Billah and Ahmad Sirhindi in India and Muhammad ibn Idris in North Africa initiated a move to restore orthodoxy and in the process reinterpreted the Sufi concepts and shifted their content from unity of being to unity of witnessing God *(wahdat al-shuhud)* and from a traditional Sufi path *(tariqa)* centered on a saint to a *tariqa Muhammadiyya* (the Prophet's *tariqa*) centered on the emulation of the Prophet through strict and active observation of the *shari'a.* But the threat that European colonialism posed to the Muslim movements transformed their efforts from religious and social reform to a national jihad against the invaders, which only hastened the disintegration of a Sufi worldview based on otherworldliness and ascetic withdrawal. Modern Muslim movements facing many of the same political challenges have generally been critical of Sufism and have espoused more and more a legalistic interpretation of the faith. However, despite the decline of the Sufi orders in recent history, many of the Sufi rituals and traditions survive today in individual and communal practice.

The Muslim world's understanding of its faith has constantly oscillated between the poles of excessive spiritualism and legalistic interpretation, although the existence of these poles has kept Islam from falling permanently into one or the other extreme, in the one case by preserving the spiritual dimension of the faith and preventing the reification of religious consciousness and in the other by grounding the faith in textual sources and moral activism. The great jurists and theologians have attempted to maintain a balance between these two dimensions of Islam, and despite opposition to certain elements in it, Sufism is generally seen as part of normal religious commitment. Thus, it was considered perfectly acceptable during the 1980s for the vice president of Cairo University, a noted scholar in Arabic-Islamic philosophy, to serve as the leader of Sufi circles in Egypt. Popular religion, however, has generally swung from one extreme to the other.

Transcendent theosophy or al-hikmat al-muta'li, the doctrine and philosophy that has been developed and perfected by the Persian philosopher, Mulla Sadra, is one of two main disciplines of Islamic philosophy that is very live and active even today. The expression al-hikmat al-muta'liyah comprises two terms al-hikmat (meaning theosiphia) and muta'liyah (meaning exalted or Transcendent). This school of Mulla Sadra in Islamic philosophy is usually called al-hikmat al-muta'liyah. It is a most appropriate name for his school, not only for historical reasons, but also because the doctrines of Mulla Sadra are veritably both hikmah and theosophy in its original sense and an intellectual vision of the transcendent which leads to the Transcendent Itself. So Mulla Sadra's school is transcendent for both historical and metaphysical reasons.

When Mulla Sadra talked about hikmah or theosophy in his words, he usually meant the transcendent philosophy. He gave many definitions to the term hikmah, the most famous one is: hikmah is a vehicle through which "man becomes an intelligible world resembling the objective world and similar to the order of universal existence". Mulla Sadra's philosophy and ontology is considered to be just as important to Islamic philosophy as Martin Heidegger's philosophy later was to Western philosophy in the 20th century. Mulla Sadra bought "a new philosophical insight in dealing with the nature of reality" and created "a major transition from essentialism to existentialism" in Islamic philosophy.

Existentialism

A concept that lies at the heart of Mulla Sadra's philosophy is the idea of "existence precedes essence", a key foundational concept of existentialism which was not popularized in the West until Jean-Paul Sartre in the 20th century. This was also the opposite of the idea of "essence precedes existence" previously supported by Avicenna and his school of Avicennism as well as Shahab al-Din Suhrawardi and his school of Illuminationism. Sayyid Jalal Ashtiyani later summarizes Mulla Sadra's concept as follows:

"The existent being that has an essence must then be caused and existence that is pure existence ... is therefore a Necessary Being."

For Mulla Sadra, "existence precedes the essence and is thus principle since something has to exist first and then have an essence." This is primarily the argument that lies at the heart of Mulla Sadra's philosophy. In Islamic philosophy, whereas previous methods of philosophical thought held that "essence precedes existence", a concept which dates back to Avicenna and Shahab al-Din Suhrawardi, Mulla Sadra substituted a metaphysics of existence for the traditional metaphysics of essences, and giving priority ab initio to existence over quiddity. Mulla Sadra affected an entire revolution in the metaphysics of being by his thesis that there are no immutable essences, but that each essence is determined and variable according to the degree of intensity of its act of existence.

In his view reality is existence, differentiated in a variety of ways, and these different ways look to us like essences. What first affect us are things that exist and we form ideas of essences afterwards, so existence precedes essence. This position referred to as primacy of existence (Arabic: Isalat al-Wujudý). Mulla Sadra's existentialism is therefore fundamentally different from Western, i.e. existentialism of Jean-Paul Sartre. Sartre said that human beings have no essence before their existence because; there is no Creator, no God. This is meaning of "existence precedes essence" in Sartre's existentialism. Therefore existentialism of J.P. Sartre and Mulla Sadra are significantly different teachnings.

Substantial Motion

Another central concept of Mulla Sadra's philosophy is the theory of "substantial motion" (*al-harakat al-jawhariyyah*), which is "based on the premise that everything in the order of nature, including celestial spheres, undergoes substantial change and transformation as a result of the self-flow (*fayd*) and penetration of being (*sarayan al-wujud*) which gives every concrete individual entity its share of being. In contrast to Aristotle and Ibn Sina who had accepted change only in four categories, i.e., quantity (*kamm*), quality (*kayf*), position (*wad'*) and place (*'ayn*), Sadra defines change as an all-pervasive reality running through the entire cosmos including the category of substance (*jawhar*)." Heraclitus described a similar concept 20 centuries earlier (panta rhei - "everything is in a state of flux"), Gottfried Leibniz described a similar concept a century later.

Islamization in this context should not necessarily be understood as synonymous with conversion, at least in the first instance. At this stage the word conversion is best avoided, for it has connotations of an individual choice of one religion rather than another on largely theological considerations such as one finds motivating religious change in the modern world, at least in the individualistic west. But were such unmixed considerations always the determinant factor? Is it not likely that religious change was gradual, and came about after a long process of association between local peoples and Muslims, beginning with curiosity, followed by a perception of self- interest leading eventually to attachment to and finally entry to that religious community, rather than a response on an individual basis to the preaching of a message? In the light of such considerations, my idea of the primacy of the mystical dimension of Islam in the Islami-zation of Southeast Asia needs re-consideration, and along with it a number of tacit assumptions as to the nature of Sufism and its relation to Islam more generally that lay behind it.

The end of the thirteenth century, which saw the earliest physical evidences of an Islamic port city in North Sumatra, marked the beginning of a strong forward movement of Islam in the region. By this time had become great international corporations, and were playing a major role in maintaining the unity of the Islamic world after the fall of Baghdad to the Mongols in 1258. In fact a process was in train -which by the eighteenth century led Gibb to remark "membership of the religious orders was practically synonymous with the profession of Islam" [Gibb and Bowen 1957: 76]. When Ibn 'Arabi died in 1240, the monistic theosophy of the Sufi tradition was well articulated and widely diffused. This, together with the fact that the earliest extant MSS from North Sumatra, albeit some three centuries later, showed evidence of a strong concern with such a theosophy seemed to suggest a causal relationship between the development of theosophical Sufism and Islamization in our region.

This was after all a view to which my early research on Sufism in Sumatra during the Seventeenth century [Johns 1957] disposed me. I had at that time an enthusiasm for the theosophy of Ibn 'Arabi, doubtless imperfectly understood, for which such generalizations seemed to provide an acceptable social context, and was intoxicated by the writings of Nicholson and Massignon. Ibn 'Arabi's visionary Sufism is indeed intoxicating.

His philosophical monism expressed in the term *walJ,da al-wujud* (the Unity of Being) transforms the emanational ideas of Islamic Neo-Platonism into an extraordinary system of aspects and relation- ships, generated by the lines of force inherent in the Ninety Nine most Beautiful Names of God, vehicles of His power and being, names such as al-Ra1:lman (The Merciful), al-I:Iayy (The Living), al-Qayyum (The Self-Subsistent) and al-Muhaymin (The Guardian). Even so such religious concepts were for a spiritual elite, not for every Muslim, and even with this qualification, they were not universally accepted. Islamization is a word with a variety of meanings, depending on the mix of trends and tendencies within the world of Islam at anyone time. Such trends and tendencies are responses to the internal and external challenges that Muslim communities have faced since the religion was first preached in Arabia, and which still continue. The division between Sunni and Shi'a, as a response to different views concerning the leadership of the community, is one example, but there are others which sometimes led to schism, at others resulted in no more than a shifting distribution of varying emphases in the formulation of doctrines on which all Muslims agreed.

Examples of such issues can be seen in debates as to whether the interpretation of the Quran was to be literal or allegorical, whether rationalism or Gnosticism should be the dominant characteristic of the religion, whether the Law or spiritual insight should have the primary role in determining its norms and ideals. The spiritual dimension of Islam was from the beginning a central concern in my research. It lies at the heart of the development of what was later to be called Sufism. Central to this dimension is the longing for an experimental awareness of God, in Quranic language, a yearning to see His face. This yearning in the history of Sufism is expressed in different ways and associated with varying styles of spirituality and spiritual taste.

They range from the severely ascetic and sober, based on techniques of self-scrutiny, to the ecstatic, induced by recitation of the Quran accompanied by music and dance leading to exuberances of theosophical expression. But these differences are not mutually exclusive, and there is a distribution of emphases within them and between them. Such modes of spirituality are part of the general history of the Islamic peoples, Southeast Asia not accepted. This area of the world, however, presents special problems to Islamicists. One of the reasons is that Islamized Southeast Asia is a region without a stable urban tradition and in which the oral tradition is stronger than the literary. It is therefore difficult to bring to it the philological and historical methodologies developed in the study of Islam in the Middle East or the Indian subcontinent.

Thus scholars concerned with the traditional Islamic disciplines found little there of interest to them compared to the intellectual excitement to be derived from the literary traditions of South and West Asia. And many of the scholars who devoted themselves to the study of the history and society of Southeast Asia lacked a wider knowledge of the world of Islam, let alone an effective mastery of the Islamic disciplines, and tended to overlook the role Islam played in many areas of local life. The result was in many writings, a prominence given to issues such as "syncretism" and the "conflict" between adat and Islamic law, suggesting that these were distinctive of Islam in the region and not encountered elsewhere in the Muslim world. In fact, the presence and role of Islam in Southeast Asia has been consistently underestimated.

This is in part because in a number of critical regions, Central Java being a case in point, many cultural forms of the pre-Islamic past still have a vigorous life, notably the shadow theatre and the gamelan orchestra. Moreover, in the search for a classical tradition (every country has to have one!) the pre-Islamic archaeological and literary culture represented by monuments like the Borobudur and the retelling in old Javanese poetry or prose of episodes of the Hindu Buddhist epics from the pre-Muslim past have exercised a stronger appeal for philologists and scholars of religion than the living tradition of Islam, which for many lay unobserved.

In addition, thanks to the tendency to regard Central Java as representing the core of insular Southeast Asian culture, Islam appeared to lack any legitimacy and cultural status, and was seen as a cultural blight that put an end to the splendour of Hindu Java. The presence of Islam was noted, and needed cursory reference, but often scholars were uncertain as to how to handle it, and so looked the other way. This attitude was compounded by the currency of such terms as the heartland and the periphery of the Islamic world to refer to the Middle East and the Indonesian islands respectively-as though the further one got from Mecca the weaker Islamic faith and practice inevitably became. Such are the ways in which we are made captive to metaphors of our own creation!

A corollary of this has been that what passes for conventional wisdom concerning Islam there ranges from the bizarre to the patronizing. It is said, for example, that Javanese Muslims are tolerant, and do not exhibit the aggressive characteristics of Middle Eastern Muslims because pre-Islamic beliefs are still strong, the implication being that the Javanese in revealing this dimension of tolerance are not behaving as Muslims at all, or that a tropical climate with its heavy rainfall, has dampened religious enthusiasm. It is difficult to exaggerate how widespread such generalizations are, or how superficial. Tolerance and intolerance are not distributed geographically. There are in Egypt and Pakistan, for example, Muslims with a far broader range of religious sympathies than many Indonesians.

There are Indonesians with a far more narrowly scripturalist understanding of the religion they profess than some Saudi Arabians. The reverse of course is also true. If such were the views simply of European non-Muslims, it would be bad enough, but in fact one finds similar attitudes among Muslims in the Middle East who speak patronizingly of their co-religionists in Indonesia or Malaysia, as though to say, due to their distance from the Holy Land, they are not really Muslims, or at best, that their way of being so is so distinctive that there can be no strength of identification with them as fellow-members of the Muslim community. A different perception, however, follows almost immediately from the adoption of a perspective other than that provided by the dichotomy between the heartland and periphery of the Muslim world, one that takes as its starting point a consideration of the active engagement of Southeast Asian Muslims in the commonwealth of Islam.

It is necessary, by way of example, to take account of their observance of the daily ritual prayer, the passage rites of circumcision, marriage and burial, and alongside these, those areas of life in which Islamic Law of the Shafi'ite school is applied, and the great annual events such as the Fast and the Pilgrimage. One should consider, likewise, their participation in revival movements such as that of the Wahhabis, or the reformist movement initiated by al-Afghani and Muhammad Abduh, or in the radicalization of Islam in modern times by Mawdudi, Sayyid Qutb and Khomeini. One has to appreciate the part they played in the transmission, development and vernacularization of the Islamic disciplines in their part of the world: their knowledge of Arabic, the manuscript copies they made of authoritative Arabic texts before the advent of printing and acceptance of its use for religious works, and their competence in the Islamic disciplines. In addition, one can look to their association with outstanding teachers in other areas of the Muslim world, the part they played in the Islamic common-wealth of religious scholars, and their preparation of text books for local conditions, making their own contribution to such disciplines as Quranic exegesis, dogmatics, jurisprudence and eschatology.

Not least one should be aware of the implications of their adoption of the Arabic script to write their own languages. Finally one should take account of the establishment of Islamized forms of the state, and the role of sultanates in the region in the days before sultans were forced to give way-at least in some areas, to Colonels and Presidents. It is only in such a wider context that the more specific question may be asked: how did they participate in the various Sufi traditions known in other parts of the Muslim world, share in and make their own contribution to the mystical dimension of Islam? It is in this context that one may ask whether there were any aspects of Sufism that facilitated the spread of the religion, or may have predisposed Muslims in the various areas of what is now Indonesia to being Muslim in one way rather than another. In this respect, the word "Indonesia" as the name of a modern nation state is an obstacle to a clear understanding of the processes of Islamization in the region. It is easily overlooked that the word had no political content before the early twenties of this century.

The fact that it is an over-arching term does not imply any homogeneity in the regions it subsumes, and certainly does not wipe out a millenium and more of the histories of a variety of languages and cultures all important in their own right. People in different areas of what is now Indonesia naturally participate in the Islamic world in different ways.

It is from such a perspective that one should attempt to highlight the various aspects and emphases in the Islamization of the region from the time that it began. Self-evidently, it cannot be separated from the trading system of the Indian Ocean. As soon as Muslims took part in that system, and eventually they were to dominate it, a discreet, silent process of Islamization began, as Muslim trading communities became established at focal points along the northeast coast of Sumatra and on the Malay Peninsula, the north coast of Java, Borneo and the Celebes. Such points were convenient stopping places to exchange goods, to take on water and firewood and wait for a change of the monsoon, either to journey on to China for silks and porcelain, or to take on board spices and locally produced goods.

How long these communities had remained silent and discreet before appearing on the pages of history with a political profile there is little way of knowing, any more than whether they formed settlements in areas largely uninhabited, to which they attracted other traders, or whether they formed autonomous quarters in already existing centres of population and trade. At any rate, as Muslims, they had their networks of international contacts within which business confidence was secure, due to the writing of contracts according to Muslim Law. Business confidence is infectious, and the association of non-Muslim peoples in the trading enterprises of Muslims with contracts written according to Islamic Law, followed by the growth, stability and prosperity of Muslim communities is a widely recognized mode of Islamization. Now if Muslim communities are to function effectively as communities, they require the presence of *'ulamii:* those individuals trained in Islamic jurisprudence who understand the principles of contracts-whether for trade or marriages-, who can work out legal solutions to the conflicts that arise in any community, and who can perform the necessary astronomical calculations to determine the times for prayers, the approach of the fasting month, and the pilgrimage season.

Such an elite and a class of scholars, have their own networks, both among themselves, the teachers from whom they had studied and acquired their legal expertise, or from whom they had been inducted into one or another of the great ariqa. Once these things have occurred, there is already effective participation in the world of Islam, even if, in the thirteenth century, as far as Southeast Asia is concerned, documentation is sparse. But there is another development to take into account. By the thirteenth century, the new institution of the sultan had become well-established. The first ruler whose coins bear the title Sultan was apparently the Seljuq Tughril Beg 1055.

From his time on, Sultanates sprang up like mushrooms in the Middle East, the Indian subcontinent and Southeast Asia. Once the precedent had been established, any leader of a community who had established an adequate power base could, when he deemed the time ripe consolidate that power base by declaring himself sultan and claiming an area of territorial jurisdiction. A sultanate, barring coups and/or assasinations is a hereditary institution and given a measure of stability, and a succession of able rulers, is able to expand its area of authority. At some stage, this happened in Sumatra, and it is the culmination of a process of silent Islamization that is marked by the first evidence of a sultan in Sumatra, the grave stone of Sultan Malik al-Saleh at Pasai with an inscription giving as the date of his death a year corresponding to 1225 or 1307, depending on how the inscription is interpreted was a harbour principality, and it is the establishment of such harbour principalities under a sultan with their religious and mercantile orientation across the Indian ocean that provide the political and economic mechanism for the further expansion of Islam.

It is likewise this institution that provides the means of a closer relationship with other Muslims, and creates opportunities in the structure of the state for the establishment of religious schools, the participation in teaching of foreign with local *'ulama:* and the creation of libraries. If one asks whether during this period there is any direct evidence of Sufi involvement in the Islamization that had reached the level at which the leader of a Muslim community might declare himself Sultan, the answer is no. But if the question is put differently: what is the likelihood of individual traders and *'ulamti'* law brokers essential for business confidence being members of *tariqiis?*, then by the thirteenth century, the answer must be that it is high, particularly if the trader, as so many of them were, was from Indian subcontinent. There is indirect evidence in the traditional stories that are elaborated in the court chronicles which attribute the coming of Islam to the preaching of itinerant holy men from abroad, one of them commissioned by Muhammad himself. But such stories are largely *ex post facto* fabrications.

There is evidence that the Pasai court was aware of personalities and events in other, older established centres of authority in the Muslim world. Fatimi, using information provided by Hitti, has drawn attention to the possible significance of the name of the Pasai Sultan, Malik al-Saleh (as it is usually spelt in histories of Indonesia) mentioned above. This name, Fatimi points out, eponymous with that of the Ayyubid ruler al-Malik al-Salih, who restored Jerusalem to Islamic rule in 1244. Might this not have been a reason for him on becoming or declaring himself Sultan, to adopt this name? It is possible to see a similar motivation in his naming of two of his sons Malik al-Zahir [sicJ and Malik al-Mansur [sicJ, both eponymous with two near contemporary figures in the Middle East. al-Malik al-Zahir Baybars was the fourth Mamluk sultan. He aspired to be a second Salah al-Din, and played a major role in blocking the Mongol's advance towards Cairo. Al-Malik al-Mansur was likewise a great anti-crusader and the most outstanding Mamluk figure after Baybars.

He achieved such renowned that even the ruler of Ceylon sent an embassy to his court with a letter no one could read!

The correspondence of names may be coincidental, but it is not inherently unlikely that the Pasai Malik al-Saleh was sufficiently in touch with events across the Indian Ocean, mediated perhaps through trading contacts, perhaps through Pasai pilgrims or a Pasai community in Mecca, to be aware of these three famous names from the Middle East, and to be heartened by reports of Muslim victories against the crusaders. After all, events there would have had economic consequences for Pasai. At the very least, Fatimi's implied point that to be a sultan was to become a member of an exclusive club of Muslim rulers is important. It is not until the late sixteenth century that local MSS sources from Sumatra become available.

All are written in the Arabic script, adapted to indicate those sounds in Malay that have no counterpart in Arabic, and all show a significant stratum of Arabic loan words and a number of features of syntax that could reflect Arabic influence. Although relatively young, it is clear that they belong to a tradition that is much older and are evidence of a long and close participation of local peoples in Islamic life and culture. The earliest example is the poems, the Malay quatrains, of the Achehnese Hamzah Fansuri (d. 1590). He is an author belonging to the theosophical tradition of Ibn 'Arabi mediated by the Iraqi al-Jill (d. circa 1408). His rendering of numbers of Quranic verses into Malay and interpretation of them as they are under- stood in this mystical tradition, no less than his vernacularisation of Arabic words and concepts, is extraordinary. His writings show an ecstatic passion for union with God, and include a brilliant tangential allusion to al-Hallaj's identification of himself with the burning bush in the vision of Moses, by an identification of himself with the tree that is burnt to yield camphor. By the seventeenth century, it is possible to demonstrate a close relationship between religion and political authority in the Acheh sultanate (1496-1874).

This relationship is evidenced in a number of ways: through the investiture of the ruler Sultan IskandarMuda (1607

- 1636) in a Sufi by his Shaikh al-Islam, (perhaps a conscious use of an Ottoman title) Shams al-Din. It is also seen in this Shaikh al- Islam acting in a political role as foreign minister and in addition Vicegerent when Iskandar was incapacitated by bouts of insanity. This combination in a single individual of the roles of Sufi adept, *murshid* to the ruler, and holder of two senior positions of state is striking. The position of Islam in the state is likewise illustrated by reference, in a nonchalant and unstudied manner, to two well-known mystical verses of Ibn 'Arabi in a Malay work published under the title *Hikajat Atjeh* a lengthy fragment of a panegyric to Iskandar Muda.

When a remote ancestor of Iskandar finds his future bride in a clump of bamboo, to quiet her alarm at this unexpected discovery, he says to her: God has made manifest today our former hidden union (in the knowledge of God, before individual existents were differentiated one from the other). In this allusion there is both reference to the predestined greatness of Iskandar, and a highly sophisticated sexual conceit, the product of close, even playful familiarity with the formulations of the central doctrine of Sufi theosophy, that of the Unity of Being. Chance allusions of this kind are more revealing of the currency of religious ideas than the fact that Shams al-Din wrote a number of treatises in Arabic, still extant, and in fact was an early, if not the earliest Sumatran on record to have written in Arabic.

The writings of Shams al-Din moreover demonstrate that there has been a shift in the provenance of religious thought popular in court circles from the Iraq/Iran tradition of al-Jili represented by Hamzah Fansuri to one that derives from Muhammad b. Fadl Allah al-Burhanpuri, a north Indian teacher who wrote in 1590 a work outlining a system of seven grades or manifestations of Being-a theosophical system that, while based on the same concept of the unity of being as that espoused by Hamzah, expresses it in a different formal structure. It should be remembered that acceptance of the Ibn 'Arabi tradition represents only one way of participation in the mystical life of Islam, and that other models are represented in fragments of works in Javanese from the late sixteenth century, dealing 3) The lines in question are: We were lofty sounds unuttered held in the highest peaks of the hills am you in Him, and we are you and you are He All is He in Him-ask those who have attained. For a Malay commentary on these lines by the Achehnese 'Abd al-Ra' uf see with dogmatics and spirituality, from one or another of the north coastal towns of Java.

These works have little to do with the monistic theosophy of the Ibn 'Arabi tradition but are based largely on the ethical mysticism of al-Ghazali. These examples are sufficient to demonstrate the independent net-working of groups of religious teachers with varying spiritual taste at the various centres of trade and authority in the archipelago, and the discrete character of local traditions all over the archipelago. By the mid-seventeenth century, a fuller documentation of this participation becomes possible, with evidence in Arabic sources of the presence of Sumatrans in Mecca and Medina and their attatchment to a particular teacher. This is sufficiently important to present is some detail.

We are able to put together a Kurdish scholar, Ibrahim al-Kurani (1615-1690) who was affiliated to a number of *tanqa,* and a *khalffa* of the Shattariyya order, who settled in Medina; 'Abd al-Ra'uf, an Achehnese who studied with Ibrahim in Arabia 1640-1661, and Yosuf a Makassarese who was in Medina with 'Abd al-Ra'uf for some years; and Ibrahim's pupil al-Hamawi, who wrote a biographical dictionary *Fawa'id al-IrtifJ,al wa Nata'ij al-Safar* (The profits of travel and the gains of journeying) a biographical dictionary of the *'ulamii'* of Mecca and Medina, in the eleventh Islamic century (seventeenth century CE) with an entry on his teacher Ibrahim and the Sumatrans who studied from him, reporting what they said to Ibrahim and what Ibrahim said to him about them. In this entry Hamawi says: Our Shaikh (Ibrahim) told me that one of our Jawi associates-and he was reading with him the [work entitled] *al-TufJfa al-mursala ila rilfJ al-nabi* while we were present-told him that this treatise and the matters it treats of was popular and well-known in the lands of the Jawi, and that it is read in their religious schools.

Ibrahim had a special relationship with Jawi students, foremost among them 'Abd al- Ra'uf whom he designated as his *khalifa* to spread this *tariqa* in Sumatra when he returned. They asked him questions about the correct understanding of the work, referred to by Hamawi and the system of seven manifestations of being that it set out. It was in response to their questions that Ibrahim wrote a major work on the topic, entitled *Ithiij al-Dhaki.* In his introduction to his work he refers to the Sumatrans and the questions that they put to him: We have reliable information from a group of Jawi that there have become widespread among the inhabitants of the lands of "Java": some books on Realities and esoteric teachings by men attributed with knowledge because of their study and the teaching of others, but who lack any understanding of the Law of (Muhammad) the Chosen, the Elect.

He continues: They told me that among the best known of books among them was the compendium entitled *al-TulJ,fa al-mursala ila rillJ, al-nabi* (the work by Muhammad ibn Fadl Allah mentioned by Hamawi in the biographical entry referred to above), and more than one of them has asked my humble self to prepare a commentary upon it to make clear the conformity of the questions (it discusses) to the basis of the principles of religion, confirmed by the noble Book, and the *Sunna* of the Lord of the Messengers. What kind of a man was Ibrahim? What did his teaching communicate to 'Abd al-Ra'uf, and how did it contribute to the participation of his countrymen in Islamic life and devotion? In other words, what was the range of learning and the kind of spirituality to which he attracted them?

In the introduction to his work *ItlJilf al- Dhaki,* he plays on the most beautiful names of God as though they were a musical instrument with the compass and resonances of a great organ, "God is the First and the Last, the Outward and the Inward: the First before whom nothing was, the Inward beneath whom nothing is more hidden." He justifies the seeking of inward meanings in the Quranic verses and *lJ,adith,* but condemns any abandonment of their literal meaning, quoting from al-Ghazali's *Mishkat al-Anwar,* al-Ghazali's use of the tradition "Angels do not enter a house in which there is a dog," to condemn the *Batiniyya.* To discover an inward sense to the *J,adith,* i. e. that the word "house" may signify heart and "dog" the spirit of anger, and thus that it means "angels do not enter a heart in which is the spirit of anger" does no violence to the words of the Messenger. It would only do so were one to claim that the only meaning of this *Jadith* is the inward one.

Knowledge of such an inward meaning however, does not exempt the believer from the duty of obeying the literal sense of the words. But, Ibrahim says, the Sufis do not do this, rather they affirm the outward sense of the words, and in addition understand them in whatever inward way that Allah reveals to them, for there is nothing impossible in God giving to anyone of His servants He chooses an understanding of meanings in His Book and the sayings of his Prophet that are not explicitly expressed. What was he like as a teacher? There is an anecdote told in a biographical dictionary: Ibrahim used to say: the *FiitifJ,a* should be recited at the end of every meeting. There was once an old *faqih* who said: I married a young woman when I was advanced in years. Her family loved me and trusted me, but secretly, she disliked me because of myoid age, and only pretended affection for me for the sake of her family. Now one day a woman friend visited her, and I listened to them talking without their knowing it.

Then the woman visitor made to leave, but said: "not until we have recited the *Fiitifa* together, as do the *faqih* and his friends when they part." So the pair of them recited the *Fiitifa,* and I wrote that down too, as they recited it. Then I told her brothers all that she had said about me, and said to them: do not make her stay with me, for I wish to divorce her. They were displeased with her and reproached her, but she denied everything I had accused her of having said against me. So I said: here is the paper on which I wrote everything down as you were saying it. And there was nothing on the page except the *Fiitifa,* and so I realised that the *Fiitifa* had blotted out every evil thing she had said.

A number of maxims are attributed to him. They include: "It is better to reconcile two conflicting points of view rather than to choose one of them or the other"; "Truth lies at the mid-point between excess and inadequacy" and "The philosophers got close to ultimate truth, but did not quite succeed in attaining it." And what of 'Abd al-Ra'uf? He lived for 30 years in Acheh on his return from 20 years in Arabia. He exchanged letters with Ibrahim across the Indian Ocean. He was supported by the court, by the Sultana Safiyatu'l-Din. He wrote prolifically, and his contribution to the vernacularization of Islam in Malay is remarkable. He wrote a treatise, on the orders of the sultana, on that branch of *jiqh* known as *al-mu'a: malat* called *Mir'at al-ullab-* a work of 600 pages in Ms; he prepared a Malay rendering of the ta/*sir* of al-Jalalayn that is still in use today and is regularly reprinted. He wrote a lengthy treatise on the spiritual exercise of *dhikr* called *'Umdat al-multajin* and a theoretical work on the concept of the unity of being, which may be summarised: the world is from God.

Everything is The Reality, *al-lfaqq,* but not as it is here and now. Being is one, but only at the level of non-manifestation in the knowledge of God. 'Abd al-Ra'uf's concerns were broad. He brings together the exterior and interior disciplines (as did his teacher Ibrahim). He writes on *ta/sir* without reference to the mystical dimension of exegesis. Yet he also writes on the spiritual exercise of *dhikr,* and on the unity of being. As a teacher, he inducted many individuals into the Shattariyya order, and was responsible for its popularity in Java. This is the first occasion in the history of

Islam in the region in which it is possible to bring together such a constellation of facts and sources of information: concerning a Sumatra scholar, 'Abd al-Ra'uf; the ruler of Acheh, Safiyatu'l-Din, who was his patron; the Kurd, Ibrahim al-Kurani, who was 'Abd al-Ra'uf's teacher in Medina, and the biographer of Ibrahim, Hamawi who refers to the presence of Sumatrans in the circle of Ibrahim's students. In addition, we have works that they produced.

We can put our hands on their writings and in some cases MSS of the letters they wrote to each other across the Indian Ocean. Another, later instance of such a constellation of elements occurs in the mid- eighteenth century under the aegis of the Sultanate of Palembang in south Sumatra. It is possible to document the relationship between 'Abd al-Samad (1703-1788) of Palembang, and Arab scholars in the Holy Land, including the Egyptian Azharite professor Ahmad b. 'Abd al-Mun'im al-Damanhuri who visited Mecca in 1763, and Muhammad b. 'Abd aI-Karim al-Samman (1719 - 1775) who founded the Sammaniyya *ariqa.* 'Abd al-Samad was inducted into this *ariqa,* and through his students in Mecca returning home to Sumatra, it was established in Palembang where it flourished within the founder's life-time.

Palembang was a centre of Muslim learning that deserves detailed study. Within a period of 50 years or less, Malay versions of such works on dogmatics as Ibrahim al- Laqani's (d. 1631) commentary on the rhymed credal statement *jawahariit al-Tawlid,* works of ethical mysticism as the *lfikam* of Ibn 'Ata Allah, and the *Risiilat fi'l-TawlJ,id* by Raslan al-Dimishqi enlarged by the Cairo author Zakariyya aI-Ansari (d. 1520) and later 'Abd al-Ghani al-Nabulusi (d. 1731) a Sufi text that lays greater emphasis on inner worship, purity of motivation, and the spiritual stages of *shukr, rida* and *sabr,* than on absorption into the Divinity. Then most important of all, 'Abd al-Samad's rendering into Malay around 1788 of *Lubiib ilya' 'ulilm al-din,* an abridgement of al- Ghazali's *Ilya' 'ulum al-din,* by al-Ghazali's brother Ahmad.

Here again is documenta- tion of a Sumatran scholar who spends years in Mecca, his association with Arab and Egyptian scholars, his induction into a *ariqa,* his spreading of this *ariqa,* in Palembang both personally, and through the students who came from Sumatra to study with him in Mecca, the major contribution he makes to the vernacularization of Islam with a work that is still reprinted, and the role of the Palembang court in supporting religious learning *[ibid.:* 36 - 37J. A nineteenth century example is furnished by the career of al-Nawawi al-Bantani. He was born in 1814, went to Mecca in 1829 and lived there the remainder of his long life. He wrote on the various disciplines of *Iadith, fiqh tafsir* mysticism grammar and rhetoric. He was teacher and guide to many generations of Jawi in Mecca over 40 years. Snouck Hurgronjc met him in 1885 and in his book *Mekka in the latter part of the 19th century* notes that he was acknowledged as head of the Jawi community; and had just published, on the newly established Mecca Press, a two volume commentary on the Quran. Al-Nawawi was the author of over 100 works in Arabic, a number of them still in current use in religious teaching institutions, regularly reprinted in Mecca, Cairo, and a number of major cities in Indonesia.

His two volume *tasir, Mariilf Labid* deserves special mention. In an introduction he lists the authors and their works on whom he depends. They include Fakhr al-Din al-Razi (d. 1209), Shirbini (d. 1570), and Abu'l-Su'ud (d. 1574). In fact about 70 percent of his *tasir* is selected from Razi's great work *Mafiitilf al-Ghayb,* giving his own compilation, following in Razi's footsteps, a markedly rationalist character. Moreover, following Razi, he omits many illustrative stories to the Quranic text that Razi rejects, which modern Muslims dismiss as Isra'iliyyat. Thus Razi's influence on him is highly significant, an influence that he passed on to thousands of his students from the Indies over a period of forty years, and in these respects anticipated and facilitated, the rapid spread of Muhammad 'Abduh's reformist ideas there. Indeed, by way of a digression, Lowe Nawawi, a great personal debt, for it was through him discovered Razi, and found a new career in Raziana.

These examples are far from exhaustive. They are, however, sufficient to show that reference to Sumatra and Java as part of a remote periphery of the Muslim world is misleading. Rather the islands of Indonesia were linked to the Arabian Peninsula by the Indian Ocean, not separated from it. Modes of participation varied from place to place. During the silent years of Islamization preparing the ground for the appearance of Islam with a political face in the region, the Sufi dimension was present, both explicitly and implicitly at appropriate levels in Muslim communities. In my giving a primacy to the Sufi movement in Islamization, the issue was wrongly put, but the putting of it was not wholly wrong.

If the generalization that the Indies became Islamized due to the spiritual appeal of Sufism was too broad, it is not necessarily wrong to say that many, if not a majority of the *'ulamll'* who played a role in the establishment of Muslim communities in Southeast Asia had Sufi affiliations. By the same token, it is certainly' overly simplistic to speak tout court of Islam being brought to the Indies by traders without reference to the *'ulamii '*. During the early years of Islamization, local evidence is so scarce that it is necessary to proceed by inference. Nevertheless it must be recognized that we have to do not simply with local peoples encoun-tering Muslims, and eventually adopting a new religion in a particular geographical area, but with their involvement in a wide-ranging international community through a variety of networks comprising related ethnicities, merchant groups, religious teachers and *tariqas.*

All this was a continuing process that by zealous net-working at an individual level *pari passu* with the expansion and contraction of political authority at the level of the ruler, extended the domain and depth of Islam in the region, particularly when the Muslim ruler allied himself with (or fought against) another local Muslim ruler. During this period (eleventh -eighteenth centuries) Sufism should not be thought of as distinct or separate from the vast body of jurisprudence which it complemented and alongside which it grew out of the primary sources of the Quran and the *sunna,* notwithstanding that the house of Islam has long been divided in its attitude to the Ibn 'Arabi tradition of theosophical Sufism. The Sufi Shaikhs were not necessarily to be thought of as individuals or a class separate from the *·ulamti'*. It is in part the anti- *tariqa* stance of the reformists of Muhammad Abduh's generation that have exaggerated this tension which they have projected back anachronistically, and a number of Western scholars have followed in their wake.

The Sufi movement is a dimension of Islam, and in so far as it has a separate identity, represents only one aspect of Islamization. There are many others which complement and support each other. Among them is story-telling, especially as represented by local retellings, adaptations and enlargements of Quranic presentations of scenes from lives of the prophets, *al-anbiyti.* (Stories of the Prophets) which long before the Germans invented the term *heilsgeschicht,* established a widely socialized perception of a universalistic salvation history from Adam to Muhammad. My examples have been limited to Acheh, Palembang and Banten, and they are far from exhaustive. One could refer to other centres and periods with similar kinds of documentation. But this brings us to a paradox: of how intensely local such communities and centres of trade and culture are, and how the religious elites were embodied in these communities, in a way that presented a fusion of universal forms of Islam with local beliefs and life-styles.

This is indeed true of Indonesia today, with its distinctive styles of fusion of local elements with the universalistic doctrines of Islam in say Acheh, Minangkabau, Central lava and the Celebes, but it is certainly not peculiar to Indonesia and its neighbours. Lapidus' great work makes this abundantly clear. What it amounts to is that the processes of

Islamization in Southeast Asia and the results of those processes are more like than unlike what happened elsewhere in the Islamic world; in the so--called polarization between what is called *shari'a* and adat law, we are only seeing the same processes that were to yield the so--called classic formulations of Islamic Law-a bringing together and infusing with an Islamic spirit and norms, a whole range of practices in familial, commercial and criminal law, administrative regulations, bringing in Persian, Byzantine and Hellenistic maxims, elements of the canon law of the orthodox church, Talmudic and old Babylonian law-bringing all into conformity with God's will.

Equally, "syncretism," no matter how this troublesome word is understood, is a phenomenon well attested in all parts of the Muslim world. Sufism then had and has its role in a variety of styles of Islamization in different regions and periods in combination with many other things besides in Southeast Asia. It is a dimension which offered a variety of modalities of participation in the universe of Islam according to the spiritual taste, cultural traditions and Zeitgeist of those parts of Southeast Asia that were to become part of the domain of Islam. So let me conclude: the role of Sufism in our region is not all that different from that of Sufism in other parts of the Muslim world.

There is little reason to regard the Muslims of Southeast Asia overall as being necessarily more legalistic, more mystical or more prone to "syncretism" than other peoples of the Muslim world. From Morocco to the Moros the Domain of Islam includes a mix of shared emphases, and a varying distribution of emphases within that mix. Indeed, a major challenge to Southeast Asianists is to learn to recognize that the presence of Islam as a living, functional component permeating the diverse traditions of the region is far greater than conventional wisdom up to the present has allowed. To echo the Quranic words: ... *Sibghata 'lltih! Wa man alJ-sanu mina 'lltihi* ... as the dye of Allah! And who better than Allah can spread the tincture of a dye? This 'dye of Allah' is more widely and deeply infused than many have realized.

Islam's Great Mystical Movement

Islam at the beginning was primarily a legalistic religion and placed before its adherents little more than a code of ethics combined with a set of rituals. The faithful observance of these was deemed sufficient to satisfy every man's religious quest and ensure him a place in heaven. There was no demand for spiritual regeneration through a rebirth experience and the indwelling of the Holy Spirit as in the Christian faith, nor for a highly spiritual form of devotion through which the worshipper could draw near to God in a personal way and discover the knowledge of his grace and favour. During the Ummayad period, after Islam had made direct contact with Eastern Christianity and other oriental religions, a deeply mystical movement arose within its realm, in many ways, perhaps, indebted to the influence of these faiths for its motivation and principles, but nonetheless an independent theosophy developing purely within the framework of the Islamic society and heritage.

The movement is known as Sufism (*tasawwuf*) and its followers are known as Sufis (pronounced "Soofies"). The word *Sufi* almost certainly comes from the Arabic *suf*, meaning "wool", and implies that the Sufi is a wearer of a woollen garment. In pre-Islamic times ascetics often dressed in wool as a symbol of their particular course of life and the early Muslims who practiced austerity were duly nicknamed "Sufis". Later on the name was adopted by those who sought to obtain knowledge of God through various stages of spiritual self-denial as asceticism in Islam gave way to mysticism.

Sufism is principally a quest for a living knowledge of the Supreme Being. To the orthodox Muslim Allah is the Lord of the Worlds, unique in his essence and attributes, ruling over all the universe and quite unlike anything in his creation.

To the Sufi, on the other hand, "God is the One Real Being which underlies all phenomena". He is everything and there is nothing but Him. Man's purpose is to lose his natural sense of a separate identity from his Creator and to be absorbed instead into his knowledge until there remains no distinction of consciousness between him and God. Through a series of stages (*maqamat*) and subjective experiences (*ahwal*) this process of absorption develops until complete annihilation (*fana*) takes place and the worshipper becomes *al-insanul-kamil*, the "perfect man".

The Sufi concept of a God who is "all in all" differs radically from the orthodox conviction that the further he is placed from his creation, the more he is glorified. Historically it is a marvel that Sufism grew out of the bedrock of Islam but its development will not surprise Christians who believe that man was made in the image of God and that his highest glory is to be conformed to the divine image and be partaker of the divine nature through the indwelling Holy Spirit. The mystical quest in Islam was perhaps to be expected for, as it has been put, there is a "God-shaped vacuum" in every human heart that no religion based purely on ethics and formal rites can ultimately fill. To become a Sufi a Muslim must attach him to a *tariqah*, one of the Sufi orders, and submit himself to a pir or master as we have seen. Only when this master adorns the disciple with a *khirqah*, a robe inducting him into the order, does he become a recognised Sufi, and only then can he embark on a valid pilgrimage through the various stages towards his goal of union with God.

Accordingly, whenever an unknown dervish comes into a convent or wishes to join a company of Sufis, they ask him "Who was the Pir that taught thee?" and "From whose hand didst thou receive the *khirqa*?" Sufis recognise no relationship but these two, which they regard as all-important. They do not allow anyone to associate with them, unless he can show to their satisfaction that he is lineally connected in both these ways with a fully accredited Pir. The covenant by which the disciple is initiated into the particular order he enters is known as a *bay'ah* and it attaches him to his master and the *silsilah* (chain) from which the master himself derives his power (*barakah*) and authority (similar to the "apostolic authority" conferred on Roman Catholic priests through a progressive laying on of hands said to go back to Simon Peter himself).

The initial Sufi experience is not, as it is for true Christians, a rebirth experience in which the man, once born of the flesh, is now born of the Spirit, has a totally new relationship to God and knowledge of him, and can through his unity with God in the Spirit develop the relationship. Rather the Sufi really seeks only "to become aware of what one has always been from eternity (*azal*) without one's having realised it until the necessary transformation has come about". The major Sufi orders are the *Suhrawardiyya* (founded by one as-Suhrawardi), the *Qadiriyya* (attributed to Sufism's most famous personality, Abdul Qadir al-Jilani), the *Chishtiyya* (its master Mu'iniddin Chishti who is buried at Ajmer in India), the *Shadhiliyya*, the *Mawlawiyya* (a Turkish order founded by Jalaluddin Rumi who is buried in Konya in Turkey), and the *Naqshabandiyya* (which is prominent in Iran and other parts of Asia).

Sufi Stages and Experiences

The goal of the Sufi is to reach a personal knowledge of his Creator until knower and known are one and there is no awareness of any distinction of personality between them. Like all orthodox Muslims Sufis reject the concept of incarnation (*hulul*) and do not believe that God can become man. They also resist pantheistic tendencies, carefully distinguishing between God and his servants, while nevertheless teaching that man's aim must be to attain to such a high state of consciousness of God that his personality may no longer be distinguished from God's essence and character. Man does not have this knowledge by nature, however, and each prospective Sufi must prepare for a course which will take him through many stages and experiences before he completes his journey.

Of course the Sufis never tire of emphasizing that the end of Sufism is not to possess such and such a virtue or state as such but to reach God beyond all states and virtues. But to reach the Transcendent beyond the virtues, man must first possess the virtues; to reach the station of annihilation and subsistence in God, man must have already passed through the other stages and stations. The Sufi who sets out to seek God calls himself a 'traveller' (*salik*), he advances by slow 'stages' (*maqamat*) along a path (*tariqat*) to the goal of union with Reality (*fana fi'l-Haqq*). The Sufi's 'path' is not finished until he has traversed all the 'stages', making himself perfect in every one of them before advancing to the next, and has also experienced whatever 'states' it pleases God to bestow upon him.

The early mysticism of Islam sought only a path of self-purification, a character renewal, until the personality was conformed to the divine image. Later it was believe that such growth must be accompanied by deliberate ecstatic experiences, confirming the progress of the soul. The decline Sufism in later centuries can perhaps be attributed to the interest of the masses purely in the experimental side of Islamic mysticism and the desire for emotional excesses. The early mystics of Islam, however, devoted themselves primarily to the first of the three stages, that is, Purgation. To the mystics, *at-tariq* (the Pathway) was a method of self-purification acquired through the cleansing of the senses and through bodily discipline. Gradually the Sufis began to develop the second stage i.e. the Illumination.

Al-Muhasibi (A.D. 781-857), who pioneered with his disciples in the pathways of Purgation, was one of the first to declare that as purification brings freedom from the attachments of this world the Sufi might expect to arrive at the stage of Illumination and thence proceed to the unitive life in God. Pure Sufism, however, sincerely seeks the fulness of the knowledge of God. Nevertheless it has been universally believed for centuries that such a search must accompanied by external manifestations. The goal will be obtained when the worshipper sees God alone in all that he contemplates and at the same time feels a total and ecstatic sense of his presence.

The whole of Sufism rests on the belief that when the individual self is lost, the Universal Self is found, or, in religious language, that ecstasy affords the only means by which the soul can directly communicate and become united with God. He then can be the Perfect Man, one "who has fully realized his essential oneness with the Divine Being in whose likeness he is made". On the path towards this goal, therefore, he must no only go through the progressive stages of self-annihilation but must also have trance-like experiences in which his normal consciousness is to be lost in ecstatic contemplation of the Divine Being alone. These experiences are the *ahwal* (singular *hal*) mentioned earlier and authenticate the developing discovery of the ultimate light and truth.

In the Sufism of the orders this ecstasy or trance-like 'state' is called a *hal*, though in Sufism proper a *hal* more strictly refers to the succession of illuminations, through experiencing which the Sufi progresses a further 'stage' (*maqtam*) towards the goal of spiritual perfection. Such experiences are, to the Sufis, not to be regarded as hypnotic phenomena to which the human spirit is susceptible in appropriate circumstances but rather gifts from God confirming the Sufi's striving for his presence. Each stage reached by the disciple is the result of his own effort, each experience is a token of the divine favour upon the endeavour - "the *hal* is a spiritual mood depending not upon the mystic but upon God"

A Christian must surely be affected by the whole nature of Sufism. True Christianity is by nature mystical and anyone born of the Holy Spirit will not only seek to become conformed to the image of his Lord but will also surely experience many proofs of the Spirit's presence in his soul. Indeed it is a New Testament principle that where such a relationship between man and God truly exists, the formal restraints of legal ethics and rituals have no binding effect as the believer has the motivation towards truth and right-living within him. It is hardly surprising that Sufis have often sought to break away from the dull strictures of formal Islamic law and have, in orthodox eyes, often shown scant respect for it.

And so for all the actions of life: no outward law regulates the Sufi in regard to them, whether the one way or the other; only the Golden Mean and the General Happiness. A prominent Sufi in Islamic history, Sari as-Saqati, who lived in Baghdad at the same time as Islam's arch-conservative theologian, Ahmad ibn Hanbal, and was strongly opposed by him, made a profound distinction between the legal formalism of the Muslim masses and the spiritual quest and path of the Sufi elite:

"The way of the multitude is this", said Sari, "that you observe prayer five times daily behind the imam, and that you give alms - if it be in money, half a dinar out of every twenty. The way of the elect is this that you thrust the world behind you altogether and do not concern yourself with any of its trappings; if you are offered it, you will not accept it. These are the two ways".

There is a remarkable similarity here between the old and new covenants, the former legalistic, the latter based on "grace and truth" which came through Jesus Christ. Islam can hardly be regarded as a stepping-stone to Christianity but Sufism definitely is, and it is this writer's conviction that genuine Sufism is Islam's only endeavour to raise itself towards the glory of the Christian revelation. The difference between the two is this - the Sufi seeks in himself to attain to the knowledge of God through a series of spiritual stages; the Christian acknowledges that his natural tendency towards sin and separation from God prevent him from ever attaining such a goal, and he submits rather to God's redeeming grace in Jesus Christ and the regenerating work of the Holy Spirit within him to enable him to know God fully and become like him.

Different Stages in the Sufi Quest

It is not easy to define the various stages of the Sufi path, especially as there is no universal consensus as to the exact identity of each stage or even of the order in which they are reached. It is generally agreed that the goal is *al-Haqiqah*, "the True Reality", also known as *fana*, self-annihilation" or absorption in God. Very prominent in the Sufi stages is *ma'rifah*, "knowledge" of God, or the gnosis of his essence and presence. In some cases it is set forth as one of the stages towards the goal, in others it is identified with the haqiqah as the object of the quest. These two, together with the initial *tariqah*, "the path", constitute the three great stages of Sufism. A Sufi must attain to these after graduating from the basic laws of Islam which are set forth, Sufis believe, as a principal code for the unenlightened Muslim masses. The foundation of the *shari'ah, the law, and the three ascending Stages of Sufism towards the goal of complete union with God through a loss of self-consciousness is* defined as follows:

Nasut is the natural human state in which one lives following the rules of the *shari'a;*

Malakut is the nature of angels, to reach which one treads the *tariqa*, the path of purification; whilst

Jabarut is the nature of power, to attain which one follows the way of enlightenment, *ma'rifa*, until one swoons into *Fana*, absorption into Deity, the State of Reality (*Haqiqa*), often called in the order literature *'Alam al-Ghaib*, 'the (uncreated) world of the mystery'.

Famous Sufis have individually been responsible for identifying and emphasising different stages making up this threefold gradient and we shall mention some of them and their respective contributions later in this section. In time these became integrated into the catalogue of stages in the Sufi quest and we shall speak briefly of some of them. One of the initial stages is said to be an attitude of indifference towards good or bad fortune. The Sufi believes that adversity, causing discomfort, depression or discourage is brought about through God's deliberate "contraction" (*qabdh*) and that prosperity, joyful circumstances and the like, come from his "expansion" (*bast*). He humbly resigns himself to both, seeking not to be affected by his circumstances but to fix his devotion purely on his Lord and Master. Quranic sanction is found for these contrasting acts of God and the Sufi's willingness to abide in them.

The Sufi has submitted himself to God, who says "God contracts and expands" (*Quran* II: 245). Thus, whether he gives contraction or expansion, the Sufi only desires what is desired by his Beloved. One is reminded of Paul's words in Philippians 4.11-13. Another typical stage is that of "gathe-ring" (*jam*) in which the Sufi begins to turn away from the state of separation from God (*tafriqah* - "dispersion"), the distinction being between God himself and the world of everything but God. There are many different stages, too many to cover in detail here, but perhaps some attention should be given to the ultimate stage - *fana* - for all the intermediate stages are different forms of disassociation from all that is "under the sun", to use a Biblical expression (from Ecclesiastes), in the cause of being absorbed into the consciousness of the Supreme Being. (Alternatively, the Sufi seeks to shake off the identity of his *nafs*, his individual soul with all its ungodly tendencies, similar to the concept of "the flesh" as it is set forth in opposition to the way of the Spirit in the New Testament, especially the eighth chapter of Paul's Epistle to the Romans).

Fana is the ultimate goal - dissolution of the Sufi's consciousness of his own identity through a total absorption in the knowledge of God. "As a technical term in Sufism, the word annihilation signifies the annihilation of the attributes of human nature and their transformation into Divine Attributes. In the state of annihilation, the Sufi is completely immersed in the contemplation of the Attributes of God and oblivious to his own self". It should again be emphasised that this does not lead to a pantheistic theosophy, for Sufis, true to the Muslim faith, are always careful to distinguish between

God and his servants. The union comes in the realm of consciousness and spiritual perspective. The distinction is well set forth in this comment: "The mystic does not become one with God; he becomes conscious of his oneness with Him".

It is true to say that the Sufi should never be able to proclaim that he has reached this stage for his complete absorption in God and self-annihilation, his *fana fit-tawhid, fil Haqq* ("Union with the Unity, the Reality"), will surely make him lose all consciousness of his own identity and personal state. The highest stage of *fana* is reached when even the consciousness of having attained *fana* disappears. This is what the Sufis call 'the passing-away of passing-away (*fana al-fana*). The mystic is now wrapped in contemplation of the divine essence.

Let us briefly look at one of the ways in which Sufis seek to induce a state of ecstasy. Though a means is employed to create this state, they insist that the experience itself is from God.

Dhikr - The Remembrance of Allah

The commonest means of inducing a state of ecstasy is the *dhikr* ceremony. A group of Sufis will gather together and begin a series of chantings, any of the ninety-nine names of Allah, or just simply of the name of Allah himself, until the devotees collapse in a state of trance. The famous "whirling dervishes" obtain their name and fame from this very ceremony. Today it has become customary for numerous adherents of Sufism, who know nothing of true Sufism or a deep spiritual quest coupled with acts of self-discipline to attain to a higher state of spirituality, to seek purely the supposed state of "ecstasy" that can be obtained through regular concentration on and recitation of the name and attributes of Allah.

After an experience of nearly thirteen years of close contact with Egyptian Moslems, I have no hesitation in saying that, as to the bulk of the population of Egypt, their real religion is Sufism, as represented by the *dhikr*. They know practically nothing of the philosophic Mysticism of their books, but through tradition they know something of the spiritual achievement of their saints; and in the *dhikr* they attempt to realize the ultimate experience of the Sufi saint by a physically induced ecstasy, ignoring the fact that these saints only reached their experiences by a long and painful road.

The Quran commends the remembrance of Allah in these words: *Wa aqimis-salaah ... wa lathikrullaahi akbar* - "and establish prayer ... and the remembrance of Allah, which is greater" (Surah 29.45). Orthodox Muslims take this verse simply to mean that prayyer without a consciousness of Allah has a very limited value. Sufis interpret it to mean that the practice of *dhikr* through repetitions of Allah's name and attributes is greater than the formal acts of the prescribed *salaah*, the basic Islamic form of worship.

According to some this means the mentioning, or the remembering of God constitutes the quintessence of prayer; according to others it indicates the excellence of invocation as compared with prayer. A dhikr ceremony is something to behold, though Christian observers can be excused if they become bored after a while with a monotonous repetition of religious cliches, e.g. *la ilaha illullah* - "there is no God but Allah", which supposedly bring the devotee into the realm of God and a conscious awareness of his presence simply because they result in a trance-like state. In all religions there are those who seek, through various means, to enter into such trances and these means are all very similar to one another. The end result seems to be a self-induced, hypnotic state rather thhan a God-ordained experience.

The Quran and Hadith

If Sufism is a later development within Islam, how does it reconcile itself with original Islam, the religion of Muhammad as set forth in the Quran and Hadith? The Sufi answer is that this original Islam has the germs of Sufism and that both the

Quran and Hadith contain numerous passages indicating the deeper nature of true Islam, that which later blossomed out into its great mystical movement. Expressions such as these in the Quran are produced by Sufis as proof that Islam is, at heart, a spiritual religion: "To God belong the East and the West: whithersoever ye turn, there is the Presence of God. For God is All-Pervading, All-Knowing" (Surah 2.115); and "We are nearer to him (man) than his jugular vein".

Although Muhammad himself could hardly be described as a mystic, let alone a Sufi, there are verses in the Quran which do at least support the Sufi contention, prompting one scholar to say: "however un-favorable to mysticism the Quran as a whole may be, I cannot assent to the view that it supplies no basis for a mystical interpretation of Islam". As the Quran is believed to be the uncreated Word of God it is little wonder Sufis seek to authenticate their movement with reference to its teaching and it is not surprising that they make much of these verses. "For these mystical texts are the chief encouragement and justification of the Sufi in his belief that he also may commune with God".

Another verse cherished by the Sufis is this one: "To God we belong, and to Him is our return" (Surah 2.156) as it seems to synchronise with their whole philosophy that man's objective and duty on earth is to strive spiritually until he comes back to the knowledge of his Creator. The "return" must therefore be one in which the soul can be re-united with its Maker through a thorough spiritual devotion. The Sufis claim that the whole of Sufism is summed up in this verse, and it is often chanted at their gatherings and sometimes repeated a certain number of times on a rosary; and in fact, although every believer is necessarily 'for God' in some degree or other, the mystic may be said to be 'for God' in a way which the rest of the community is not.

The Hadith contain certain "hadith qudsi" (divine sayings of Allah), allegedly reported from Muhammad himself which contain mystical elements even closer to the heart of Sufism than the verses quoted from the Quran. A famous saying of this kind is:

My slave keeps on coming closer to Me through performing Nawafil (praying or doing extra deeds besides what is obligatory) till I love him, so I become his sense of hearing with which he hears, and his sense of sight with which he sees, and his hand with which he grips, and his leg with which he walks; and if he asks Me, I will give him, and if he asks my protection (Refuge), I will protect him.

One writer comments that "the whole of Sufism - its aspirations, its practice, and in a sense also even its doctrine - is summed up in this Holy Tradition, which is quoted by the Sufis perhaps more often than any other text apart from the Quran". Another similar saying is: I was a hidden treasure and I desired to be known; therefore I created the creation in order that I might be known. These traditions are, for the Sufis, their motivation for earnestly desiring to know God and their belief that he does indeed desire that his servants should thus seek him. One writer says of the last saying:

This is called the "self-revealing" (*tajalla*) of Allah and is only really intelligible through the mystical contemplation, which sees all things in God, as it sees God in all things.

There is, of course, the possibility that the hadith quoted are symptomatic of later developmenta in mystical Islam, just as many legislative traditions betray evidences of an advanced juristic process in Islam as we have seen. Accordingly they may well have been invented. Nevertheless, for the Sufis, they authenticate Islamic mysticism, enabling them to trace it back to statements allegedly reported on the authority of Muhammad himself.

There are a number of Sufis who stand out in the history of Islamic mysticism, all of whom have made their contribution in one way or another to the development of Sufism. One of the most famous of the early Sufis was Junayd, the head of a large body of disciples, who died in Baghdad in 910 AD. He "was the greatest exponent of the 'sober' school of Sufism and elaborated a theosophical doctrine which determined the whole course of orthodox mysticism in Islam". Junayd, being one of the early Sufi masters, was not given to excesses in his mystic devotions and sought chiefly through a process of self-denial to discover the way to God. The following saying, which seems to be far more Christian than Muslim in origin and emphasis, is attributed to him: "Sufism is that God makes thee die to thyself and become resurrected in Him". It was this very principle of dying to self that later became the foundation of the Sufi concept of *fana*, being lost in the consciousness of God, and Junayd was one of the first to use this expression.

At the other extreme we find the famous Persian Sufi master Bayazid al-Bistami, "first of the 'intoxicated' Sufis who, transported upon the wings of mystical fervour, found God within his own soul and scandalised the orthotox by ejaculating, 'Glory to Me! How great is My Majesty'". Sobriety was not at the heart of this man's mystic experiences. He not only established the concept of being so united to God that the identities of the Creator and creature become one but also gave the ecstatic character of this experience its impetus. As was to be expected, he was highly unpopular with the orthodox Muslims of his day. He is credited with many bold and daring statements, of which the one quoted above is an example. Here is another:

> For instance, one day Bayazid was in his cell.
>
> Someone came and said, "Is Bayazid in the house?"
>
> He answered, "Is there anyone in the house but God?
>
> (Nurbakhsh, *Sufism*, p.53).

He also greatly emphasised the ultimate state of *fana* but gave it a far more experimental character. He is accordingly regarded as the founder of the "drunken" school of Sufism, a description implying that a true falling away of the separate consciousness of the believer in his Lord would be manifested through a state of spiritual intoxication. From Bayazid's example grew the interest in Sufism in outward manifestations of the inward experience.

Some Muslims say that a true Muslim on pilgrimage will see the Ka'aba the first time, the Ka'aba and the Lord of the House the second and only his Lord on the third. Bayazid went further:

"The first time I entered the Holy House," stated Abu Yazid, "I saw the Holy House. The second time I entered it, I saw the Lord of the House. The third time I saw neither the House nor the Lord of the House".

This experience illustrates the whole meaning of the fana state - a lost consciousness even of God himself as the Sufi pilgrim becomes one with him. Another symbolising this same concept is:

One day someone came to Bayazid's door and knocked. The shaykh said, "Who are you seeking?" The man replied "Bayazid". Bayazid then answered, "Poor Bayazid! I have been seeking him for thirty years but have found no sign or trace of him".

Another famous mystic from the golden age of Sufism was Abu Sa'id ibn Abul-Khayr, a prominent member of the group of early masters who emphasised the doctrine of losing one's human consciousness and subsisting in the knowledge of God alone. These men all believed that by renouncing earthly pleasures, by mystical hours of devotion, and by seeking out the higher virtues of the soul, one could walk the road towards this goal. Self-love had to be replaced by a disinterested love for God alone. Abu Sa'id followed in the footsteps of Bayazid, making many bold statements calculated to antagonise the orthodox. On one occasion he told one of the *fuqaha*, the Muslim jurists, that he could read his thoughts (many anecdotes have been recorded of his alleged power to discern the thoughts of men).

The jurist had thought to himself that he could not find

Abu Sa'id's teaching in the seven-sevenths of the Quran (that is, the whole Qur an). Abu Sa'id replied that his doctrine was contained in the "eighth-seventh" of the book, meaning a special revelation given by God to his favourite servants. This concept of an independent revelation given to a Muslim after the revelation of the Quran is diametrically opposed to the Muslim doctrine of the finality of prophethood.

Here Abu Sa'id sets aside the partial, finite, and temporal revelation on which Islam is built, and appeals to the universal infinite and everlasting revelation which the Sufis find in their hearts. As a rule, even the boldest Mohammedan mystics shrink from uttering such a challenge.

Among the great mystics of Islam was a woman, Rabi'a al-Adawiyya, who lived in Basra (in Iraq) in the very early days of Sufism. Her chief contribution to the growing mysticism of Islam was her insistence that God should be loved, not out of fear of wrath or for the prospect of reward, but purely for himself. One of her sayings was: "O God! If I worship Thee in fear of Hell, burn me in Hell; and if I worship Thee in hope of Paradise, exclude me from Paradise; but if I worship Thee for Thine own sake, withhold not Thine Everlasting Beauty!" She was once seen carrying a burning torch in one hand and a bucket of water in the other. When asked why, she replied: "I am going to set fire to Paradise and quench the fires of Hell so that men may worship God for his own glory alone".

Of Rabi'a her biographer wrote that she was "on fire with love to God", and she was one of the first among the Sufis to teach the doctrine of disinterested love to God. She was asked if she hated Satan, and answered "No", and when asked if she loved the Prophet, she said, "My love to God has so possessed me that no place remains for hating aught, or loving any save Him". The most tragic figure in Sufi history is al-Hallaj, one of the "intoxicated" mystics who was also inclined to complete indiscretion in making bold statements which outraged the orthodox. He openly claimed *ana'l Haqq* -

"I am the Truth", and for refusing to recant was brutally dismembered and crucified. (It is striking to find that he suffered the same fate as Jesus Christ who made exactly the same claim, albeit more worthily).

Later Sufi mystics considered him a true martyr even though many at the time disowned him. They charged him with teaching *hulul,* i.e. incarnation, in that he suggeated that God himself joined in union with man in all his essence rather than that man attained to a state of identifying with God in his attributes and personality. The later Sufis, however, endeavoured to interpret al-Hallaj's doctrine as distinct from the concept of hulul and "they have also done their best to clear Hallaj from the suspicion of having taught it. The general line taken was that he was right in his teaching, but that he ought not to have published abroad the secrets of Sufism, a proceeding for which he deserve to be put to death.

It must be remembered that later Sufis left out many of the distinctive features of Hallaj's doctrine. They discarded the term *Hulul,* and they replaced his view of the union of the human soul with God by a doctrine of monism, in which all created things including the souls of men, are merely mirrors reflecting one or other of the attributes of God. Although Abdul Qadir al-Jilani is held to be the founder of the Qadariyya, the greatest school in Sufism, and is so venerated that he "has very nearly displaced Muhammad himself in the eyes of the Sufi-worshipping public", the extent of his devotion to Sufism cannot be ascertained fully. He was a dedicated follower of the legalistic school of Ibn Hanbal and many myths surround his life. Nevertheless he is universally regarded to this day as the greatest of the early Sufi masters.

After the heyday of Sufism in the early centuries of Islam the movement began to lose credibility and it took the great Islamic scholar Abu Hamid al-Ghazzali to give it a more sober image and respectability among the general public. Al-Ghazzali was a renowned orthodox theologian and, after a period of cynical agnosticism and depression, he declared himself a champion of Sufism, claiming to have found peace and purpose at last through a personal experience of refuge in God alone. His mysticism was chiefly of a less emotional kind than his predecessors, concentrating on intellectual insight and understanding, and it is therefore not surprising that "he is not regarded as being a practising Sufi by the ecstatics and gnostics". Yet it was he who reconciled Sufism with orthodox Islam and a fine example of the way he did this is found in his definition of the four stages of the knowledge of *tawhid*, the "unity" of God, in his greatest work:

> The first stage is like the outer cover of a cocoanut, the second stage is the inner cover of a cocoanut, the third is the kernel of a cocoanut, and the fourth stage the oil of the kernel. The first stage of Tauhid is to utter by tongue "There is no deity but God". The second stage is to confirm it by heart. The third stage is like kernel which can be seen by inner light or by way of Kashf. The fourth stage is like oil in kernel. He sees nothing but God.

Here the orthodox dogma is almost imperceptibly fused with the whole foundation of Sufism. Al-Ghazzali's chief contribution to Sufism was to remove its stigma in the eyes of the orthodox by tempering its character and bringing it more into line with fundamental Islam. The influence of al-Ghazali in Islam is incalculable. He not only reconstituted orthodox Islam, making Sufism an integral part of it, but also was a great reformer of Sufism, purifying it of un-Islamic elements and putting it at the service of orthodox religion.

Not only did he save Sufism from extinction by softening its dramatic character but at least one writer considers that he also delivered orthodox Islam from the dead-weight of formalism: "Had not mysticism in the course of time acquired a place in official Islam, chiefly through the influence of al-Ghazali, the Muslim religion would have become a lifeless form". Sufism is a remarkable phenomenon in Islam and

Christian readers must, after reading this section, have recognised how similar it is to Christianity in so many of its facets and objectives. In many ways its spiritual character is far more consistent with Christianity than orthodox Islam. The Christian witness to Islam has here its greatest potential for making its message heard and understood.

Bibliography

Ali, Syed Ameer. *The Spirit of Islam: A History of the Evolution and Ideals of Islam,* with *a Life of the Prophet.* London: Chatto & Windus, 1978.

Bloom, Jonathan and Sheila Blair. *Islam: A Thousand Years of Faith and Power.* New Haven, CT: Yale University Press, 2002.

Booth, E. *Aristotelian Aporetic Ontology in Islamic and Christian Thinkers.* Cambridge, 1983.

Burrell, D. *Knowing the Unknowable God: Ibn Sina, Maimonides, Aquinas* (Notre Dame: 1986).

Cook, Michael. *The Koran: A Very Short Introduction.* Oxford, UK: Oxford University Press, 2000.

Daniel, Norman. *Islam and the West: The Making of an Image.* Oxford, England: Oneworld, 2000 (reprint ed.).

Davidson, H.A. Proowson. *An Introduction to Islam.* New York: Macmillan, 1994.

Druart, T.-A. "Philosophy in Islam," in *The Cambridge Companion to Medieval Philosophy* , ed. A.S. McGrade. Cambridge, 2003.

Elias, Jamal J. *Islam.* Upper Saddle River, NJ: Prentice Hall, 1999.

Esposito, John L. and John Obert Voll. *Makers of Contemporary Islam.* UK, Oxford University Press, 2001.

Esposito, John L. *Islam: The Straight Path.* New York, Oxford University Press, 3rd ed., 1998.

Esposito, John L. *The Oxford Encyclopedia of the Modern Islamic World,* 4 Vols. UK, Oxford University Press, 1995.

Fakhry, M. *A History of Islamic Philosophy* , 2nd ed. New York, 1983.

Gutas, D. *Greek Philosophers in the Arabic Tradition.* Aldershot, 2000.

Hodgson, Marshall G.S. *The Venture of Islam,* 3 Vols. Chicago, IL: University of Chicago Press, 1974.

Keller, Nuh Ha Mim, trans. *Al-Nawawi's Manual of Islam.* Cambridge, UK: The Islamic Texts Society, 1996.

Leaman, O. *An Introduction to Classical Islamic Philosophy.* Cambridge, 2002.

Lewis, Bernard, ed. *The World of Islam: Faith, People, Culture.* New York: Thames and Hudson, 1992.

Marmura , M.E. (ed.), *Islamic Theology and Philosophy.* Albany, 1984.

Morewedge, P. (ed.), *Islamic Philosophy and Mysticism.* Delmar, 1981.

Nasr, Seyyed Hossein. *Islam: Religion, History, and Civilization.* San Francisco, CA: Harper San Francisco, 2002.

Nasr, Seyyed Hossein. *Islamic Spirituality I: Foundations.* New York: Crossroad, 1987.

Nasr, Seyyed Hossein. *Islamic Spirituality II: Manifestations.* New York: Crossroad, 1991.

Nasr, Seyyed Hossein. *The Heart of Islam: Enduring Values for Humanity.* San Francisco, CA, Harper San Francisco, 2002.

Newby, Gordon D. *A Concise Encyclopedia of Islam.* Oxford, UK, Oneworld, 2002.

Peters, F.E. *A Reader on Classical Islam.* Princeton, NJ: Princeton University Press, 1994.

Qadir , C.A. *Philosophy and Science in the Islamic World.* London, 1990.

Ruthven, Malise. *Islam in the World.* New York: Oxford University Press, 2nd ed., 2000.

Schimmel, Annemarie. *Islam: An Introduction.* Albany, NY: State University of New York Press, 1992.

Tayob, Abdulkader. *Islam: A Short Introduction.* Oxford, England: Oneworld, 1999. University of Chicago Press, 1986.

Waines, David. *An Introduction to Islam.* Cambridge, UK: Cambridge University Press, 1995.

Watt, M.W. Islamic Philosophy and Theology. Edinburgh, 1962, revised ed. 1985.

Watt, William Montgomery. *The Formative Period of Islamic Thought.* Oxford, UK: Oneworld,1998.

Watt, William Montgomery. *What is Islam?* London: Longman, 1970.

Williams, John Alden, ed. *The Word of Islam.* Austin, TX: University of Texas Press, 1994.

Wolfson, H.A. *Studies in the History of Philosophy and Religion* , ed. I. Twersky, G.H. Williams, in 2 vols. Cambridge, MA, 1973, 1977.

Wolfson, H.A. *The Philosophy of the Kalam.* Cambridge, MA, 1976.

Ziai, H. "Islamic Philosophy," in *The Oxford Companion to Philosophy,* ed. T. Honderich. Oxford , 1955.

INDEX

A

Abyat, 147, 150, 151, 152, 153.
Aguéli to guénon 99.

B

Baqa, 67, 241.
Book trade, 137.

C

Certified shaikh, 76, 78.
Chishti order, 188, 238.
Classical sufism, 189.
Contemporary sufism, 219.
Contented soul, 66, 266.

D

Dhikr, 36, 76, 183, 196, 210, 211, 214, 215, 218, 222, 243, 263, 277, 278.
Divan poetry, 119, 125, 126, 127.
Divine presence, 55, 173, 178, 179.

E

Early ottoman prose, 127.
Early translations, 97.
Ecstasy, 153, 160, 219, 239, 273, 277, 278.
Embodied perception, 108.
Epic tradition, 121.
Essence of man, 60.
Existentialism, 247, 248.
Extinction, 67, 286.

F

Fana, 67, 163, 241, 270, 272, 275, 276, 277, 281, 282.
Five pillars of Islam, 40.
Folk poetry, 118, 119, 122, 125, 136.
formative years, 212.
Future movement, 132.

G

Great mystical movement, 279.

H

Hadith, 41, 83, 173, 194, 221, 242, 280.
Hadith-e-ihsan, 173.

I

Islamic aesthetics, 103, 104, 105, 110, 111, 114.
Islamic traditions, 104.

K

Khalwa, 196.

L

Later academics, 102.
Light of quran, 82.

M

Meditation, 26, 67, 173, 174, 176, 182, 189, 196, 215, 216, 218, 220, 221
Mystical path, 67, 140.
Mysticism, 11, 14, 16, 23, 24, 25, 26, 31, 51, 55, 56, 70, 89, 102, 110, 158, 163, 164, 167, 202, 203, 220, 229, 232, 237, 242, 260, 264, 265, 269, 272, 279, 281, 283, 285, 286.

N

Naqshbandiyya order, 180.
National literature movement, 133, 135.
New literature movement, 131.

O

Orders and lodges, 213.
Orthodox sufism, 163.
Ottoman literature 124, 129.

P

Performative aesthetics, 110.
Poems of uftade, 153.
Popular religion, 164, 172.
Post-independence literature, 133
Pseudo-Sufis, 68, 220

Q

Quranic roots of sufism, 62.

R

Religious message, 139.
Reproaching soul, 66.
Rituals and practices, 214.

S

Shaykh, 62, 69, 99, 121, 136, 165, 166, 167, 169, 170, 189, 199, 238.
Signs on the horizons, 2, 3, 5, 6.
Spiritual mentor, 61.
Spiritual union, 221.
Stations and ascension, 67.
Substantial motion, 248.
Sufi, 11, 13, 14, 15, 16, 19, 20, 21, 26, 27, 31, 32, 33, 36, 90, 96, 97, 98, 99, 100, 101, 241, 242, 243, 245, 246, 247, 248, 249, 250, 253,

269, 270, 273, 274, 275, 276, 277, 278, 279, 280, 281, 282, 283, 284, 286.
Sufi festivals, 160, 161.
Sufi literature, 73, 213, 217, 233.
Sufi music and dance, 219.
Sufi practices, 220.
Sufi Quest, 275.
Sufi saints, 51, 53, 143, 160, 162, 195, 202, 215, 238.
Sufi spirit, 158.
Sufi stages and experiences, 271.
Sufi theosophy, 164.
Sufi thought, 125, 157, 223, 230.
Suluk, 65.
Sunnah, 7, 8, 10, 28, 32, 70, 71, 72, 76, 78, 82, 84, 86, 87, 179, 184.
Sunni mystics, 220.

T

Teachings and tenets, 216.
Tenants of sufism, 52.
The covenant of allegiance, 76, 81.
The third way, 46.
Theosophical Sufism, 241, 242, 245, 250.
Turkish literature, 117, 118, 120, 121, 122, 123, 130, 131, 132, 133, 134.
Turkish mystical poetry, 117.